BORN READY

EUGENE PAUL SEMMENS

BORN READY

THE LIFE OF EUGENE PAUL SEMMENS

CS Development Group Fort Payne, AL

Copyright © 2022 by Eugene Paul Semmens

All rights reserved. No part of this book may be reproduced in any manner whatsoever without written permission except in the case of brief quotations embodied in critical articles and reviews.

First Printing, 2022

PREFACE

COL Eugene Paul Semmens, 1995
Commander, Army Space Command

"If I were to begin life again, I should want it all as it was. I would only open my eyes a little more." Jules Renard

CHAPTER ONE

CHILDHOOD, 1946-1964

<u>I am writing this book for my boys and anyone else who might be interested in my life. I have considered several outlines-chronological, thematic etc. including using the questions from a book called A Father's Legacy. I had trouble deciding, so this narrative may (will) wander a little.</u>

My Dad wrote a family history in which he was bluntly honest, and I hope to do the same. Know that I have enjoyed writing this, it's brought back many memories of accomplishments, failures, friends but mostly of my family, my greatest treasure. It's been fun, I hope you will enjoy reading it.

I have been writing this for over a year now and already debates have ensued about the accuracy of what is contained in this book. So be it; what is in this book is what I remember and if there are inaccuracies, the family can sort them out later, if you desire.

<u>I named this book Born Ready as my life was one where I tried to take on every challenge put in front of me; sometimes successfully and sometimes unsuccessfully. I will end with advice for my grandson, Grant, and future grandchildren and I hope someday that he/they can learn from his Grandfather's mistakes and accomplishments.</u>

Ft Payne, Alabama, 2022

What did I enjoy as a child? I really loved to play outside. I played outside from the age of 4 or 5 until I graduated from college. I either played sports or from the age of eight until I was 10 or twelve, we would play war with our wooden rifles. I would maneuver my "men" around the battlefield with great intensity. Dad told me once we were pretty good.

I guess I was quite the organizer when I was little. In addition to raising and "training" my Army when we were in Washington, I organized a 3-team football league. We were the Eagles and we played in two neighbors back yards that were not fenced. We all had helmets and shoulder pad with distinctive black jerseys with gold on the top. The problem with our field was there was an 18 inch drop off on the 50-yard line. Since we ran the ball mostly it was very advantageous to be going downhill for second half. It was during this league play that I chipped my front tooth. I would love to say it was from a vicious forearm shiver, but I chipped it one day when we were moving a swing set which acted as the goal posts.

(Point of clarification: as a child, we moved from California to Ft Bliss Texas, then to San Antonio Texas, Germany, Ft

Leavenworth Kansas, Washington D.C. and then back to Colorado for Dad's last 10 or so years in the Army.)

We moved from California when I was a year or so old. WWII ended in 1945 and everyone was discharged except for the regular Army officers, mostly the West Pointers. It took Dad about a year to get back into the Army and we were assigned to Ft Bliss around 1947 and then Fifth Army Headquarters in San Antonio, Texas. I was named Eugene after my Uncle Mervin Eugene (Dad one day suggested that he was going to name me Mervin and my Mother who was barely five feet tall and came up to just above my Father's waist replied, "No kid of mine is going to be named Mervin." And so, it was. I never liked Eugene, but it sure beat Mervin. I was named Paul after my Dad, Clifton Paul, and my Great Uncle Paul whom I met only a few times, but he was a prince of a guy.

I don't remember our house in San Antonio but when were assigned to Ft Bliss we lived on Dickman Road in a duplex. I played outside a lot and the son of the next-door neighbor who was nine (I was four or five) delighted in beating the hell out of me. Dad returned from a trip and after hearing what had happened, he went next door to talk to the kid's dad. When the Dad refused to let Dad into talk, Dad kicked the door down and finished the conversation. I never had trouble with that guy again. I heard God's voice for the first time on Dickman Road. This clear voice kept saying Paul over and over. I remember frantically looking around as I didn't have anyone to play with that day. Needless to say, no one was physically there.

Next, we went to Germany in 1952; we originally were stationed in Munich and later in Hanau Germany. In Munich we lived in a mansion, a house off post where General Eisenhower had stayed right after the war ended. We had a German maid and I played with German kids all the time and apparently got pretty good at speaking German. We then moved to Hanau where we lived on Fleigerhorst Kaserne in a duplex. Nana became very familiar with the Catholic post chaplain, Father Dadish, and since he didn't have any altar boys, he trained me to do the Latin Mass and when I was nine, I was confirmed.

One day at Hanau, my brother Mike and I were digging around in the back yard of our quarters which butted up on a farmer's field. My Mother deserved to go to heaven just for the aggravation of washing our play clothes which were always filthy and torn. Anyway, we came across something shiny and started digging it up. Nana came out and almost had a nervous breakdown-we were digging up an unexploded German 88mm round. Nana called the Explosive Ordnance people who were there right away and dug up the munition.

We were assigned to Washington DC in 1955 and lived on Truman Avenue in Arlington. We had a great house; it had four levelsl a basement and a main level; a third level that had a bath and two bedrooms and then a fourth floor that had a large dormitory where Mike and I lived. It was here in the neighborhood that I had most of my military "successes" and where I played for the Eagles. Our housing development was new but there was lots of woods and empty space where we roamed. Today, I am sure you can't turn sideways in Arlington, its wall-to-wall houses. My Dad rode to work in the Pentagon with Colonel Severe.

I became great friends with his son Pete and when the Severes were reassigned his Dad wouldn't let him take his baseball card collection which he had organized into wooden boxes. He had a box for every team including the Yankees who I admired. CBS owned the Yankees so in 1955 the game of the week every week was the Yankees. And boy did they win! Hard to lose if you roster has players named Mickey Mantle, Roger Maris, Yogi Berra, Tony Kubek and Bobby Richardson. Pete asked me if I wanted them, and I said sure. When we left, my Dad had me throw them away. Who knew Mickey Mantle rookie cards would be valuable one day? I think I had five of them.

Dad's work always interested me, especially when we were in Hanau. His unit would have family days and I would get to sit in a Duster, a 40mm Air Defense gun mounted on a tank chassis. The most enjoyable thing was to sit around and listen to the war stories. All Dad's friends were Colonels who had fought in WWII and Korea. They would tell hilarious stories and they would talk shop. I knew from a very early age that I wanted to be a soldier.

Mom was always a stay-at-home Mom except when we were in Washington. Because the cost of living was so high there, she took a job as a secretary in the Georgetown University Athletic Department. We sometimes would get to meet her at work, and it was always cool.

My favorite sport was always football, but I enjoyed Basketball and baseball as well. I pole vaulted in High School and 10 days before the state meet, we obtained a fiberglass pole to replace our aluminum ones. Dad had been a great pole vaulter and had held the California State High School record for over a decade. Dad vaulted with a bamboo pole and went 13'6" in 1936. The world record at that time was 14'6". Dad gave me plenty of coaching. My best vault with an aluminum pole had been about 10'. I started jumping with the new pole and after I got used to the delay before the pole snaps up, I was clearing heights over 12'. Our bus broke down on the way to the state meet, we arrived late, and I could never get my steps right. I failed to qualify at the opening height; I was two feet above the bar but kept falling on it.

In Colorado Springs, we played football continuously in the street when I was a teenager; sometimes we would have 16-18 kids in a game. I played football for a rec team my 9th grade year and tried out for the Wasson JV team the next. I was playing guard and I thought I was doing well but when I went into the locker room the first day of school my locker had been cleaned out and the head coach told me I had been cut. I asked why and he replied, "I didn't know you." Later that year in a PE class, the line coach who had coached me in fall camp before the season asked me how football was going. When I told him what happened, he replied it was a mistake. I played guard and I would knock the starting guard on his butt in one-on-one blocking drills. It was unfair, but life is unfair, and you just must keep pushing forward.

My junior year I was not allowed to play football because I got a 2.99 GPA in school and Dad had made a rule that we needed a 3.0 GPA to play sports. It broke my heart and I suspect, his. My junior year, I transferred to St Mary's High School, and I sure wanted to play ball to give the new guy (me) some status. It was not to be. My senior year was my second year at St Mary's, and I went out for football as a senior and made the team. I mostly played center at 160 lbs. (our offensive line average was 180), a little defensive end and one of the 2 middle linebackers in our 4-4-2 defense. My junior year, the leading pass receiver on the team had 5 catches for the SEASON, so our defense was stacked to stop the run. Late in the season I was playing center against St Francis and at halftime, coach told me to move to middle linebacker. I had never practiced being a middle linebacker, but Sam Zavatti, the other middle linebacker told me what to do.

The was a running back for St Francis who naturally had this grin on his face all the time. He infuriated me. One play he carried the ball on a sweep right in front of our bench and I knocked the guy flying almost taking out our defensive coach. It was a lucky but spectacular hit. Coach looked at me in shock and I was the middle linebacker the rest of the year. Our last game of the season was against Cheyenne Mountain, a much larger school who was undefeated and had a prolific offense including two backs who were on their way to playing college ball. Coach had put in several trick passing plays, and we tied them 20-20, the only blemish on their record. They went on to win the state championship. It was a special game for me as Dad had just gotten back from Korea and he got to see me play. I had a fumble recovery and helped block their last extra point. We controlled them. We lost 2 games that year, but the Cheyenne Mountain win made the season a success. The day I got my football letter was one of the great days of my life. I still have my letter jacket. It's ironic that my son Michael would graduate from Cheyenne Mountain while I was at Army Space Command in Colorado Springs.

The football season was important to me as it proved I could stick to something if I really wanted it. My coach, Chuck Herring, was a daily communicant and a great guy who encouraged me through the whole process. I'm just sorry my brother Mike who followed me at St Mary's didn't have Coach Herring, as he had taken a job at Southern Colorado University. Raising a family on a parochial schoolteacher's salary was just too tough. Over 10 years later, I was officiating the pole vault at an Air Force Academy meet and Coach H was there with the Southern Colorado team. I went over and talked to him. We ended the conversation with me saying "Coach I still hate Regis". Regis High School was one of our biggest rivals and we could never compete with them. The good news was they could not compete with Mullen High School, and we could beat Mullin. It was always a three-way tie at the top. Coach, the daily communicant replied to me, "That's good Paul, that's good."

Growing up my faith life was like any other kids. The only prayer I remember practicing regularly was the Guardian Angel prayer which Mike and I said with our Mother every night. Like my Dad, I always felt I was ok with God but all that would crumble and reemerge later. Mama instilled great faith in us by her example. She truly was a Saint on earth.

Dad's mom was Nell Fedderson, who was married to my step grandfather, Tom Fedderson. Tom was German, spoke with a heavy German accent and was a strong powerful man. Gran-Gran was always good and loving with me and Mike, but we learned later she had a rough time in her early life. She was raised in Cripple Creek Colorado during the gold rush in the late 1890's and could tell stories about that life until the cows came home. Tom and I worked together one summer in a lumber yard in California, it was a happy time for me. Every time Gran-Gran came to visit us in Colorado, we would go to the melodrama in Cripple Creek. One-time Uncle Paul came along, and he and I discussed hitting left-handed on an abandoned baseball field there that I will never forget. Nobody on Dad's side of the family kept their hair in the front except my brother, Mike. We all ended up half bald.

Mom's Dad was Arthur Fogarty or Archie. We never saw Mom's relatives that much as we were moving around, but

Daddy A, as we called him, would get in his Plymouth Valiant and come see us. Daddy A had been a mechanic his whole life. He had repaired train locomotives during which they had to create the repair parts for the engines. He built ships during both WWI and WWII and as part time work when he worked for the Savannah Fire Department, he would fix people's car under a tree next to the fire department. He was one of the original "shade tree mechanics". Late in his life he repaired boat and small engines. Mama was on him all the time when he visited us. Daddy A was a fun loving, full of life guy who was in no hurry to get anywhere. Daddy A's second wife was Anna who was a beautiful, sophisticated woman and they never got along.

Mom's side of the family was all Irish and Gran-Gran was an O'Brien before she married. He only mistake was marrying this guy Semmens (who was English not Irish) who was an oil field entrepreneur. He fought in WWI and is buried in Ft Logan Veteran's cemetery in Denver along with Mom and Dad. Dad and his brothers had a tough time growing up. At one-point Gran-Gran had to put them in a foster home to insure they would get 3 squares a day. This home put a real emphasis on keeping things clean and orderly, something that stuck with Dad until the end which he passed on to us. Being Irish is something I was always proud of and like the saying goes if God had not invented liquor, the Irish would rule the world.

We always had people in our house. Frequently they were Catholic Priests, a practice that I have continued to this day. As I mentioned earlier, having dinner parties for mom and Dad's friends and the Pryor's, Goettle's, Lewis's all became surrogate parents to us. When I was in High School, they all lived on Meyers Avenue in Colorado Springs, so it was not hard for any of them to get home. Early in my life Mama cooked good wholesome food. When we were in Colorado Springs, she took a gourmet cooking class and the fare really changed. That was okay, as I was off to College.

I'm kind of bouncing all over the place but I wanted to mention our family trips. We were not big travelers. Dad, or Gomp-Gomp after Rob's early attempts to say Grandpa, after retirement was sort of sedentary. I remember he would spend his days sitting at the kitchen table up on the mountain reading Louis L'Amour novels all day. He had every Louis L'Amour novel ever written; I think. I love his stuff and to this day I am still reading L'Amour's stuff digitally now. But there was something about reading his books in paperback.

Anyway, the only place we seemed to visit was El Paso and Uncle Skee and Aunt Liz. When he retired, Uncle Skee worked on being a professional golfer-I think he played 6 days a week. Aunt Liz was a good golfer too, she was a tall, very beautiful woman. When I was in High School, and we were in Colorado we would all bundle up in the car and drive the 10 hours to El Paso. Uncle Skee had just gotten cancer which essentially eliminated him from becoming a general and he was bitter about it. So, there were some tense moments; things at times got a little argumentative at times, visits but Mom and Dad handled the situation with grace and charity. I always loved Uncle Skee and Aunt Liz. Early in my career when we kept getting reassigned to El Paso, we always stayed with them until we got settled. After that, we saw them frequently. Aunt Liz made the best Mexican food I have ever eaten.

Aside from when we went to Germany, we never visited Mom's family very much. I remember sitting on the front porch of Daddy A's house with Grandma O'Gorman when we were going to Germany in 1952. She was in her late 90's, she had terrible arthritis and cataracts and to read the newspaper she had to use a magnifying glass. She had been a child when Sherman marched to the sea during the Civil War and if you ever mentioned Sherman to her or Mom, you were greeted with a string of blue profanities which were so unique to these holy, Catholic women. I remember visiting Uncle Bill and Aunt Erma Fogarty just a few times. They were super people. They came to Colorado when I was teaching at the Air Force Academy, and I got to give them a tour which included places that most visitors couldn't go since I was on the faculty. Uncle Bill was always full of wonder, he was a great guy and Aunt Erma was a quiet saint. You have to remember, even as late as the 70's air travel was expensive so to get anywhere one had to drive at 55-60mph. We saw our family when we could.

We were very faithful in going to Church. Mom was an ardent Catholic and Dad was a man of great faith. He had asked Jesus to cure him when he had cancer the first time when I was about 4 years old. The Lord did cure him and Dad from that point on was focused on raising his boys to be tough, responsible men. By the way when Dad had cancer the first time, I stayed in Mobile Alabama with my Aunt Babe and her lifelong friend, Aunt Neal. They were both in their 80's and I remember talking walks with Aunt Babe holding her hand. They were just awesome with me.

Daddy A came to visit us in Mobile once, and he and I went crabbing in the Mobile Bay. I remember I couldn't understand how we were going to catch crabs without a hook. Daddy A attached string to the ends of several pieces of rope and tied meat in the strings and we just threw the ropes over the sides of the dock. The timing mechanism to pull them up was when

Daddy A finished a beer. We wrapped it up when the six pack was gone. He was a great, fun loving guy. Nana set the example for all of us for our faith lives.

CHAPTER TWO

COLLEGE, 1964-69

I decided to attend Colorado State University. I visited CSU and the University of Colorado. We had to attend an in-state university because of the cost. When I was a junior in High School Nana told me that a lady who often came see her, a Mrs. Pape, could get me into West Point. I was an average student in High School and terrible in math because I never studied and the step-by-step process that math required was boring to me. Mrs. Pape was the widow of General Pape and had been at Pearl Harbor on December 7th, 1941. She had a lot of pull and later in my life I became convinced she could have gotten me into the Academy. I took several math classes in college and did well because I studied. Had I gone to West Point I am sure I would have been placed in the bottom math class, as they section or group students in the hard science and math classes based on ability. When I taught at Air Force years later, I saw how the faculty worked with students who were struggling, and I became convinced I could have made it. I guess I have a little regret about not going to Army, but one of the 10 proudest moments of my life is when my son Rob entered with the class of 1998.

I went with him to R-Day (registration). We were marched in the gym, given an orientation on what was going to happen that day and then a cadet wearing a red sash walked out and said: "Class of 1998 you have one minute to say goodbye to your parents." I turned to Rob, and he had crocodile tears in his eyes, my always self-reliant brilliant son. We talked later about R day later and he did fine. At the end of the first day the new plebes take their oath of office. My heart fluttered when the Commandant explained to the kids that the oath, they were about to take was not the one used in the active Army, but the same as the one taken by Lee, Grant, Pershing, Patton, and MacArthur on that exact same field. The plebes then paraded by, and I was amazed at how good they looked. Rob excelled at West Point; he had a few occasional disciplinary problems as I surely would have had. I always felt close to West Point from an early age when I would watch a television series called West Point until the present day. Beat Navy!

God had a plan; CSU was perfect for me. I majored in history studying under the embryonic history faculty that was just expanding to cover the growing number of liberal arts students. CSU had been a civil engineering, vet med, range and forest management school and they were recognized for their excellence in those areas. I had some great profs-Art Worrall, Jim Jordan, and others. They taught me the fundamentals.

I enjoyed college, I was a member of the Phi Kappa Alpha fraternity and lived off campus in a big old stone house with 10 or so other guys. I made some dear friends there. In the spring and summer, we would play volleyball in the yard. CSU basketball was great as we went to the 32 team NCAA tournament twice when I was there. I saw may future professionals play, both football and basketball. Oscar Reed played RB for the Vikings, Lawrence McCutcheon played for the Rams, Lonnie Wright was a phenomenal athlete who played professionally for both the Broncos and the Nuggets, Bob Rule played for the Supersonics and led the league in scoring one year and many others.

I dated a lot when I had a car which was only when I could pay for the gas and the insurance and late my junior year, I met Marilyn. She was a responsible, organized person who was exactly what I needed at that time. She was fun to be around as well. We dated until we both were in graduate school, and we were married in 1969. She had already started grad school as I was finishing my senior year. So, the result was when we were married, I had one quarter to finish my degree as she had already graduated. Her father Glen was a prince of a guy who was clever with both money and working with his hands. He had a kind heart. Although we divorced later, I will always respect Marilyn.

After I went to college my reliance on God and regular attendance at mass was spotty. God Bless Marilyn, who converted to Catholicism, she got us to mass regularly after the boys were born. One of my real regrets was I didn't help her very much; my faith example was real poor. I regret that to this day.

Another of my regrets was my treatment of my brother. I was 4 years older than him and most of our childhood, I could easily beat him, so I considered him a nuisance more than anything. I remember the day we got into one of our weekly fights and he held his own. Life would be different from now on. We visited Mike several times, usually in conjunction with a move. He and his wife Cheryl were always very gracious. Mike had become a Vice President at Braddock Dunn and Mac-Donald, a defense contractor. Mike and Cheryl started in D.C. and then were transferred to New Mexico where Mike supervised the company's skunk works-the division that regularly took on new and unique challenges. Mike when on to become the President and CEO of an energy company in Austin Texas and then continued his career as the President of Imprimis Inc, a Cyber Security Company. I always thought Mike was dumb when we were kids. He sure proved me very wrong, he would earn a master's degree in mechanical engineering and have incredible success in his professional career. Mike has that trait that I preached to every officer I counseled: persistence. My brother will patiently and tenaciously grab hold of a challenge and stay with it, regardless of the cost, until it is accomplished.

Fear is part of life, as is failure. But you don't know what you can do or not do until you try. If you fail, learn from it, and move on. When I was in the Army, I really made an effort to counsel my officers. I was honest with them, to the point of telling them where I would place them in my senior rater profile. The attribute I preached repeatedly was persistence. Try and if you fail, ok, get better. When Rob got the scholarship to Stanford, he asked for my advice, and I told him "Follow your heart". That move really cost him personally, but it ended up a great experience. When my son Sean wanted to go to Kaiser University to follow his golf dream, I was happy to support him even though I thought his curriculum didn't seem very college like. Short swing fundamentals does not seem like a college class to me although if you are playing golf, it's necessary. All my boys are examples of following their hearts and doing it their way, as I did. My greatest legacy is my boys.

After Mom, Dad, Mike, and I lived in Washington DC we always had a dog. In DC we had a boxer whose name was Rex, Dad seemed to like that name and later he would name a Lab we had in Colorado, Rex. The Washington Rex was a sweet dog and very disobedient. When I went to college, we adopted a stray mutt at the Fraternity house who we named Lucille. Lucy was a saint but when keeping her in the fraternity house became an issue, she found a new home with Mom and Dad. So, for a while Nana and Gomp-Gomp had two dogs. When we were assigned to El Paso in the early 1970's Lucy went with us. She was old by that time. The night Rob was born I came home late from the hospital and couldn't find Lucy. She had curled herself up by a 10' brick wall in our back yard and died. She was a joy. By this time Dad had the Lab Rex who was a sweet old boy and who loved to wander the woods around Dad's house. Rex tried to fight off the bears that raided Dad's trash cans with minimal success. Rex left a legacy in our family as my brother and I each have had several Labrador Retrievers. They are the best.

Fighting was just part of our lives especially when we got into our teens. One time when a friend and I were walking home from a football game, three guys drove by us and stopped, it was clear from the start that they were looking for a fight. I decided 3 against one wasn't very good odds so I just stood there. My friend had run. One guy took a 2x4 and hit me over the back; they then ran off. When I got home, Dad was furious that I didn't fight back. I learned my lesson. We fought all the way through high school, sometimes even in class. After I had graduated, I was at the St Mary's – Cheyenne Mountain football game. College was still a week away. I was in the stands enjoying the game as we were winning, when a guy came up to me and said there were some Cheyenne Mountain Seniors fighting with my brother. Mike was a freshman and had been one of the last cuts from the varsity. He went on to be a great end for St Mary's. Anyway, I flew out of the stands, down the hill behind the stands and saw this guy talking very loudly with my brother. He didn't have a chance. I came out of the blue and knocked the guy on his butt. Mike was furious with me. That was probably the last fight I had.

Mike and I were both growing teenagers and our favorite thing in the world was to sleep. But every Saturday morning, Dad would get us up at 0800. We would eat breakfast and get to it. Dad was a real handyman and our chores included everything from sweeping to helping him build a cabin in the mountains. I didn't like working with Dad and I am now regretful that I didn't learn more from him. It seemed like we worked to time, not to an objective where we could stop when the job was done. One thing I did admire about my dad is he would try anything. He finished our basement in every house we lived in, and he loved to successfully tinker. I always tried to give my boys tasks to complete rather than pinning them down for a certain amount of time. They may debate that.

After we got into High School, we were encouraged to get a job. The situation became serious my senior year of High School when I was informed that I had to make the money for my spending money in college. I dug ditches for $2 and hour for about 6 weeks and then I waxed cars in the neighborhood for $10 apiece. The waxing business was hard work. You really had to rub to get that paste wax in. Business was pretty good.

After my Freshman year in college Mom found me a job with the City of Colorado Springs reading utility meters. Being a meter reader was a great job. Our supervisor Mr. Tevebald was a great guy. After about 2 weeks on the job my partner, Greg Johnson, and I, got pretty good. Since we were temporary help, we would split the book of accounts that a regular guy would have. We always were done in less than 4 hours, sometimes less than an hour. Our first time we had taken the books in when we were finished at 10 in the morning, and we got chewed out for coming in so early. So, our practice became to finish and then show up at my house to play wiffle ball or to go to Greg's and lift weights. I read meters all through college, it was a great job. I can still read an electric meter with all its dials.

Well, the good old days so to speak were gone. High School had been great; had a car (it may have been 15 years old, but it ran great), a nice girl friend Nancy Cook who dumped me after we graduated and I got to play a lot of sports, not well, but I got to play. I enjoyed Colorado State University. I did well academically, and I really enjoyed my studies. I loved history, assimilating lots of facts and then developing trends from them. I especially liked military history which would serve me well later. I loved going to basketball games and football games. CSU was ok in football and my junior year we beat Wyoming with a trick play. Wyoming was the #4 team in the country and had an all-American halfback named Jim Kiick who would later play for the Miami Dolphins. Our basketball teams were good; they were invited to the NCAA tournament 3 of the years I was there. My junior year, 1967, they won three games in the tournament and had they beaten Drake in the 4th game, they would have played UCLA and Lew Alcindor for the national championship. In 1966, they played Texas Western University twice. They lost to them in Ft Collins on a miracle shot by Bobby Joe Hill at the buzzer. One of my fraternity brothers, Jim Favor, was an announcer for the CSU radio station and he got a van, and we all went to the game in El Paso. We picked up Uncle Skee and watched our beloved Rams get pulverized. Texas Western was good, and it gave me satisfaction to see them win the national championship. Life in the fraternity was great and I made some lifelong friends, Daryl Youngstrum, Jim Cowsert and Louis Bragaw.

My junior year I met Marilyn Foster. Several of the brothers in the house had recommended that I ask her out. She was a lot of fun, a very determined woman. We got along great, and I would rely on her judgment for a long time. She was Scottish and she had a common sense that I needed.

We were married in 1969, in Long Beach California by one of Mom and Dad's friends, Father Stegman, a Franciscan priest. I had known Father for years and loved him; he always had a twinkle in his eye and laughed all the time. We then went on our honeymoon up to San Francisco where we took in a Giants game. It was bitterly cold, and I think we left the game early, but I got to see the great Willie Mays play, even though he struck out 4 times in the game. Marilyn didn't mind going to baseball games and one time we saw the Braves play the Dodgers. Henry Aaron hit a home run off Al Downing who was the same pitcher he would later hit his historic 715th home run off, breaking the record for home runs set earlier by Babe Ruth who hit 714 in his career.

CHAPTER THREE

FORT BLISS, TEXAS, 1970-71

Package Training

Marilyn and I reported into Ft Bliss after the honeymoon. Because I went on active duty as a First Lieutenant, I never went to the Officer's Basic Course instead joining an activating Chaparral-Vulcan battalion that would conduct its initial training at Ft Bliss and then deploy to the 3d Armored Division in Germany. We first attended about an 8-week course that included some tactics and a great deal of hardware training. At first, I was okay on the hardware training, but struggled to see the big picture sometimes when we were crawling around on the guns. I would take a correspondence course later and get good on the Vulcan and Chaparral. What was missing in that training was a clear picture of what we could do for the division; it seemed like all we were going to do was chase tanks and hope for the best. So, life in the battalion became ultimately a test of obedience in the sense there were very few lanes established to operate in. Upon reflection, I am convinced nobody knew what they were doing.

Because I had accrued rank in graduate school since I was a regular officer, Major Lord our executive officer decided to make me the adjutant. I begged to go to a battery even agreeing to have a junior officer as the Executive Officer ahead of me. Lord said historians can write, so the S-1 I became. It would be my last job outside operations. After we graduated from the Automatic Weapons course, we trained for 12 weeks in the desert north of Ft Bliss, driving around and feeling very proud of ourselves. The last 2 weeks of our collective training was spent preparing for a mounted review where all the vehicles in the battalion would pass in front of the reviewing stand. We trained and trained and trained for this review. I remember as the adjutant I had to strut from the right front of the formation to its center on foot, about 200 yards. It seemed like it took me forever. We then passed in review and our Battalion Commander LTC Partridge, attempting to one up the previous battalions, had a Vulcan, a Chaparral, an APC and a M48 tank charge the reviewing stand at the end of the ceremony, symbolizing Air Defense joining the Combined Arms team in the 3d Armored. We had borrowed the tank from the museum at White Sands, New Mexico as there were no tanks at Ft Bliss. The old girl had driven the 50plus miles south to Ft Bliss, and after the ceremony it was parked in the battalion motor pool. When it came time to return the tank, it wouldn't start. It had done its job. We tried everything but we didn't have a recovery vehicle big enough to pull it. Armor officers from all over Ft Bliss attempted to apply their magic to no avail. So, when we cleared post, we just left it out on the pavement. The inspectors asked our property book warrant, Mr.

Robinson who owned the tank, and Robbie replied "dunno". In my subsequent assignments I always wanted to check to see if the tank was still there, but never got around to it.

CHAPTER FOUR

BUDINGEN, GERMANY 1970-73

We took some leave and went to both our homes. We were flying out of Newark NJ. We shipped our car and then went to the military airport. It was a military commercial flight, and we were required to wear our Class "A" uniform. The overheads were tiny, so there was no place to put our blouses or wheel hats (no one had told us we could have worn service caps which would have been a lot better). We arrived in Germany exhausted and were bused to Budingen where we were assigned.

Budingen is located about half -way between Fulda and Frankfurt in a northeasterly direction. It was a nice enough town but in the early seventies the attitude of the Germans was they were sick of us. The Russians hadn't come, and the Americans occupied some prime real estate. I would work this very same problem at USAREUR almost 30 years later but by then Americans had become so much a part of the German economy that they were writing letters and petitioning us to stay.

They bused us to the officer's club which was an old house with an adjoining clay tennis court. We all met in the dining room. We had sent an officer ahead with money for deposits to get us apartments. The 9th Cavalry Squadron also occupied Budingen and when the artillery battalion that we replaced moved out, the Cav took over all the quarters. Marilyn and I were told since we didn't have kids yet that we were at the bottom of the priority list and our temporary quarters was a bedroom upstairs. Marilyn cried most of the night, it was a miserable night exacerbated by a roaring welcoming party downstairs.

We found an apartment within a week, one of the NCOs gave me a tip. It was in a little berg about 5KM from post. Our landlords spoke no English and we spoke no German. It was an amazing demonstration of how you can communicate with sign language and a few words. Our two-room apartment and the kitchen were on one level and the bathroom was in the basement. That bathroom was not heated, and we took many a cold shower. Our landlords were great people and we hated to leave them after about six months. We had been assigned quarters on post, a two-bedroom apartment right outside the front gate. It seemed like it was palatial. We lived happily there for 2 1/2 years.

We had a chance to travel a lot that first tour. We went to France, Spain, Greece, and Switzerland. In Budingen, we were always treated courteously but I always had the impression that they considered us the ugly Americans. We went to dinner frequently in the local area and played double tennis at the club in the summer. We socialized with the other couples in our apartment complex and the big adventure was with the American dollar being worth over 4.5 German marks, one could get stuff cheap. Almost everybody bought a Triumph, MG, Fiat, BMW, or Volvo. Marilyn and I bought a Porsche 914 for $3300, brand new. We went to pick it up and were told they had to finish detailing the car, which for Germans is a big deal. They had a candy apple red Porsche 911 in the show room. It was so beautiful I almost drooled over it. I started dreaming, but $9300 was a fortune in those days. Our Porsche was a great car; it was rock solid at 95mph on the autobahns and had a surprising amount of trunk room. I sold it to another officer at our next assignment at Ft Bliss and he kept it for over 20 years. The problem was that 70mph was just between 3d and 4th gear. Maintenance was super expensive as well.

As I started out my career, I had very few life goals. I just wanted to be all in at being an Army Officer no matter the personal cost. I worked constantly-I was even in the top 10% of my Advanced Course and at the Command and General Staff College. On weekends when the boys were younger, I would come home exhausted. I wanted to be the first one to work and the last one to leave. In some ways it felt unnatural, and I really didn't think about how I was alone in the office, and no one noticed, so it really didn't matter. I just wanted to be ready. I have never been professionally happier that when we were at US Army Europe in Heidelberg. On weekdays, I got up at 4:30 AM and usually got home at 8PM. I worked every weekend except for a handful. By working a weekend, I mean 9-5 on Saturday and 12-5 on Sunday except when we had a deployment. When I was at USAREUR we had one a month for the 18 months. I had a secure telephone in my quarters and everyone in European Command knew that number and they did not hesitate to call at any time day or night. I just loved it. I didn't realize my balance was totally gone, but it was what the job called for.

My first boss, MG Dick Davis came in my office one day and told me that he was being considered for command of a Division. General Davis was a great guy, very humble but the finest staff officer I have ever known. He humbly told me that he didn't think he would be selected, but if he was, he would like me to be his Chief of Staff. An Air Defender as the Chief of an Infantry Division! It was the highest compliment I was ever paid in the Army. Well, he didn't get it, but I admire him to this day.

Balance is the key to life. We need to balance our mental, spiritual, and physical requirements. I think I did ok with the mental and I did continue to work out, but I didn't get enough sleep and spiritually, other than halfhearted attendance at mass, I had no spiritual life. I found it hard to have fun to relax without drinking. Many times, Marilyn would want to do something on the weekend, and I would fight her as I was just too tired. She eventually said to heck with it, and I was given the option of staying alone at home or going with the rest of the family.

By the end of my first 5 years in the Army, the officer core underwent 3 Reduction in Force (RIF) initiatives. The Army was over 600,000 men but the size of the officer corps was disproportional as many officers were hold overs from the Vietnam War. The first RIF came a year after we arrived in Germany. We had 4 Battery Commanders and the S-3, the operations officer, eliminated from the service. I was the new guy on the block, but trying to learn from everyone I met, most of these guys left a lot to be desired in terms of being a leader and officer. So, I guess I wasn't surprised. Our battalion was only authorized 14 Captains and 2 Majors so the elimination of 5 officers really hurt us. The Battalion Commander took the guys with the most experience and moved them to command batteries. The S—3 shop was empty except for our operations NCO, Jim Hunt, who was one of the best NCOs I had ever served with during my career. Fortunately, we had a promotable Captain assigned to the battalion. LTC Partridge tried to get him frocked or authorized to wear the rank before he was promoted, but he was at the bottom of the promotion sequence list and estimates were it would be over 3 years before he was authorized to wear the new rank. If he had been within a year of promotion, getting him frocked might have been more successful. Anyway, I was moved to the S-3 shop as the Assistant S-3 and sat in a desk opposite MSG Jim Hunt who spent his days teaching me what I should know from basic military skills to how to run an S-3 operation.

Our S-3 was a nervous guy, his hand shook a lot and he chain smoked. About this time, we got a new battalion Commander, LTC Dick Jewett, who was an awesome guy. A few months after he took command, we got tasked with supplying a Major to Frankfurt for 6 months. Our S-3 was the only guy available so off he went. LTC Jewett called me in the day he left and told me I was the S-3 and to move out.

I don't remember doing anything spectacular as the S-3 as we didn't train very well in the post-Vietnam Army. Viet Nam was a terrible war for the Army. My battalion was not trained well; sure, we would drive around a lot, but we were not a cohesive force; we really didn't know what to do. In Viet Nam, the guys adapted to the situation and tried to make the best out a very poor political strategy. The objective became body counts instead of pacification and winning the hearts and minds of the people. So, we crashed through the jungle and didn't get much done. When the North Vietnamese Army did show itself like during the Tet offensive, we kicked their tails. I wasn't conscious of it at the time, but I had a feeling that something wasn't right. That would all be rectified in the 1980's.

When it came time to transfer to my first battery, I re-inventoried the equipment that I was signed for in the S-3 shop. I had been very careful with my initial inventory as I had just completed an investigation into millions of dollars of missing equipment in the battalion from our move to Germany. When we arrived in Budingen, the plan was to take 30 days to carefully up pack the Conex containers that we used to ship our stuff to Germany. When LTC Partridge reported to the division headquarters for the first time he was told that 30 days was way too long, and we needed to be combat ready in less than 2 weeks. Guys just ripped stuff out of the containers and worked late into the nights. The supply system was a little undependable then, so if a unit was short something, they would just "borrow" it from a sister unit. I got tasked with the survey as I was the only guy in the battalion that was not missing anything. I discovered that the Conex's were unattended for a while when they were in port and the Army wrote all the losses off.

Anyway, back to my property survey as the incoming Assistant S-3. In my initial survey, I discovered that a tent on the books that we never used, had a liner and the liner was missing. Trading was big in those days; a bottle of bourbon could get one a part for an APC (which I did once) or I hoped a tent liner. I had no luck finding anyone interested in bartering. So, my driver and I drove our jeep with a covered trailer into the

USAREUR supply depot and threw a GP small tent liner into the trailer and waved to the guard as we left.

In retrospect, I should have been in the Infantry or Armor. I liked the way they talked, their direct manner, their toughness. I served 3 years in the 3d Armored Division and 5 years in the 24th Infantry Division, went on over a dozen rotations to the National Training Center where I had to interface with combat arms guys all the time. When I was in the Pentagon where we didn't wear branch insignia, everybody thought I was an Infantryman. I recommended to both my older sons that they go into the Infantry and they both did and served well with 6 combat tours between them.

Back to Budingen. Just as I was ending my tour in hell as the S-1, I applied to go to Airborne school. US Army Europe had an airborne school in Mainz Germany where the 3d Brigade of the 8th Division was stationed. The 3d Brigade was an airborne brigade and they needed a place to get their replacements jump qualified. I spent every free minute before going getting into shape, running in boots, and working on my pullups. I showed up in Mainz with an only slightly broken in pair of jump boots. I was a Captain and there was one other Captain in the class and since he was Infantry, they made him class leader. Every morning at formation he would report the students ready for training and he had to exchange places with a Black Hat NCO who was on the right flank of the formation. Our Captain was an in-shape guy. The Black Hat NCO appeared to be overweight but for three weeks in a row, he beat the Captain switching places in the formation which were about 10 yards apart. The Black Hat should have been playing in the NFL, he sure had the size and speed.

Jump school went as it always did. Ground training in week 1; week 2 was tower jumping and week three was jump week. We did not have 250' towers in Mainz that they had at Fort Benning, so we doubled our jumps out of the 34' tower. We were all cinched up in our harnesses; we waddled around like ducks. We would jump out of the tower and then waddle to the Black Hat instructor who was sitting in the shade in a little hut. We had to report to him precisely: "Roster number 61 Sergeant" (can you believe that I still remember my roster number from jump school). The instructor would then tell us our head was up and our feet apart and our response was "Clear Sergeant, Airborne". Any failure to respond correctly resulted in 10 squats as we couldn't do pushups in our harnesses. The 10th day in jump school was a big day as it was the last chance for some of my classmates to do the 6 pull ups. The Black Hats were a little lenient and everybody qualified to jump. On our 10th morning we ran 5 miles at an airborne shuffle pace. I was glad when it was over, but some guys suffered. Remember, PT was just coming back in the Army, we wouldn't run regularly as a unit until I was a battery commander.

Jump week was exciting. We had guys from Germany, England and several other countries who came to jump with us and get their American jump wings. There was a British NCO who had over 800 jumps, impressive.. Before our third jump while we were waiting on the tarmac to load the plane, I sat opposite a German Sergeant Major. Making nervous talk I asked him how many jumps he had; he replied: "not many", around 125. I then asked him when he first jumped and he replied "Crete, 1942". The Germans had jumped into Crete in WWII, and it was a blood bath. So, I said to him "Tough fight, huh?", to which he responded with a head nod in the affirmative.

We were jumping in the fall; the leaves were starting to turn, and it was chilly at night. On my first jump, being a Captain, I was the stick leader, the first dude out the door. When we reached the drop zone the jump master had me stand in the door even though it would be a while before we jumped. Our class leader, the Infantry Captain was in the opposite door. The jump master grabbed me, and I almost jumped, but he held me back and told me to look at the lights in the door and when the green light came on to jump. I looked down and could see the features of the terrain below. It was raining but at 800 feet, the rain was snow. The light turned and I jumped. I guess my training hadn't been ingrained in me because I forgot everything during the first four seconds which are important in a parachute jump. One wants to count to 4 as a reminder your chute should be deploying, and you want to ensure that your feet at together so the prop blast from the airplane doesn't spin you around and get your risers tangled.

Due to the grace of God, my chute popped, and I had the presence to check around me. The 6th guy from my stick, an Infantry Lieutenant named Jesse Johnson, had what they call a Mae West; his risers had wrapped over his chute so it couldn't open. It was his first jump; he had no idea how fast he should be falling. I looked down and saw the ambulance headed towards where he would land. We all started screaming "Pull your reserve" and nervously continued to watch our classmate. Jesse finally understood what was happening and popped his reserve. They taught us that one had to feed the reserve out until it caught the wind. Jesse's reserve just popped out; he swung to the left, then the right and hit the ground. He was fine.

With Jesse safe I returned to my own situation. I was 125 feet from the ground. At this point of a jump, we were taught to cock our parachutes into the wind to slow our descent a little. We were jumping with T-10 parachutes the same ones used in WWII and they were designed to get a trooper to the ground as quickly as possible, hopefully safely. The Mainz jump school prided themselves on not popping smoke on the ground as they did at Ft Benning so the students could know which way the wind was blowing and cock their chutes appropriately. I looked at my feet and thought I should pull on my left riser; when I did, I realized I was with the wind, gaining speed. As I let it go and started to grab my other riser, I hit the ground hard, but I did a parachute landing fall, a technique we were taught to lessen the impact of the fall. The ground was wet, it was raining and just down from a little plateau that I had landed on, our class leader was screaming in pain: he had broken his leg in three places. What a start.

Our second jump the next day was uneventful except for an Infantry Lieutenant who had barely passed the pull up requirement on day 10, checked the canopy on his chute just after he exited the plane and noticed that his chute was starting to tear apart from the apex of the chute down. He pulled his reserve, and he was fine. On our third jump, we had a hung jumper; the guy jumped out of the plane and his chute didn't deploy so he was flying along with the plane. The Black Hats tried to pull the guy back in but when they couldn't they just cut him loose and told him to pull his reserve. He was fine.

Our fifth jump finally came. It was a beautiful sunny day. I was in the back of the stick and when I jumped everything was just perfect: I kept my feet together, checked my chute when it deployed and slipped the correct way as I approached the ground. There was almost no wind and I landed softly and perfectly. I stood up, patted myself to insure I was all still there and then screamed "Airborne." I got my wings at graduation and quickly had then sewn on a uniform. The first time I saw LTC Partridge he yelled out "Airborne" and enthusiastically greeted me. Jumping was only part of being airborne I learned as I studied airborne operations later. Airborne guys were tough and couldn't be beat despite the circumstances. I always tried to have that attitude. Airborne school for me was a big step forward in my maturation as a soldier. I had faced danger and had overcome my fears.

I took command of A Battery, replacing a guy who was an Airborne Ranger which was unusual at that time in a non-Infantry job. I guess the best way to describe the situation is the unit had low morale. So, I started talking to everyone, starting with my 1st Sergeant, Al Conrad. He came into my office and bluntly asked me "Well Captain, how are we going to run this thing". I replied that I was going to command the battery and he was going to run the battery, a statement which prompted a long conversation. The problem was in those days, the First Sergeants were the administrators of the Army. They did the morning report every morning which accounted for every soldier in the battery. 1st Sergeant Conrad was a super administrator, so I didn't want to mess with that arrangement. After studying the personnel of the battery and talking around I discovered I had 2-3 Sergeants who were presently squad leaders who would make great platoon sergeants. 1st Sergeant Conrad was getting ready to retire so I decided that I would appoint a "Field" 1SG, the guy who would get things done outside of the orderly room. I selected PSG Alphonsus

Irving, a mountain of the man 6'4" and probably weighed over 270 pounds. PSG Irving had a sunny, happy disposition and he was a man who could laugh about himself. But when it came time for disciple, he did not hold back. The NCOs would run that unit and I was blessed with some real good ones.

US Army Europe, in fact the whole Army, was addressing the black acceptance issue. Remember, we were less than 30 years from WWII where black troops were totally segregated into separate units, where many of them performed heroically. We took some sensitivity classes which focused primarily on understanding terms that offended black people. I got the battery together, told them I would not tolerate any offensive conduct towards anyone and reaffirmed my belief, taught to me primarily by my grandfather and mother that everyone would be treated the same. I was fortunate, I had 16 talented black soldiers and I did not hesitate to put them in leadership positions. 1SG Irving was black, two of my four PSGs were black, my training NCO was black as well as my APC driver. I made it clear that if a soldier had a problem, I wanted it brought up the chain of command. We never had racial problems that some of the other units had, and I thank the black soldiers in my unit for doing what was right.

The big emphasis was on administration. There was a Best Company program in V Corps; the outfit that we belonged to which had 75,000 soldiers assigned to it. To prepare us for this inspection, LTC Jewell started a best battery program to prepare us for the Corps inspection. I was in command for 20 months of best battery inspections and my battery won it 16 times; HQ, B, C, and D batteries won it once each. When the Corps boys showed up, we won it for the entire Corps. The boss was excited.

We didn't train much and when we did, we just followed tanks around on the paved roads to avoid maneuver damage. The biggest training event is when we went to Todendorf, which was a firing range on the North Sea to fire our Vulcans. We were up there for two weeks. The first week we practiced and the second week, guys from USAREUR would come evaluate our shooting which was called Annual Service Practice. The Vulcan is a gatling gun and makes LOTS of noise when it fires. We had no guidance on hearing protection and one day on the range, I felt something sticky on the side of my face. I reached up and it was blood, I was bleeding out of my right ear. The Army got smart about hearing protection soon after that but for me the damage had been done.

Our schedule was routine day-to-day in the battery, so we played football and lots of softball after work. Marilyn and I had plenty of time for leave and we visited Paris, Spanish Beaches, Greece, Berlin, Switzerland, and Austria. I almost starved in Greece as there was nothing on a Greek menu that appealed to me. I finally discovered a noodle dish with cheese on the top and I lived on it the rest of the trip.

When it was time to go back to the states, we had to first drive our cars to the port of Bremerhaven where they were shipped. We got all our paperwork together and five of us drove in convoy up to the port with a great guy Ted Boss, who had a big old Mercedes that would carry us back to Budingen. We showed up the night before and left our cars in line and went to have dinner. We had heard about contractors who were guys hired to ship cars did some pretty shady things at the port. So, I decided to sleep in the back of Jim Starkey's Peugeot station wagon. When I went to sleep our first car was number 35 or so in line. When I woke up the next morning, it was number 75! What had happened is during the night the contractors had brought in more cars. The original line had been parallel, one care behind the other. The contractors took cars they had in line and re-parked them diagonally so they could get 3 cars into the space of one. We were very upset, but our anger evaporated when they opened the gate and we learned there was one line for contractors and another for servicemen who were with their cars. We moved into the right line, and we started at number 3 in our line. We all checked in the office where the paperwork was processed, and keys turned over to the Army for shipment. Four of us were done but the last guy in our party, CW4 Ted Doderline had forgotten his orders. He had all the other paperwork, but he had forgotten to include his orders which was the authorization essentially to ship the car. I never forgot the professionalism of the NCO who was taking care of the paperwork. He reached under his counter, pulled out a large manila envelope and started writing on it. He handed it to Ted and said "As soon as you get home, put two copies of your orders in this envelope and mail it to me. I will hold your paperwork until your orders arrive. Your car will be on the same ship as your buddies." We all stood there dumb founded and relieved. What a great example of professionalism, the overcoming of obstacles to reach the objective.

    The big thing about coming home is we got to fly commercial. It was great, civilian clothes, booze, we were very comfortable. On the flight home, I reflected how much the world had changed in the less than 20 years since I had been to Germany. When we went to Germany in the 1950's, the only way to get there was by ship. We took old troop transports-the *Randal* one way and the *Darby* the other. I remember being cramped on the trip and a little bored, but the Captain knew that so one day he had us all come to the bridge. We were in the North Sea and there was some turbulence, and the bow of the ship was actually dipping under water and we took on the big waves. It scared me to death until the Captain assured me that we weren't going to sink. My other memory is we had an abandon ship drill both going and coming. Everyone had to be trained on where to go if the ship was sinking. The families were positioned in the middle of the ship where the lifeboats were. Between the families on either end of the ship were two sailors with Thompson sub-machineguns. I asked Dad why they were there and what their job was, and he explained that the families had priority for the larger lifeboats and the sailors would use life rafts which were positioned towards the ends of the ship. The sailors with the guns were there to ensure no sailor tried to get in a lifeboat. If one tried, he would be warned then shot. I was sure glad we didn't sink either way. I remember coming home from Germany and we arrived at night. We sailed right into New York city, right past the statue of Liberty. It was quite spectacular.

Anyway, we got home landing in Newark, NJ. The Porsche made it through fine. I washed it before our trip west, worried about salt getting into it from the sea voyage. The trip to Colorado and California went fine except for the fact that 70MPH was between 3d and 4th gears. I was either revving the car's RPMs way up or I was clogging along. That fact plus the expensive maintenance costs were cause for me to sell it once we arrived at Ft Bliss. It was a great car. In Wyoming, where the maximum speed was 75MPH, it did just fine.

We had a nice visit with Mom and Dad at the cabin as we called it-it was over 4000 square feet. I remember watching TV and this new station had been created called ESPN. They talked to coaches and players and gave game highlights on Sports Center which was super. The rest of the time they had programming that included ping-pong tournaments, bowling, and a bunch of other bizarre stuff. I would remember this different ESPN programming in 2020 during the COVID pandemic when there were no sports for a time and SC covered corn hole championships and wrestling once again.

Marilyn's parents, Glen and Marge were fine. Glen had been the secretary-treasurer for an electric company and was a shrewd investor. He had bought two lots in Marina Del Rey, a block from the beach and had built a neat house on the first property. Glen and his wife Marge lived on the 2d floor which I remember being about 2000 square feet. They rented an apartment below and had a 2-car garage in the back of the house. Glen would eventually sell those two lots when he retired after Marina Del Rey was in full recovery and became a desired location and retired. Glen always had a project going. He was an incredibly patient man who planned meticulously. I remember after they had moved, he was planning a fence around their new home, and his design was amazing. Marge was the perfect housekeeper who insured all in the house was ship shape all the time.

CHAPTER FIVE

FORT BLISS, TEXAS, 1973-76

It's amazing what you can remember and can't remember. We got to Ft Bliss and moved into a nice rental house on Chateau street in El Paso. Marilyn worked and I went to the advanced course. That 9 months was a great time; made a bunch of good friends and we studied and partied together. My biggest recollections from the advanced course were when about half done, Col Jim Kilgore the Director of Tactics, who I would work for later, called us all in to announce that the advanced course would now be dedicated to preparing us to be battery commanders. He asked for a show of hands of how many guys had commanded before. 72 of 75 hands went up. Of those guys who had commanded over 60% had been relieved. Back then this wasn't fatal as I know some of those guys that had very successful careers-many got promoted to LTC. Air Defense did eat its young back then.

The second recollection was the announcement that since they didn't have enough coursework for us to do, they decided that we would all become Prefix-5 qualified, meaning that we would be trained in nuclear fallout prediction, amongst other things. I remember the course being several months. Our instructor was a Greek chemical corps Captain who had a great sense of humor. I stumbled with the math at first, but then I broke down and bought a Texas Instruments Calculator and all went well from there. The nuclear threat was real back then and would not dissipate until the 1990's.

They really didn't have enough to keep us occupied so they announced one day that we were all going to take a class at the University of Texas at El Paso to begin our master's degrees. Well, I already had a Masters, so I signed up for tennis at UTEP. I was told that was a no go, so I signed up for auto mechanics at the community college. I was told that was not possible either, but I asked to see the Division Chief of the Leadership Division, an LTC, to appeal my case. After several days I saw him and after arguing the Army was all about maintenance, I got permission to attend the class. Unfortunately, in the interim, the class was closed.

Since I had to take something, I signed up for a management class at the community college. I went to the first class which was held in one of the barracks buildings on Logan Heights and we were asked to write down a little on our backgrounds and then we turned in the papers. After the class, the instructor, "Red", who was a CSU grad, asked me to see him for a second. He asked what are you doing here? I told him and then he said, tell you what, you have an A in the class, and you don't have to come again. Well, I wanted to learn so I asked him if I could come to class and that I wouldn't give him any trouble. He said ok, and I got an A.

After the advanced course, I was assigned to the Tactics Department as a Forward Area Weapons instructor. Back then officers with experience in Chaparral/Vulcan were still rare. General LeVan had moved the Tactics Department from the headquarters, building 2, to building 1 a block down the street that had been General Pershing's headquarters at Ft Bliss where he staged before going to chase Poncho Villa. We were really squeezed in. All the instructors, probably 50 of us were on the same floor. They brought in 4-foot-high dividers to divide the sections. You could easily see what everyone else was doing with one glance. Privacy was not important until later in my career. At ROTC advanced camp, I had lived in a WWII barracks where there were 40 guys on each of the 2 floors in an open bay. The bathrooms were the same way-all the toilets and showers had no dividers or curtains to provide privacy.

Once one was assigned as an instructor, the first thing you had to do was pass a murder board before you taught. You picked the subject and after graduating from the Instructor Training Course, you put together and pitched the class. I picked Reconnaissance, Selection and Occupation of position. I didn't want to pick a Tactics subject as I didn't want to get into a debate. RSOP was clear; it was pretty much black and white how you did it.

I finally was ready after hours of practice. I had my attention step and felt pretty good. Normally the Chiefs of the Tactics and Leadership Divisions, 2 LTCs were the audience. As we were preparing to start, in walked MG LeVan. As I gave my class MG LeVan was fidgeting and mumbling. I just drove on through. At the end of the class, he talked to the two LTCs for a long time. I passed and later learned that that was my audition to become a briefing officer.

I taught tactics to the advanced and basic courses. It was a great time of my life as I was assigned as the FAW briefer for the Commanding General (who was a close friend of my Uncle's and Dad). Major General LeVan was trying to reinvent tactics for the newly formed Chaparral and Vulcan battalions. In retrospect, the General was using our briefing rehearsals to formulate ideas, so what was good one day was trash the next. So, when I would give a briefing there would be several guys in the back to record what the CG said. After the briefing, we would go back to the Tactics Department and go over the comments one by one. We finally got the brief close and one day the CG scheduled another practice. These sessions were General LeVan's thinking times and we often had others brief on concepts that the CG was interested in. Despite the fact these were practices, everything had to be polished and first class. One day, a young officer from the Directorate of Combat Developments briefed and he had very simple slides. LTC Jim Webb, my boss's boss, attended every briefing with me to provide top cover and the two of us were cringing at the briefer's informality. When he was done, the CG said: "Thank you for your effort". LTC Webb and I immediately looked at each other and said: "What the hell?" We had borne a lot of not so nice criticisms when we had done exactly what the CG said he wanted. We later learned the CG had been told that day that he was going to be promoted to LTG. Everything I learned from those tactical briefings I taught on the platform to the students. This whole effort gave me great satisfaction and was the basis for my interest in ADA tactics my whole career.

We had a great time on this tour. Marilyn and I bought a house in northeast El Paso and regretfully moved out of the house on Chateau. Our new home was a cute place and as I recall, it was about 1800 square feet-huge! By this time, we had sold the Porsche, and I was driving a 396cc Chevy Chevelle. We also had a nice Oldsmobile, so we were very happy and comfortable. That house will always be special as it was the house that we brought Robbie home to. One of the nice things during this time - period was Mexico was still open. We would drive into Juarez, have a very nice dinner with a few beers and we would buy a bottle of Rum on the way back to Texas. The whole night would cost about $10. We were living high on the hog. My pay had risen from about $750 a month as a First Lieutenant to over $2300 as a Captain.

Rob's birth was quite the event. Marilyn and I had gone through classes to enable me to help her with her labor (LeMas?) When we got to William Beaumont Army hospital, we were placed in a room with another lady with only a curtain dividing us. The other lady was in great pain and was moaning and occasionally crying out in pain. I coached Marilyn through, and she did great having Rob without any anesthetic. It was a proud day we brought him home, one of many times I would be proud of him later. My experience with Marilyn and Rob would serve us well 2 ½ years later when Mike was born.

Well, 1976 came around and I was due for an assignment. Branch called me and told me I was going to be assigned to Safeguard, a Strategic ADA System that had just been fielded in multiple sites in North Dakota. Marilyn, my California wife, was not happy. She finally calmed down when I agreed to buy a 4 - wheel drive vehicle. She was not happy though. In the meantime, I was working hard to get out of this assignment. I asked the Director to call branch and tell them of all the guys in the branch, I was not a scope dope, I was a forward area air defender. It did no good. Then one day I had a thought and I called branch. I talked to my assignment officer and told him that I was happy with Safeguard (a lie) but did he notice if I took the assignment when I was done, I would have 10 years in the Army without a short, or unaccompanied tour. There was a long pause of the phone and the guy told me he would get back to me fast. The next day he called back and told me I had been assigned as a Battery Commander that was taking a "package" of 30 operators and mechanics to Korea to convert Korea from basic (vacuum tube technology) to "Improved Hawk", solid state technology. I knew nothing about Hawk, but I knew I was going to learn fast.

CHAPTER SIX

KOREA, 1976-77

The packages, or groups of about 30 officers and enlisted guys, were training at a base camp called Tobin Wells, which is about 5 miles north of main Ft Bliss. The accommodations reminded me of our setup when we were standing up the Chaparral Vulcan battalion five years earlier: WWI buildings, no frills, lots of dirt and dust everywhere. They had concrete pads for the equipment and my package had our own dedicated system. I was riding a small Yamaha motorcycle and if I went to work in a car, since our new house was in northeast El Paso, I would have to drive all the way into Ft Bliss and then come back 5 miles north to get to the wells. Instead, I found a place on Railroad Drive in El Paso that had a crossing for maintenance work. I just hopped the tracks and took the tank trails, kind of cross country, into Tobin Wells every day on the Yamaha.

We trained for several months, and I spent my off time learning the system. When I was in my 70's, years later, I learned that I was an explorer, my primary motivation being to figure things out. I learned that the maintenance people had schematics of the system, so I often found myself in the maintenance shed going over the schematics. We passed our final crew drills and passed the evaluation of our ability to move the system at night, a skill I knew we would not need in Korea, where all the sites were permanent. You fought and died from you site. Dumb.

The package went to Korea a week or so before me. I left Marilyn and Rob with her parents in Los Angeles and took off.

I flew into Seoul and was met by the battalion commander who took me to Reno Hill where the battalion headquarters was located. The battalion commander told me that we were at DEFCON3; a few days earlier an American Army Major had gone into the DMZ to cut down a tree that was blocking the field of fire of a firing position. They had axes and other tools with them, and they were met by a larger party of North Koreans. Words were exchanged and the American Major was hacked to death by one of the North Koreans. We were collectively upset. Later, I saw the Corps Artillery plan for any offensive operation that might be considered. Artillerymen put a little one inch by one inch + on every target that they registered. The advantage of doing this is the firing solution-the azimuth and elevation of the gun had already been calculated and it saved time. When one looked at the map with the artillery plan for the DMZ, you could not see the map, there were so many +'s. We would have pounded the daylights out of them.

That night I had a few beers with the boys and came away very unimpressed. The next day my First Sergeant, Eddie Price came to Reno Hill with my weapon, helmet, and web gear. The Defcon 3 situation was suddenly very real. My jeep didn't have a spare tire on it-so I knew there were challenges ahead.

We got to Quan Duk where the battery was located. We had an administrative area with about 30 Quonset huts, and three permanent buildings-the BOQ, the E-7 and above hooch and the motor pool. We had a barber shop, small PX, a site maintenance facility with Korean government employees to man it, and a nice mess hall. It was a little city.

Up the hill from the admin area was the Tactical Site, located on the highest hill possible to eliminate clutter from entering our radars. The Pulse Acquisition radar was on the highest point on the site and the low altitude detection radar (CWAR) and the tracking radars (HIPIRS) were on the next ring down. The launchers were on the lowest level along with the dog training area.

Life in Korea for a commander was the wild, wild west. The Improved Hawk equipment arrived, and we transported it up to the Tac Site and we deployed the basic Hawk battery equipment to the end of the runway at Osan AFB, which was the headquarters for not only our Brigade but also for the Air Force boys in theater. Osan was about 30km from Quan Duc.

The situation in the battery when I showed up was bad. The battery had to be immediately ready for and air attack at any time, having the system ready to fire immediately for one week per month. The other three weeks were spent training and doing maintenance. With the current crisis, we were being asked to be ready as much as possible, which was a challenge. There were two lieutenants in the battery. One of them Jerry Noonan, had been living on the hill as the second officer, a West Pointer, could not pass the test to become a

Tactical Control Officer, the guy who directed the system in battle. All the soldiers in the basic battery were to stay in the battery until their time for reassignment came due, including the officers. Lt. Steve Gerhart, who came with me from Ft Bliss was an excellent TCO and along with Noonan, that gave me two good TCOs. We were under great pressure to become operational with the new system and the boys worked into the night for weeks, 7 days a week to make it happen. When the improved battery was operational, I would have to man it with a TCO 7 days a week, but we could shut down the battery at the end of the runway at Osan. I worked every day from the day I arrived in Korea in July until Christmas Day.

The maintenance warrant officer for the basic battery was CW3 Sam Pignatella. Sam was a character. He was TCO qualified, but maintenance people, while certainly capable of operating the system, had not been trained on the tactics determining when to engage a target. Sam had somehow become a certifier for TCOs. He and Noonan were really hurting pulling duty every day especially with Sam having to fix the equipment. I visited the site at Osan every day. One day Sam suggested that I do a graded prep for action crew drill and become certified. I said fine.

Basic and Improved Hawk were very similar and very different. For one thing in Basic Hawk there were no headsets, so everyone just screamed out what they were doing to insure they were heard. Also, in Basic when one ran a prep for action drill, the firing lights were real, that is if you pushed one you would fire a missile. In Improved Hawk, the firing lights would come one to check the circuitry, but an additional step was needed to make the missiles operational. Doing a prep for action crew drill in basic Hawk was a very different feeling.

I had run many Improved Crew Drills at Ft Bliss and had taken the Tactics test. Sam suggested we walk through a practice drill before we 'went for record." The screaming and the Fire Control Operators actions (they put their hands on their heads when the firing lights were lit) just unnerved me. I told the Chief we ought to do it again, but Sam said I was ready. We ran the drill with the Chief telling me what to do and say every step of the way and I passed which gave us three TCOs and the Chief in reserve. Life got a little better.

About two weeks after I took command, I got a call from my friend, Captain Terry Monrad, who was the S-2 of our battalion. Terry had been one of General LeVan's aides at Ft Bliss and I had gotten to know him a little bit there. Terry came into my office, sat down and then said "I hate to do this to you, but your mess hall is under investigation". What had happened was that our site was so remote, the mess sergeant had stockpiled canned goods to ensure that everyone had something to eat when driving on the roads became impassible. I appealed for mercy for my cook and the battalion commander decided just to move him and not punish him. Here I am pulling state 30 km away every other day and now I got problems in the mess hall.

Well, the Lord immediately sent me an answer. A few days after the decision was made, SFC Jim Ward walked into my office and reported. We made small talk, but Ward looked really irritated. I asked him if something was wrong, and he responded: "Sir I was here 20 years ago". I responded, here, Quan Duk? He replied: "No sir in a company mess hall". I responded so where are you coming from, and he replied: "The 7th Corps Mess Hall IG inspection team." Anyone on a Corps level inspection team was the best of the best. I said wow and made a deal with him. I told him if he would stay with me for a few months, I would support him going anywhere he wanted. He agreed. Mess hall issue was at least temporarily solved.

Two days after Sergeant Ward took over, the First Sergeant came in and said: "Sir we have a problem in the Mess Hall". Next thing I knew Sergeant Ward stormed into the office, almost forgot to report, and told me we needed to fire all the Kitchen Police, who were civilian government employees. I asked why and he told me they were stealing salt. What the KP's were doing was they were taking a napkin, pouring a little salt in it, and carrying it out the gate. On the outside, that little bit of salt was worth several dollars. Black marketing was a booming business in Korea in the mid 1970's, just as it had been for Dad a decade earlier. Dad had a pilot light stolen out of a furnace that was turned on! They were creative. We had a little helipad just outside the installation and it had PSP or metal planks on it so the pad would have a firm base despite the weather. A Korean told me if I gave him the PSP, he would concrete the pad. I was real interested until the 1SG told me the guy would make a fortune off the scrap metal on the black market. We straightened the PSP and painted it, OD of course.

Back to Sergeant Ward. As I was talking to him, the head KP came in and the 1SG came into my office with a smile on his face. When he told me that the KP wanted to see me, I very dramatically said in a loud voice "If he is on this post in the next 5 minutes, I am going to have him shot." Next thing I heard was the screen door flapping. The Civilian Personnel Office came to see me arguing we had plenty of salt. I replied they were fired. We went back and forth two or three times and I finally agreed to bring them back if a letter of reprimand was placed in their records and if the CPO agreed that any future problems would result in their immediate dismissal. SFC Ward was happy.

The 38th Brigade had a best mess competition every month and SFC Ward won it 7 months in a row. During the last inspection that we had before I returned to the States, I walked down the mess hall to see how things were going. I found SFC Ward explaining the mess regulation to the food service warrant officer who headed the team, the guy who was inspecting him! After the inspection, Chief came up to the office and asked if I would support Ward going to Brigade. I said I would, I had promised, if that is what he wanted. I talked to SFC Ward, and his reply was "F--- 'em sir. They didn't want me when I arrived here and I am damn happy where I am." SFC Ward was a great NCO, he got promoted to E-8 shortly after he arrived, and when the 1SG wanted to get away for a few days, he would take the battery, including running all the formations. He loved it. His breakfasts were to die for: eggs cooked to order, pastries, hot and cold cereal, pancakes, waffles, and fruit-all for 25 cents! His number 2 cook SP6 Luther Webb was a baker, and his donuts were so good the Commanding General would fly a helicopter through our site to pick up a couple dozen of Webb's donuts for VIP events.

The 38th Brigade had units spread out from the DMZ to the extreme southern tip of Korea. My battery was the closest to the head shed so when VIP visitors needed to see a real Hawk site, they came to A/1-44. We worked out a little dog and pony show for visitors and we had about 2 visits per month. One visit was from the Chief of Staff of the Army, General Rogers. Rogers was a big standardization guy, he was trying to get discipline back into the Vietnam Army, to the point of taking the beret away from the 82d Airborne Division. He was a big people guy. When he came to the site, I was told he would only visit the TAC site but as a precaution, I asked the 1SG to make sure the admin area was ship shape. Well General Rogers came, visited the TAC site, and then asked to go through the admin area. We waited for 15 minutes for the Korean who ran our closet sized PX to open it up and then the COS went through every building in the admin area. We were preparing for our Annual Service Practice, where we fired a live missile and to build spirit, we had special red baseball caps made for the ASP team and any other battery members who wanted to buy one. We were told over -and- over again NO ASP hats when the COS came. All was going well, when Gen Rogers went to the mess hall and SFC Ward came out and smartly reported to him wearing his ASP hat. The Brigade Commander looked at me with a look that could kill, but General Rogers said nothing and then went in to enjoy some of Specialist Webb's donuts.

    1SG Price rotated back to the states around Christmas time and I appointed SFC (P) Bill Huffman as the 1SG. Sergeant Huffman was a tracking radar mechanic, but a go getter and he did a great job and taught me a lot. About a week after he took over, he came into my office and said: "Sir why don't you trust the NCOs?". I was shocked at first, then I got a little mad, and replied "What do you mean?" He told me I was micromanaging what was going on and while my interest was good, the boys were spending too much time dealing with me and not enough time doing their jobs. He made some suggestions and by that point I was about to boil over. I responded with clinched teeth "Ok, we will try it for a few weeks and see how it goes." Let me tell you, it went SUPER. In my first battery I had to be involved in everything, teaching, and encouraging my NCOs. By the time of my command of the Hawk battery, the NCO Education System had started, and the NCOs were much more capable of leading and doing maintenance, which I knew very little about for a Hawk battery. Trust-Bill Huffman taught me that and the battery almost ran itself for the last 6 months of my command.

Since we were so close to the Yellow Sea, up on the highest hill in the area, in the wintertime it got cold, especially in January and February when the wind blew 30 MPH+. One winter day the Pulse Acquisition Radar broke, which was located on the highest point on the site. Chief Warrant Officer Roland Matta and Jim Coots were both superb guys who would stay with a problem until it was fixed, sometimes for 24 straight hours. Well, we were having a time diagnosing the problem with the PAR, so I went up there and just stood around to show my support. It was the coldest I have ever been in my life, but I just stood there with my hands in my pockets to provide moral support for the guys. They were touching freezing metal and the energy they maintained was truly outstanding. An Army consists of men and women on the front lines who deservedly get most of the headlines. But the great majority serve behind the lines and demonstrate the same commitment and service as those up front.

We were really isolated in Kwan Duc; it took an hour by dirt road to get to a paved road and almost an hour from there to get to Osan or Camp Humphries. One Friday night, I was asleep in my bunk when my MP sergeant came into the BOQ and pounded on my door. I asked SSG Hudson what was happening, and he just told me to get to the gate ASAP. I threw on some jeans and a t-shirt and headed for the gate. We had two 10' high fences around the admin area and there were about 30 Koreans standing outside the gate talking loudly. I asked one of our Korean contract guards, who spoke a little English what was up, and he told me that an American soldier had assaulted a Korean and cut him with a coke bottle. I had the soldier brought to me and asked him what happened after reading him his rights. We were in State 6, the only week of the month when we didn't have a crew on the hill. We worked pretty much a normal day. The only guys on the hill were our MP dog handlers who let the dogs run free on the Tac Site.

What happened was my soldier was bored and had wandered into downtown Quan Duc to buy a coke. There was a Korean nearby who was almost unconscious from drinking very potent, homemade, Korean wine. He confronted my soldier and had charged him. My guy instinctively held his hands up in front of him, holding the glass coke bottle which was in his hand. The Korean head butted my guy, broke the bottle, and cut his head badly. The Koreans outside my gate were angry as an erroneous story was circulating around the 'ville that my guy assaulted the Korean. I went to the battery headquarters and gave battalion a call.

When I got back to the gate, the victim was lying inside the fence on the ground. One of the Korean guards had let him in. He was obviously very drunk, to the point he was not controlling his bodily functions. I asked where our medic was, SP5 Smith and was told he was in the club. Great! Smith came out and I asked him how he was, and he said fine. Smithy had been a Viet Nam medic, which meant his experience was quite broad-in fact he had delivered a baby. He took the victim to the aid station with the help of a couple of the guys.

I told the folks outside the gate that I would investigate what happened (which I had already done), we were patching up the victim and there was nothing more to do: I told them to disperse. A roar ensued and I was told the Mother of the victim HAD to go the aid station to ensure Specialist Smith didn't put any evil spirits in his head. I let her in.

I told the crowd again to disperse and they stood fast. I called the hill and asked who the head dog handler was on duty. It was Specialist J.W. Smith, a Texan, who was as wide as he was tall. Perfect guy for the mission. I told him what to do.

We had 6 dogs on the site, and they would growl and bark when you approached but universally if you told them to shut up with a loud voice, they would cower away. They were all cowards. The MPs had to do gunshot training monthly with them where the MP would fire blank rounds near the dog, so they could get used to gunfire. During that drill, one of my dog heroes would eat rocks and make himself sick every time. The dogs were all show and no go when things got tough.

Harper and his partner drover a 2/12-ton truck down the hill to the gate where they had to make a sharp right turn to get into the admin area gate. I had the outer drive through gate opened. When Harper and his buddy stopped at the inner gate, Harper and his dog, Ned, and his partner with his dog came roaring out of the back. Ned was the loudest, most vicious appearing dog I had (but also the biggest coward). The dogs barked loudly and flashed their teeth. The crowd dispersed like an explosion had gone off in the middle of them and we did not see them the rest of the night. The "Mayor" of Quan Duk came to see me the following morning protesting the dogs. I told him if he ever had a complaint, he was welcome to come see me and I would fairly investigate his complaint but if he came with a crowd again, I would escalate my response. We had no more civil - military issues and the mayor and I became good friends after I gave him a bottle of bourbon.

I got promoted to Major. I had been selected for Major "Below the Zone" on my first look, so I was a promotable Captain for the entire time I commanded the battery. It was cute; when I first took command, I had to set the record straight. Many of the soldiers thought that because I was promotable, I could give Field Grade Article 15s-nonjudicial punishment which carried double the punishments of a company grade Article 15. The men were greatly relieved when they learned that although I was almost a Major, I only had the authority to give Company grade Article 15's since I was commanding a company.

Two months before I was scheduled to go back to the States, I got a call from the personnel people in Washington DC. Now you need to appreciate the technical challenge this phone call represented. My assignment officer Major Murray called the switchboard in Korea, he was then patched to the switchboard at Camp Humphries which was about 20 miles east of us as the crow flies, an hour by dirt road; they patched the call to my battalion headquarters which forwarded the call via microwave radio to me in Quan Duc. I had just gotten up at 3AM waiting for Kim Il Sung to attack us one more time. When we were in State 2, we had the system ready to fire and a full crew in the van. All the soldiers slept except for the Tactical Control Assistant and me the Tactical Control Officer. After we stayed "up" for 2 hours so around 5AM, I had gone back to the Crew hut where the TCO had a room and a bunk.

So, the phone rang-the phone was a TA 312, a field telephone. I answered the phone Captain Semmens since I hadn't been promoted yet. The voice said "I'm looking for Major Semmens" to which I replied this is Captain, *almost* Major Semmens. "Give me your social" said the voice which I did.

Now that he was convinced that he had the right guy the sales pitch started.

"Do you have to go to Fort Ord?" I had been assigned to the C/V battalion there and was looking forward to the assignment because of the job and getting Marilyn to California. I replied that I wanted to go to Ord, but it wasn't imperative. He then said: "I can't hear you too well, call me back". I responded: "Sir if you can understand me this is as good as it gets." He said ok. He then asked me if I needed leave when I left, to which I replied: "no sir, what's up?" Well, he replied "how would you like to go to the Air Force Academy?" I replied to do what; and he replied to teach military history. I was in the line Army mode, I just wanted to be with units as that was all I really knew. I replied "Sir I really don't know" to which he replied "I will drop you 30 days" meaning I would be sent to the States 30 days early. I replied: "sir you got your man." The last 60 days or so of my tour was pretty uneventful-I got promoted to Major, Steve Gerhart got promoted to Captain; we had two SFCs that were promoted to E8 and a Sergeant who was promoted to SSG. All of us threw in money for a collective promotion party and we hired the best band in Korea, and they started playing at 3PM and didn't stop until 2AM the next morning.

US AIR FORCE ACADEMY 1977-80

The story behind Major Murray's strange call is the Army kept recommending non-combat arms PHDs in history to replace the Army Major who literally was the only green amongst the blue in the Department of History, or DFH as it was called. Col Alfred Hurley, the Professor, was one of the most incredible people I have ever met. He wasn't worried about the caliber of the instruction, he wanted warfighters to instill a warrior spirit in the cadets. When I reported to Col Hurley, he told me just that during our initial interview. School was about to start and that's why there was a rush to get me to the Academy. I was assigned to teach the survey military history course to sophomores. I quickly discovered that while my historiography was solid, I hadn't read the books I should have in graduate school.

We bought a bi-level house in Northeast Colorado Springs, about 20 minutes from my office (cubicle) on the Academy. We lived on a steep hill. I had an orange VW bug as my car and when I bought it, the guy gave me a pair of studded snow tires already mounted on wheels. So, when it would snow, I would put the studded tires on and go down the hill to work. With the special tires, the VW was a good snow car. The tires propelled it through anything and the belly plate on the car would let it slide along if the snow was too deep.

The great event of our family life was the birth of Michael MacLean Semmens. Mike was born at the Academy hospital which was and still is a great facility. Marilyn's water broke so we rushed to the hospital. The Doctor decided to induce labor to avoid any problems. I started doing the things I did for Rob, but something was wrong. We were moving way too fast, she wanted to push much earlier than she had done with Rob. I called for a nurse who came in and immediately called for a Doctor. Marilyn was having Mike. We went into the delivery room, and he came out crying and healthy. Holding your newly born son in your arms is one of God's great joys and one of the top 5 experiences a guy can have in his life.

Our friends were all from the Academy. Every other guy in the Department had a PHD from a well-known history school but they were all warriors. We had guys who had flown F-5s in Viet Nam, bomber pilots and a few trash haulers (cargo airplane pilots). I started to learn the lingo-B-52 bombers were BUFFs-Big Ugly Fat F-----. They were all warriors in a different sense than I had known before and great guys who could drink a horse under a table. We had a club called the Bridgers-these were people who worked in more than one Department at the Academy. There were three activities at the Academy: the faculty, the Commandant's shop that handled the military instruction and the athletic department. If you helped or worked in two or more departments, you were eligible to be a Bridger. Well, I worked as an Associate Tac Officer and I officiated track meets for the Athletic Department, so I was eligible. LTC Dave MacIssacs, who was my boss and a big time Bridger got me in. There is still a plaque in the basement of the USAFA Officer's Club remembering the Bridgers. And my name is on it.

We played softball, basketball and did other things as a Department. We partied together and just had a great time.

But the good times were in the 2d and 3d years. The first year I just prepared for class and read my butt off. I remember staying with Dad and Mom while our house was getting ready. I have a distinct memory of sitting on Dad's side porch on a 3-day holiday reading about Napoleon. What helped me is the second semester of my first year, I taught honors history. I only had 6 students, so admin time was minimal (the bane of all instructors) which gave me tons of time to read. We read Michael Shaara's Killer Angels for our Civil War reading and it was one of the best books I had ever read.

The highlight of my tour was working with Colonel Hurley. He had been a Major flying as a navigator when he was selected to be the Professor of History and immediately promoted to Colonel. He got the job because in grad school at Princeton he wrote the definitive book on Billy Mitchell, the great airpower pioneer. But Al Hurley wanted warriors more than anything else. He made every cadet read Anton Meyer's Once an Eagle the story of a good guy Sam Damon and a conniving careerist named Cortney Massingale. The book was 800 pages long and each cadet had to finish it before they graduated on his/her own time. This requirement was given with complete confidence as the cadets were accountable on the honor system. If they didn't finish the book, they were obliged to turn themselves in. I gave a copy to my brother Mike and he was so impressed with the story that he named his first son Damon, after the hero of the book, Sam Damon.

The Army guy in the Department was always different but this Army officer sometimes had strange ideas would turn heads. I enjoyed destroying perceptions. They all thought every Army Officer had an arsenal of personal weapons and loved to hunt and fish. I had a lot of fun dispelling their perceptions as I had/did neither.

The Air Force has this amazing capability to focus on the mission, the flight line. So, they didn't worry about rank, saluting or shining their shoes. Everyone knew the pecking order of the flight line. I got used to having Captains call me by my first name but toward the end of the second year they all started calling me sir. It was odd, but they were just respecting the Army tradition. As a Captain for 8 1/2 years in my wildest dreams I would never think of calling a Major by their first name although I had Majors I worked with ask me to. Another difference was instead of telling people directly, everything was communicated via the bulletin board in the little break room we had in the Department. I almost missed a staff meeting when I first got their because privates read the bulletin board in the Army; officers are told things. I got used to it and it was an effective way to communicate.

At the end of my second year, I was due to move. I had talked to my assignment officer, and he said very emphatically that I was going to the Command and General Staff College. That was fine with me. Colonel Hurley called me in and asked me to stay a third year. I explained to him that I had 2-3 years left as a Major and I had to go to CGSC for a year and I had to get a Battalion Operations job if I was going to be competitive for battalion command. He said he understood but the Army couldn't find a guy again that met his requirements. He said he would keep me informed.

I immediately called branch and told my assignment officer what was up. He told me not to worry about it. A few weeks later Colonel Hurley told me that I was staying another year. What happened is my assignment guy did push back until LTG Tallman, the superintendent of the Academy, called an old Army buddy in MILPERCEN who happened to run the place. I was cooked, the needs of the service and all that.

Every summer was divided into 3-3-week periods. The cadets could take a class during one period, they had to do something military during the 2d period and the 3d period was leave. During the first period I sometimes taught military history to 6 or 8 cadets who had failed it during the normal school year. The first-year cadets, "Doolies", just coming into the Academy began with 6 weeks of military training on the Academy grounds. The third period they marched about 5 miles over a ridge next to the Academy to Jack's Valley. There as squadrons, or as units of about 100 cadets they went through a series of stations like the bayonet assault course.

I ran a station called Recondo and we put the kids through a confidence building leader reaction course. The cadets would stop on a road next to a steep 300-meter long hill next to our position. Our cadet 1SG would suddenly yell at them and tell them to get up our hill double time. Chaos issued. As they were coming up the hill, some of my guys fired off a couple of artillery simulators and some uncertainty and fear followed. As the plebes poured over the top of the hill the cadet cadre would start hazing the plebes big time. If a plebe was special, he/she got to see the OIC, me. One time one of my guys brought me a female cadet who he accused of loafing. I looked at this young lady I saw a woman who maybe weighed 90 pounds carrying a weapon, an M1 rifle, and probably another 25 pounds of gear. I told her to get in the bleachers where we gave the orientation.

The plebes were sized so when they marched into stands the shortest cadets were on the first row, generally women. Women were just coming into the Academy and there were several male cadets who wanted to make sure they were tough enough. The class of 1979 was the last class to graduate without women. I was there from 1976-1979 so the assimilation of women was just starting. I gave the orientation, focused mostly on safety. The boys had caught a garden snake and when I mentioned the presence of snakes in the training area, I would pull the snake from my pocket, and I would have it passed down the front row. When he came out of my pocket, he would wiggle quite a bit and that snake would go down that row pronto. My cadre loved it.

I had to tell the boys several times to tone down their hazing with the female plebes. My boys had all the intel on the incoming squadron. I got my chance to teach them a lesson one day when I was told that one of the female plebes in the next squadron was a gymnast. When a cadet did even the most minor of infractions in the bleachers during the orientation, like slightly turning their heads to stretch their necks, they came down to the front of the bleachers and assumed the front leaning rest position for a couple of minutes. A couple of cadets had committed one of the "mortal" sins our guys were looking for and finally the gymnast, Miss South, twitched her nose and I had her assume the position. She maintained a perfect pushup position for almost 10 minutes, smoking four or five male cadets who tried to keep up with her. Later, I told her she had done a good thing for women at the Academy. She smiled and said: "Thank you sir, it was my pleasure." I bet she became a general if she stayed in. She turned a few heads among my boys and the intensity of the female hazing diminished. Seeing the plebes at the end of the day feeling so successful and confident was really a good feeling. Like Coach Lombardi, we tore them down to build them up.

The plebes selected the speaker at the end of summer training which marked the beginning of the academic year. I was selected to give the speech twice. The speech was given in Arnold Hall an auditorium that held 4000 people. The plebes knew they had surmounted the challenge of summer training and were feeling good. The first time I gave the speech, I walked out of the stage to a raucous crowd, and they all started chanting Recondo, Recondo. It was a great night. My last year at the Academy the plebes wanted me to give the speech again, but Colonel Hurley told me that the sup had told him "I don't want an Army officer giving this speech two times in a row" so they invited an Air Force astronaut instead. I understood and was cool with it. A week before the presentation, Colonel Hurley came into my office and told me the astronaut had to cancel and they wanted me to do it again. I said sure and gave the speech, the only person of any service to have given it two times in a row at that time. I was personally very honored but what I think appealed to the cadets was the spirit of a warrior which I tried to preach every time I had a chance.

All instructors were given use of the cadet gym which was an awesome facility. After a year or so you got a locker. It had a good weight room, an indoor track, which was useful in the winter, and a million basketball courts. I had to be careful who I worked out with as most of the Air Force guys would kill themselves just to beat the Army guy.

The spring of my second year, I applied to Pathfinder school to fill one of my three-week summer periods. Branch told me it was in the can. I loved jumping and really wanted to do it again. Right before I was set to go, Branch called me and told me that Air Defense had no Pathfinder slots so I couldn't attend. Right there on the spot I asked if I could go to the Cadet jump school they had at the Academy. I checked into the PT test for the school, and it was much more strenuous than the Army test. It consisted of 5 events that were strictly timed: 40 pushups, 40 sit-ups', standing broad jump (I think I had to jump 6' and having white man's disease it took work); 20 pullups (hands forward toward the bar) and a medium long run that required a pace of 7:30 minutes per mile to pass. That pace wasn't so bad but after 8 minutes of strenuous exercise and running at 7000 feet, it was a chore.

The day of the test came. I had been training for several months but had only done 20 pullups once. I was a little nervous. The pushups and sit-ups went fine, I broad jumped 2" beyond the requirement, and then they took us into the gymnastics room for the pullups. We did them on a gymnast's bar which gave a little when you went down and helped you spring up. I could have done 40 pullups on that bar. We then went outside for the run. We ran it on a 300-meter oval that had been painted on the tarmac outside the gym. When I started running it seemed like I could never really get going because I was turning all the time. We had to do like 8 laps, I was watching my time and was ok when on the last lap Captain

Gerry Gendron, a colleague in the Department who had been running with me asked if he could go ahead. I was ok but at 85% capacity, so I said sure, and that young bum steaked off and finished about 15 seconds ahead of me. I never went to the AF jump school, but Gerry did. Regret? Maybe but I didn't need it, school was cranking up again and I was going to be the course chairman for the survey Military History course in the fall and the Capstone military history course, the American Way of War that Colonel Hurley and I taught.

I always listed to Colonel Hurley's lectures, and he knew so much that he would make comments that floored me. For example, he once threw out offhandedly Hoyt S. Vandenberg after whom one of the cadet barracks was named, was a member of the last West Point class without running water.

One of my fondest memories of Colonel Hurley was my last semester at the Academy. We used Bruce Catton's This Hallowed Ground as the civil war reading. It was the only complete history of the civil war that the great Catton wrote, but it was 800 pages long. The cadets had about 2 weeks to read it. So, in our course organization meeting before the semester began, as the course chairman I suggested Killer Angels as the reading, a much shorter book. I was expecting push back and I got it. Colonel Hurley was a member of the core of historians who wrote the official history of the Air Force. Accuracy was everything. I asked the Colonel if he had ever read it and he replied, No, I had a copy of the book with me and said "Sir would you read it this weekend" knowing he read a book every weekend. He knew so much he would read books and just look for new information. He said ok reluctantly.

Our meeting was on a Friday and the following Monday morning Colonel Hurley's secretary came in my cubicle and told me the boss wanted to see me. I walked in his office, reported, and he threw the book across the conference table in his office at me. Being a pretty good third baseman, I fielded it before it hit the ground. Silence. Then he said. "that's the best book I have read in 5 years." We used the Angels and the cadets loved it. But I saw a quality every great leader needs to have: the ability to adapt.

We hired Doctor Russel Weigley, who wrote the text we used for the American Way of War, to come out and talk to the cadets. Dr. Weigley argued in his book that Lee was Napoleonic during the Civil War, that is he sought the offense whenever possible. During one of our classes, a cadet argued with Weigley respectfully and made some good points. Colonel Hurley, after the class told me to go to the cadet library and look in the archives for anything I could find. All the Academies share the archives from all the other Academies, so we had the West Point records. I went down to the microfiche room and with the help of a great librarian, located the West Point records from the 1830's. Colonel Hurley wanted me to look at the records when General Lee had been the superintendent of the Academy. Sure enough, I found a record of a meeting of a Napoleon club which included Lee, Burnside, and several other future generals. Several leaders of the Civil War made a concentrated effort to study Napoleon's tactics and strategy. I reported that to Hurley and the cadet and the boss sent a note to Dr Weigley.

Life at the Academy was good. It was pretty much 7-5 and it was rare that we had to work on weekends. That was good because in the Fall, we had football.

Air Force had good football teams when they first started competing in Division I in 1958. By 1976 when I arrived, they were in bad shape. To support the cadets, I became a season ticket holder. In three seasons, I saw them win one game and it was against Army.

Army-Air Force football weeks were a lot of fun. The 2d year I was there, Major Bill Dollar, who was the Army "rep" at Air Force (the senior guy) came to me and told me that he needed help in supervising the 6 Army cadets who were at Air Force that semester. The previous year the Army cadets had left a mule in the Commandant's office, and it had done its business on the Comm's brand new carpets. The Academies swap 6 students each semester and have instructors from the other services at each Academy to give the students a "joint" perspective. We only had one Navy instructor who taught G-Section math to the students who had the lowest aptitude for math as evidenced by their entrance examination scores.

I got the Army cadets together and we hatched a plan. We were given some money from the West Point Association of Graduates, and I obtained all the supplies and the kids met at our house the Sunday night before Army week to get going.

The plan for Sunday was we were going to fill the roof of the cadet mess hall, Mitchell Hall, with balloons that said: "Go Army, Beat Air Force", purchased by the grads in Denver. I borrowed a helium tank from the airfield at the Academy and then borrowed a van to transport the balloons. We started working at our house and after about 15 minutes the van was full, and we had 85% of the balloons still left. I made the command decision that we would go to Mitchell Hall and fill the balloons there. We showed up on the loading dock and were met by the Mitchell Hall supervisor, a retired Army CSM. We delayed while the CSM closed all the curtains in the hall and then we proceeded upstairs with our tank and filled the heavens with Go Army balloons.

The next morning, we all set together for breakfast in Mitchell Hall. There was a large mockup of the space shuttle hanging from the center of the dining room and it was totally shrouded with balloons. Every once and a while a balloon would run out of gas and float to the ground, and we heard these pop-pop-pops. The West Pointers were elated. The Wing of Cadets was getting angry.

Tuesday, we built a large wooden frame in sections and stapled the large billboard "Uncle Sam want you, join the US Army" and dropped it over the front of Mitchell Hall as the cadets were marching into lunch. Frustration rose as the cadets were helpless to do anything as they were in formation. Wednesday Andy Smoak, who was an Air Force pilot and an Army grad who had chosen to go into Air Force when he was commissioned, and I went on the cadet TV station and did a skit. I asked Andy if he thought Army would win to which he replied "Of course they will, they have the 12th man behind them", the corps of cadets, inferring that the Air Force football players did not. Thursday, Andy and I snuck into Mitchell Hall for the lunch meal and the CSM gave us access to the PA system. We had a cassette tape of the Army fight song, which we intended to play as soon as the cadets were called to attention at their tables. The Wing marched in, and we could hear them moving to their tables. Just when I was about to push the button Andy came screaming into the room where I was and said: "the Commandant is here!!" The Commandant, who oversees all the cadet military training, often ate lunch with the cadets.

I heard the command "Wing attention" and told Andy screw it and I hit the play button. The Army fight song begins with a little whistling and the cadets were stunned for a second but then the words of the song came "On brave old Army Team". I heard roar and suddenly all the cadets were beating their plastic bowls to drown out the sound. I poked my head out of the sound room and made eye contact with General Richards and he had a big smile on his face.

Well, the reprisals were swift. Tuesday morning, I walked into my cubicle, and it was filled up with hay (for the Army mule) to the desk level. Tuesday my whole office was moved to the third story women's bathroom intact and set up exactly as it had been upstairs (we were on the 4th floor of Fairchild Hall, the academic building).

Friday was the grand finale. Bill Dollar had gotten two helicopters from Ft Carson and one from a pysops national guard unit in Denver to buzz the wing as they were marching to lunch. It was all timed, Dollar was on the roof of Fairchild Hall in radio contact with the aircraft. The trigger point was when the 6 Army cadets broke out of ranks and ran to spirit hill, a small mound next to Mitchell Hall on the terrazzo. The Army cadets all got to the hill and unfurled a home-made sign on a bed sheet that said Go Army. Just at that moment the helicopters popped over the roof of Fairchild Hall. They were flying in a line and on one direction they had signs that said: "Go Army" and on the other "Beat Air Force". The third helicopter was a psyops bird from the Colorado National Guard and it was playing the Army fight song over a loudspeaker.

We had all the Army officers positioned near spirit hill. The Wing broke from ranks and charged spirit hill. It was like the wagon box fight; we were badly outnumbered, but we had the firepower-all the officers who surrounded the Army cadets threatened the Air Force cadets with punishments until they graduated if they even touched one of the Army kids. Order was restored but it was chancy there for a minute.

When I showed up in my office the Monday after the game, all my furniture and books had been put back in my office perfectly. All the straw was gone except for a couple of small pieces. Colonel Hurley came in to check on my situation and was infuriated that the office was not perfect. Next thing I knew there were 4 doolies in my office picking up what the other guys had missed. It took them 5 minutes, there sure wasn't much. Standards-that's what Colonel Hurley taught.

The great remembrance of that week was two of the Army cadets, Howard Belknap, and Andrea Holland. Both were great people and I kept in touch with them for a while and they were both doing very well. Andrea was a Rhodes scholar; I think the first woman from Army.

Well, we lost the game 14-9. It was the only game I saw Air Force win in my three years as a season ticket holder. Later I served with Dan Enright who was the center on that Army team. To improve the Army Football program, the Army administrators hired Lou Sabin, the father of Nick Sabin, the Alabama coach. Lou was well known. He had coached the Buffalo Bills in the NFL. Army and Air Force were both 0-7. Lou called the team together for his pregame comments. They were short: "Men we are going to find out today who the worst football team is in Division 1." After the game, when he addressed the team, he said: "Men you are the worst team in Division 1 Football." Army had played well and when the

Superintendent of West Point found out about his coach's post game comments, he fired Coach Sabin on the spot.

We made good friends at the Academy-the Wolfs, the Milingers, the Tiernan's and the Smoaks. Andy and Margie became our good friends, Marilyn loved Margie. Andy became a General, but I lost touch with them. Bob Wolf became a B-52 Wing Commander, the equivalent of an Army Brigade and died in a B-52 crash when he was an instructor pilot for a new pilot. Bob was Mr. Napoleon at the Academy and I hope his wife Nan has had a good life. Kent Tiernan and Andy Smoak and I served together at the Pentagon. Andy helped me understand the Air Staff when I worked a couple of multi-service actions. Service together always resulted in ties that lasted.

I didn't want to go to the Academy when I was assigned there; I was worried and irritated when I got extended for a third year, but it ended up being one of the best tours of my career. When I left, Colonel Hurley asked me if I wanted to receive the Air Force Commendation medal; it would be my only chance to receive that award, but I opted for a Meritorious Service Medal because it was a higher award. Stupid; I eventually ended up with 5 MSMs. The end of the tour was a sad time for me; Colonel Hurley announced he was retiring. We later learned that he had accepted the position of Chancellor of North Texas University. All professors are promoted to Brigadier General when they retire for a day, without the benefits of being a retired General. But their retired rank is Brigadier General. I commented to the Boss, "That's pretty cool, huh sir", to which he replied "Yeah, it looks good on Christmas cards." He was the first truly great man I served with in the military.

The Academy was a special place; all our academies are special places. Every year for graduation the facility was manicured. The 2 or so miles of grass islands one encountered driving into the Academy from the South Entrance were beautiful. I had several cadets ask me to swear then in the night before graduation. Sometimes it got hectic; all the guys wanted to be sworn in at a unique spot on the Academy. One time I had to run from the chapel to the gym and then to the football press box to swear 3 cadets in. I memorized the oath of office, which impressed them, and I told them each of them should internalize that oath to guide them in their future careers. The cadet chapel is one of the real monuments to God and the creativity of man. The founders of the Academy wanted the facility to have a modern, totally new, impressive look vice the storied and historic appearance of West Point and Annapolis. The Catholic chapel is in the basement of the church, and we used to go to mass there on occasion when I was a kid for several reasons. First, the Catholic Chaplin said a historically fast mass and second, we would go to brunch at the AFA officer's club which was always a treat.

One of the additional duties that I had at the Academy was being the Department representative to the 3d class or sophomore academic committee. This group consisted of a representative from every department and was headed by a full Colonel from the Dean's office. Like most universities around mid-semester, grades were issued to the cadets, called progress reports or prog as it was called there. Any cadet with a GPA below 2.0 had to see the committee and we saw everyone. Ken Hatfield had just taken over as the coach of the football team and he came in with every football player that appeared before the committee. I remember one cadet named Richardson who was the starting strong safety on the football team.

Mr. Richardson had a .8 GPA. He had taken summer school to get his cumulative grade point average back to 2.0 but with the demands of football he was struggling. Coach Hatfield made an impassioned plea to keep him, terming Richardson the "Future of Air Force football'. We listened and voted to kick him out. As with every other football player we saw, when we voted them out the Superintendent would override us and allow them to stay. Not so for hockey players, we had a hell of a time keeping the hockey team eligible.

To see all the cadets who were in academic trouble, we met often and became friendly. Our chairman decided one day that we needed to investigate why Navy football was doing so much better than Air Force football. Our Department wrote the history of the Athletic Department and in the late 50's when the Academy first started in the late 50's, AF football was good. Phil Meilinger interviewed the first Athletic Director of the Academy and asked him how the football program was so instantly good. The AD replied that from the outset, AF had some challenges. Most of the Air Force leadership in the 50's and early 60's were Army grads and despite being in the Air Force, they supported Army football like Andy Smoak did. Pete Dawkins, the Army Heisman trophy winner was heavily recruited by AF, but Army won out. To compensate for this AF recruited good players and sent them to Roswell NM Academy to improve their math and English. Phil asked the AD who paid for this, and he replied: "Son the Air Force has friends everywhere." Many of those early players also went to the Academy prep school, so it took them 6 years to earn their commission. That interview with the AD was also interesting because AF turned down Vince Lombardi and Ara Parseghian when they applied for the head coaching job in the early 60's. As the former AD stated: "Who ever heard of Vince Lombardi" (in 1960).

The results of our spying on the Navy program produced some interesting findings. Navy was having all their football players not declare a major, so they took one less class per semester. The players were also put in G sections for all their classes, regardless of their aptitudes. Lastly all the Navy players took a class in summer school which lessened their academic loads especially in the fall and gave them additional time to work out in the summer. All this was passed up the tape and AF changed their policy with athletes soon after and AF football started getting better.

I left the Academy with some remorse. It was a special place. Excellent leadership, brilliant and interesting people, and a real mission. Those thoughts were mixed with my desire to get back into the Army and to get on with my Army career. The senior major and his family were heading to Leavenworth.

FORT LEAVENWORTH, KANSAS
1980-81

Ft Leavenworth is about 30 miles northwest of Kansas City, Ks. I don't remember much about the town of Leavenworth except the people were nice and they had a Sears mail order store. We moved into our quarters which were a 3-bedroom row house in a cull du sac at the bottom of a small hill. That hill would become famous as the site of big wheel races led by 6-year-old Rob Semmens. When there was a big race, there would be big wheels lined up across the street and sidewalks, bumper to bumper. They were a sight to see. Leavenworth is in the rolling hills next to the Missouri River so not much was flat but not that hilly either. The summers were super-hot and muggy, and the winters were cold. The student newspaper carried an article every issue in the winter on how to stay warm when you ran in the winter. Remember, Gore-Tex did not exist in 1980, so the best solution I saw regarding staying warm was to wear long johns underneath your sweatpants.

We attended school in Bell Hall which was about 2 miles from our quarters. It was a huge building, three stories tall, filled with classrooms and a large library. We were organized into sections of 60 students. The sections were further divided into work groups of about 15 students who worked together to solve tactical problems and other group work. We had 2 women in our section: Major Kirsten Newberry, a signal officer and another National Guard Major who left at Christmas. Kirsten was a leader and the first female soldier that I had any contact with. I asked her why she was in the Army, and she replied that the good deals just kept on coming. She later became a Signal Brigade Commander. She was a special person who gave my attitude a big adjustment as far as women in the service went.

The core of the course was the tactics instruction which was divided into about 6 weeks on the offense and 6 on the defense. We had guys from all the branches in our class, so listening to the thinking of Infantry and Armor guys was a real education for me. General Vuono, the Chief of Staff of the Army, had also published a new training system called the Battalion Management Training System and we got a heavy dose of that which came in handy in my next job as a Battalion S-3. Each tactics exam was 4 hours long and not everybody passed. The guys who did the worse were the maneuver guys who knew what they were doing, but the key to success was just giving them back what they had taught you. Our section leader, an Army Dentist LTC named Tom Reddy, got the highest grade on the defense exam because he did just that.

We did things as a section, but the most competitive and fun drill was the school basketball tournament. The school was divided into 4 leagues and the top two teams in each league advanced to the post-season tournament. We won our first game, but our center hurt himself and would not return until the playoffs. We won two games and lost four. Our hardest loss came to the BOAPS, the nickname for another section-Bunch of Athletes Playing Sports. They were good and everybody hated them. When we played them, I got 8 quick points but then they double teamed me with two guys who were taller and better than me and my night was over. Our point guard Jimmy Shane was only about 5"9" tall but he was quick. So, the playoffs came around and three of the four teams in our division were 2-4. The BOAPS were 6-0. So, they decided they would have a playoff to go to the playoffs. We would play the other two teams with the same record. We were all pretty fed up, but our section leader gave us a big pep talk and we decided to go ahead.

We went into the first game totally loose and we won! We not only won, but we scored 70 points! We hadn't scored more than 40 all year. We had the upper hand the second game as well. Shane told me when we rebounded the ball to sprint down court and he would get me the ball. Dave Fowler our center, rebounded well and when Shane got me the ball on the wing over and over and I ended up scoring 23 points. We won again! We were into the real playoffs.

The next game was against the BOAPS and while we played them better than the last time, we lost and the season was over, thank God. It's amazing how you remember the good times and not so much the bad times. One of the BOAPS was

Major John Mayer who would serve with me again at Hunter Field in Savannah, Georgia.

Leavenworth is an historic post, lots of tree lined boulevards. We enjoyed our year there. I studied a lot and was in the top third of the class. One of our final courses was military history and I did well on the exam (duh) which propelled me into the top 10%. I met a lot of great people at Leavenworth and the tactical training I received there made me even more sensitive for my next job which was providing Air Defense for guys just like the ones I had stood around the table with at Leavenworth.

Probably the coolest thing that happened that year is every class gives the school a gift when it graduates. Our class formed a committee and they decided, after gaining consensus amongst the class, to hire an unknown western artist named Don Stivers to do a painting commemorating the fact we were the 100th class at Leavenworth, if one went back to the formation of the cavalry school in 1880. Stivers painted a scene he called the staff ride and everyone loved it. There were 2000 prints made. The class had the first crack at the first thousand prints. We paid $60 a print and everyone else who wanted one paid $80 for the second thousand. They sold out almost overnight. When we graduated, we gave the painting to the museum at Leavenworth and gave the money ($40,000) to the school library.

Branch as we called them, the assignment people, visited Leavenworth twice. My assignment officer was crazy with worry that he could get me to a line unit in time to get an OER before the LTC promotion board met. He came a second time late in the school year and let me know that I was assigned to the 24th Infantry Division at Fort Stewart, Georgia, just 40 miles from Savannah. We tried to make a swap to get assigned to Hawaii, knowing Marilyn would love that, but the deal fell through. Nana was ecstatic though; we were moving to her hometown.

My new battalion commander, LTC Van Lowe was in the command course towards the end of the year, and we invited him over to dinner. He came in wearing a Detroit Lions T shirt, jeans with no belt and tennis shoes. I was a bit underwhelmed. Van turned out to be one of the finest human beings I would ever know and his wife, Martha was a jewel. My relationship with Van documented that first impressions can be totally wrong.

FORT STEWART, GEORGIA
1981-82

BATTALION OPERATIONS OFFICER 1981-1982

When we arrived at Stewart, we first started looking around Hinesville, Georgia-the town outside Ft Stewart- for a house. There was not much available, and those that were did not pass the test with Miss Marilyn, rightfully so. We looked around the south side of Savannah and bought a place near Armstrong College and moved in.

Savannah is right on the coast and consequently it is always humid, especially in the summer. It takes getting used to. On our first staff run (which was in boots) I fell out about ¼ mile from the finish. That was the last run I EVER fell out of. It was very hot even at 6AM.

We shared a headquarters building with 2/9 Cavalry and frankly, we didn't see much of them. I had a little office with a bullpen area outside for my officers and NCOs. 1984 was the height of the Regan administration and we were super funded. We were also well manned; at one point I had 6 assistant S-3s. Most of the Captains who worked for me were guys waiting to command like Ed Gozner and Tom Trumps. I also had some Captains, all of whom were from the south and black that had asked to be assigned to the 24th to be close to home. These black officers were incredible human beings who worked harder than anyone and that is saying a lot. But they couldn't write, which significantly impaired their ability to write staff actions, a fundamental requirement for a staff officer. Years later, I had the chance to talk to General Wally Arnold, a black officer, who was the commander of ROTC command. General Arnold told me he had instituted a writing and reading enrichment program in the ROTC programs in the black colleges, and it made a significant difference. After that point, I never met a black officer who I thought was lacking in anything.

When you walked out of the battalion headquarters you walked past four of the orderly rooms and across the street to our motor pool, a huge "H" shaped building where we did all our maintenance. We had over 200 wheeled vehicles and over 80 tracked vehicles, so it was a big operation. That motor pool was the site of some amazing things, more on that later.

We went to church at a small Catholic Church fairly near us. When Marilyn went in to register in the parish the secretary commented on the different way of spelling Semmens. She asked: "Do you know Mary Kate and Paul Semmens?" Marilyn replied yes. The lady was Rita Murphy and her husband, Cade was my Godfather. They lived about 3 blocks from us, and we had many happy times together. Their daughter had a son out of wedlock and was going to put him up for adoption. It demonstrated the kind of people they were when they said no relative of theirs was going to be put up for adoption and they raised David starting in their 50's. Rita was a Saint, a wonderful caring person who had the great gift to determine when to get involved and when not to. Cade was a character. He insisted on being called and titled Colonel, even though he was retired. He'd get mad if a letter came addressed to Mister Murphy. He was a great guy and he and I had a lot of fun together. He had a time share apartment in Myrtle Beach and he and I took a long weekend and played golf all day and drank beer on the beach at night. They both were a blessing, and I am sure they are both in heaven. I don't know if Jesus calls Cade "Colonel". I'm not sure.

Rob was not as interested in baseball as much as Michael was, but he would go along with us to see the Savannah Braves play, the AA affiliate of the Atlanta Braves at the time. They played in an old ballpark which was neat. It always cost me a fortune as they both brought a buddy or two and Dad footed the food bill. There is something about a ball game that made those kids VERY hungry. Mike used to get 4 hotdogs to start, a big soda and more food as the game went on. After they had devoured the first installment of food, they would scamper down the foul line with their gloves, hoping to get a foul ball. They never got one.

Rob went to St James Catholic School, and he came home one day and told me they were looking for a soccer coach. Rob was 6 at this time, and I agreed to be the coach knowing NOTHING about soccer. I don't remember our record, but the season was in the winter, and we played in Dauphin Park. It was miserable and I don't think we were very good. The other coach and I kept telling the kids to "hit the other guy", certainly not good soccer advice unless it was done correctly.

I enjoyed coaching and would do it a lot more with the boys. I was always super busy at work, and I tried to keep contact with my boys by coaching them in sports. It was a privilege and I enjoyed it very much.

As the battalion operations officer, I took it on myself and my staff to get our training organized. LTC Lowe had told me I had decision making authority, but he would appreciate knowing what I had decided. After about 3 months he told me I had decision making authority and I didn't have to tell him what I did, though I did so anyway. BTMS had just come out and we worked hard first on identifying all the tasks that a C/V battalion had to do. We then grouped the tasks into events where the staff could evaluate the units. The key event was the Platoon ARTEP where our platoons would go to the field once a month for 3 days and be evaluated on their movement, tactical decision making and many other things. I had 2 Captains in the S-3 shop whose sole job was evaluating the platoons.

Training the battery Commanders was a chore, so when I was in command later, I went to the NTC every time one of my Vulcan batteries went and the Captain and I would talk constantly. Common tasks were grouped into what we called Combat Capabilities which was a catch all evaluation which included, machinegun evaluations, land navigation, a PT test for the battery, a barracks inspection, crew drill evaluations, a check of the recall roster and other things. We did the combat capabilities and the Platoon ARTEPS once per month. We also did an inspection monthly of the records inspected during an IG. This sounds like a lot of battalion time interfering with the units but once you got your Sierra together, it wasn't too bad. The Division gave us plenty of opportunities to train the battalion staff, we would have at least 4 Division level Command

Post Exercises or Field Training Exercises each year. We had 850 men in our battalion and no women.

I have never been so happy as I was at Ft Stewart. The battalion was in rhythm and all I did was subtle adjustments from time to time to get us back on track. We had great leadership and since we tried to do what Division wanted, life was good. There were three Commanding Generals during my time at Ft Stewart and they were all special in their own unique way.

General Jack Galvin was the CG when I arrived. He possessed a beautiful humility and appreciation for everything that everyone did for him. He had a clerk in the Headquarters whose sole job was to print 2-star notes and she was busy typing them from morning until night. He sent those notes to everyone, from privates working in a motor pool to battalion commanders. When he left the division and got promoted to LTG, he and his family vacationed for a week at Camp Blanding Florida and while there General Galvin wrote a bunch of 3-star notes, one of which I received and have to this day. It was not uncommon to find him walking down a tank trail. I picked him up several times and took him where he wanted to go.

We were alerted that we had to send a Vulcan battery to a place called the National Training Center in the desert of California in early 1982. Simultaneously, we were sending a battery with the 1st Brigade of the Division to Egypt for an exercise called Bright Star. I asked Colonel Lowe which had priority and he told me "Bright Star of course" and I agreed with him. Bright Star was a dog and pony to get the Egyptians to buy American Equipment including the Chaparral. We sent a battery to Egypt to do just that. The Egyptians did buy the Chaparral, but for the core of the US Army, the NTC would prove to be the most important activity.

The 24th Division at the time had two-line brigades, our third brigade was what was called a "round out brigade" which came from the 48th Infantry Brigade, US Army National Guard from Macon, Georgia. We supported these boys several times when we went to the NTC, and they provoked a lot of thinking on what reserve units could do and couldn't do. Back then, the reservists were solid at the company level, and not so good at the battalion and certainly the brigade levels. They were teachable and they wanted to do what was right, but so much about an Army operation is habit and they just didn't have time to build the right habits.

Our first trip to the NTC was headed by our 2d Brigade, who I thought was our best brigade. I had a Leavenworth classmate, Major Rob Thompson who was the S-3. I thought their Brigade Commander, Colonel Becker, was a thoughtful, and solid commander. LTC Lowe thought that we should go visit the rotation, so off we went.

I made the travel arrangements and since Las Vegas and Ontario, California were equidistant from the NTC, I naturally chose Las Vegas. That policy was changed on the next rotation, so one had to go to Ontario. Van and I arrived in the late afternoon and left the next morning for Barstow where the NTC was located. Our battery commander met us and gave us a situation report. The Brigade was not doing well. The NTC had a full-time opposing force or OPFOR that drove Soviet vehicles and practiced Russian tactics. They were just too clever and fast for us. We couldn't shoot well, manage our logistics or plan our individual and collective responsibilities well. We were getting our tails handed to us after the FORSCOM Commander had called General Gavin and told him to show the

OPFOR what well trained soldiers could do. We were considered the best trained unit in the United States.

We drove straight to the battlefield, to a uniquely shaped hill called the whale. I remember I stood on the whale and admired a tank ditch, or a trench which was over a kilometer wide and six feet deep and three feet wide which stretched from the whale to Furlong Ridge, 11/2 kilometers away. The battalion we were supporting had the mission of keeping the OPFOR from penetrating the imaginary line between the whale and Furlong ridge. We had a Vulcan platoon supporting the battalion, commanded by Lieutenant Chuck Dreissnack who was a West Pointer and one of the finest guys I ever served with. Chuck's mission was to defend the tank company on the whale and then fall back to support a reserve tank company on a small hill to the north called OP1. (Since the desert was so flat and difficult to navigate all the unique terrain features, mostly hills, were given names at the NTC. We had to learn the names fast.)

Van and I were on top of the whale when the OPFOR came. Over 100 tracked vehicles in perfect formation, a magnificent sight. I was locked in, enjoying the thrill of the attack, until Van rudely slapped me on the shoulder and said: "Let's get the hell out of here". We fell back towards OP1 and as we did, that impregnable tank ditch I had admired just seemed to part and the OPFOR blew through it. Our reserve tank company was eliminated, and the battle was over. Chuck had fallen back with his Vulcans, but he had not coordinated with the reserve tank company, so when these strange looking vehicles headed for OP1, our tankers just lite the Vulcans up.

After every battle, there is an After-Action Review or AAR. This was the third rotation at the NTC so many of the things that would eventually be put in place, the Star Wars building and mobile vans for the conduct of AARs, at the NTC which were connected to the Star Wars building were not in place. The AAR did not go well, the LTC evaluator reviewed each mistake with our battalion commander in a frank, positive environment. Then the Chief of the Observer Group, Colonel Shackleford, got up. We were sitting on the side of a hill. At the top of the hill was General Gavin, Colonel Becker, and assorted battalion commanders. Shackleford got up and the first thing he asked LTC Martin, was "Colonel, do you think you are capable of commanding this battalion?" Martin replied yes, in a very positive manner. Shackleford then said: "OK we'll fight the same battle over again tomorrow." Everyone was shocked as the practice was to move the location of the battle every night to protect the environment. But that's what we did, and we got our tails handed to us once again. After that battle, Van and I drove back to Vegas, and left the next morning for Stewart.

When the Brigade returned, General Galvin had a meeting for all the majors and above in the Division. He showed his greatness. He said we were going to learn from the NTC, that we were going to have an AAR after every rotation for the division leadership and we would admit our mistakes to each other so we could learn. Other Divisions were declining opportunities to go the NTC and Galvin said we would take every rotation that we could.

That started a three-year period where it seemed like we were going to the NTC all the time. But we got better and a year and a half later when I returned to the battalion as the commander, we were winning half the battles we fought and by the time I left command, we had some units that were winning every battle. Unfortunately, in the early days, the NTC was called the "National Testing Center" and failures there-and there were a lot- resulted in career ending decisions. Colonel Becker was not relieved, but he gave up command early and my classmate, the S-3 was relieved. A brigade S-3 has little to no impact on what happens at the NTC, but we needed a scapegoat. Rob did get promoted to LTC, but a promising career was ended way too soon.

CHAPTER TEN

HUNTER ARMY AIR FIELD 1982-84

When I was promoted to LTC, I asked to stay in the battalion but of course one cannot have two LTCs in the same battalion. I was sent to Hunter Field in Savannah to be the Deputy Post Commander or City Manager. My main job was to facilitate the interface between the line units and their garrison support, which got me involved in a whole bunch of stuff. For example, the post engineer sent me the plans for a new barracks for one of the battalions at Hunter. I asked for a few days to review it and send back comments and called the Victory (or garrison) Brigade CSM, CSM Jim Hart, and asked him to look at the plans. We were early in the construction project, so we had carte blanche on what we wanted. The CSM came back with all the CSMs on post, and they had radically redesigned the whole building with a special emphasis on easing the charge of quarters responsibilities so they could observe what was going on in the hallways, while monitoring the arms room at the same time. It was just amazing what those NCOs came up with.

Even though I was not in charge of anything I had the influence with the post garrison staff at Fort Stewart and the commanders at Hunter to get a lot done. One of my major responsibilities was to be the interface between the Division Headquarters and the post. It was an interesting assignment; I often would be asked to go find out what had happened; the "rest of the story". The Chief of Staff of the Division at the time, who was my connection to the division, was Colonel Horace "Pete" Taylor. Taylor later became an LTG; he was a great man. His demeanor was gruff, and stern but he had a caring, Christian heart. We did a lot of business together.

One time a soldier insulted Mr. John Goodrum who ran our gym. John was a veteran of the division during the Korean War and the brass was real upset about it. Colonel Taylor was picked to come to Hunter and apologize to Mr. Goodrum. I picked Colonel Taylor up at the airfield. He was super intense; his teeth were clinched shut, anticipating having to eat crow for something he had no control over. They met in the gym, Goodrum appreciated the apology from the division and the encounter went ok. Taylor would call me at all times of the day and night to tell me to go onto post and investigate this or that. It was exciting, but sometimes a little challenging.

It seemed like 90% of my taskers from Colonel Taylor involved one of the tenants on Hunter Field, the 1st Ranger Battalion. The Rangers were the most disciplined soldiers I had ever encountered on duty, but off duty they were wild. Aside from investigating the occasional bar fight the battalion made some questionable decisions. After they got back from Grenada (more on that later) unbeknownst to the division, they had brought an arsenal of captured weapons back to Hunter Field. We had renovated a building for a new Class VI store, and it had an attached garage, about the size of a three-car space. The Class VI didn't need the garage and Major Steve Nix, the XO of the battalion asked me if the rangers could have it. I said sure.

I got one of my middle of the night calls from Colonel Taylor. The Rangers had reported a missing AK-47 rifle. Colonel Taylor was really upset, for during that time frame the Army was big on not bringing back war trophies. I went to the facility and Nix was there and I walked into a space filled with weapons: rifles, pistols, they even had an anti-aircraft gun. The garage door had been secured with a commercial combination lock that anyone could buy at a hardware store. The loss of the weapon was discovered because the lock had been cut and a new one had been put on the door. Because of this, Nix told me "It has to be a Ranger."

I reported everything to Colonel Taylor who told me to monitor the situation. LTC Wes Taylor, the Ranger Battalion Commander, locked the battalion down; that is no one was allowed to leave the barracks and soldiers living off post had to bunk in the barracks as well. We waited for three days. The morning of the 4th day, when our Military Policeman went out early in the morning to unlock Rio Gate, a remote gate on the backside of the post, he found the weapon in a trash can. The battalion was released from confinement and the Rangers destroyed all the weapons.

I really enjoyed my time at Hunter Field as I was constantly helping people. Each month, I had sensing sessions with privates, mid-ranking NCOs and senior NCOs. I remember the first sensing session with the privates (E-4s and below) started awkwardly. After I told them what the purpose of the meeting was, the 10 privates in the room just stared at me. In retrospect I should have considered their position a little more. Here they were talking to a guy who had the same rank as their battalion commander whom they NEVER talked to. And secondly, I'm sure some of them believed their opinion didn't count for much. Finally, I said we are going to sit here until I get something. Then one of the Rangers said "Sir, the PX sucks." Well, we had just built a new PX, and everyone seemed to think it was spiffy. The regional PX manager had visited Hunter and had an office call with BG Herring, my boss. During the meeting which was sort of a brainstorming session, General Herring asked for my input, and I boldly said: "how about a new PX?" Proof positive there is a God, the guy just said OK, and we got a new PX. You can't achieve anything if you don't ask or try.

Anyway, back to the Ranger. I asked him why the PX sucked, and he told me they didn't have any chewing tobacco. Chewing tobacco is/was always popular with soldiers for at night in a tactical situation when operating under blackout conditions and couldn't smoke, chewing tobacco gave you a little lift. I asked him what he was talking about; I told him I chewed, and I bought mine at the PX. He then proceeded to list off six or eight types of chewing tobacco, snuff mostly, that was not in the PX. I adjourned the meeting and called the PX manager and asked him to stock the desired brands. He said sure and a week later, they were available for sale. At the next meeting, I asked the Ranger how the PX was, and he replied "Outstanding." The flood gates opened once the soldiers knew that I appreciated that little things made a difference, and I was really listening to them. The comments at the next session filled a legal pad.

BORN READY

The part of the job at Hunter that I really enjoyed was I was into everything from maintenance on the post, to the clinic, the club system, post security and managing the deployment facilities for the Rangers. Our clinic had 6 docs and every month I had to prepare a report for the General on activities on the post-revenues such as the number of tickets issued by the MPs, and the volume of traffic at the clinic. A couple of months after I was assigned to Hunter, we got a new head Doc, Colonel Hyland Moore who would turn out to be one of the most interesting men I had ever met in my life. Colonel Moore asked for an appointment with me right after he was assigned. We made small talk; he had married late in life to a younger lady and had 4 small children. After the chit-chat, he asked me what I reported to the General about the clinic each month. I told him I reported the total number of active duty and retired patients seen. When Colonel Moore arrived at the clinic was seeing less than 10 retirees a month.

The following month, the volume at the clinic doubled and following month it doubled again. Colonel Moore came by one day and I asked him what was up, and he simply replied: "Docs have to be motivated as well." He was just pushing them to be "all they could be." Hy really wanted to be part of the team. He came in one day and asked if the clinic could have a guidon. The clinic really wasn't a unit per say so they had nothing official, but I told him it was ok that they made one up. I asked him why he wanted a guidon and he said he was going to start to have the medics and docs do PT at the end of each day, around 1600.

I smiled and said "great". Well, I really hadn't thought it through because the clinic was on one of the major roads leading off post. At 1600, the civilian staff on post was going home using the road that the medics were running on and the next thing I knew, the Sheriff, my Provost Marshall, was in my office telling me we had to do something. There was a massive traffic jam as the vehicles slowly followed the running medics. We ended up assigning a patrol car to follow the medics on their run and they stuck to one lane on the road which made the situation bearable. Hy Moore was assigned to Ft Riley to command the hospital when he left Hunter where he died of Lou Gehrig's disease a few years later. I pray for his soul every day.

One of the great joys of serving at Hunter was working directly with General John (Jack) Gavin. General Gavin was a great man whose vision not only for the division but for the city of Savannah as well was continuously amazing. One day he called me and typical fashion, he started probing me. "What do you know about General Monk Hunter after whom Hunter Field was named. I replied: "not much sir, fighter pilot, WWII in England". General Gavin was an historian and when he learned I was an historian, he decided to use me. He said "General Hunter's sister, Jean, is still alive and lives in Savannah. We are going to see her."

The General flew in, and he and I went downtown to visit Ms. Hunter. She had never married, and her brother never married as well. She was a delightful lady and had several things that were General Hunter's. General Gavin asked if he could have those items as he was going to build a museum in honor of General Hunter in the post headquarters at Hunter Field. She said great and when it was done, she toured the facility.

The museum happened quickly, and we discovered that we had several items that we didn't have a place for. I informed

General Gavin and he had the idea of building a big bookshelf in the officer's club to display those items. Marilyn did all the designing for the display, and it was unveiled at a big dinner in the club. I remember the Rangers had the color guard and were those boys sharp.

A lot of funny stories came out of the dinner. General Doug Smith, who was a bachelor, was at a table talking to two couples who had known General Hunter. The conversation drifted around to Monk's dating habits and the ladies at the table both agreed he was quite the lady's man. One woman volunteered that General Monk slept with every woman he dated. So General Smith asked the women if they had dated General Hunter to which they replied: "Oh yes."

Once the Hunter museum and display work was done, General Gavin called me again and asked me what I knew about the battle of Savannah in 1789. Caught flat footed again, I replied I didn't know much except the patriots held the ground and that forced the British north which eventually resulted in the battle of Cowpens which was the beginning of the end to the war. General Gavin had found a dentist in Savannah whose hobby was the battle of Savannah, and the guy had a diorama of the battle. The General and I went and visited the guy, and the issue was collating the events of the battle with the current layout of the city. The only definitive point we had was a negro cemetery that had been there in 1789 and still was there in 1983. General Gavin made an educated guess where the redoubt was the patriots constructed to defend the city and I took him to see the city council. He got them to agree to build a visitor's center and he would rebuild the redoubt that defended the city.

The council was ecstatic, and construction started. We had a heavy engineer battalion at Hunter which could build anything. General Gavin told me that they needed "training" as moving dirt was one of their missions. General Gavin also worked with the city council on the design of a perimeter road around Savannah. Abercorn Street which bisected the city north-south had 7.5 times the volume of traffic that it was designed to have, and traffic was a big issue. They didn't finish it while the General was there, but it exists today. Jack Gavin was a man of incredible vision and the work ethic to make things happen.

Ft Stewart, our parent post, had the facility responsibility for maintaining the Departure Airfield Group (DAG) for the 1st Ranger Battalion. The DAG was a secure area with a headquarters building and all kinds of facilities to help the Rangers get ready to deploy – it was a secure area. One day I got a call that the Rangers had an alert order to deploy to a small island in the Caribbean called Grenada. There was a medical school there that students from all over the world attended, including a good number of Americans. There was a communist backed coup going on and we were worried for their safety. Our Ranger battalion moved to the DAG and camped around the HQ building. I drove out to coordinate with LTC Rick Childes, who was the post G3, the Director of Plans and Training. Rick told me he thought a deployment was imminent but most of us thought that was unlikely.

On one of my daily visits, Rick told me that 2d Ranger Battalion from Ft Lewis, was going to be joining our guys. They arrived and their preparedness for deployment was not as good as our guys and the post staff had to jump around quite a bit to get them what they needed. We finished their preparations late one afternoon and the next morning when I drove out to check on things, they were gone!

I went back to my office and got a call from Colonel Taylor; I was to be the post liaison with the Ranger Battalion at Hunter, and I was to be especially cognizant of the families. Everything about the operation was kept under a cloud of secrecy, so there wasn't much information to share.

The next morning, Good Morning America announced that there were Rangers in Grenada. The Battalion Commander's wife, Linda Taylor called me and demanded to know what was up. Linda was a great lady, but she was feeling a lot of pressure from the battalion wives. I called Colonel Taylor and he told me to hold a town hall meeting with the wives. We had it the next day at the post theater and I was authorized to tell them nothing; I could not confirm or deny what was happening. At the session, I was called every kind of SOB you can imagine, but I hope it made them feel better.

For the next 2 weeks I lived in my office working 18 hours a day, helping where I could. The main thing I was involved in was working the casualty messages and helping where I could. The Joint Task Force parked off the coast of Grenada. General Swarzkopf was the commander, so we were getting a little more information than others. When he got back, he told us a funny story of those early hours in the operation. The staff was sitting around on the command ship trying to figure out how to contact the students. Finally, a junior naval officer in the back of the room said: "Why don't we just call them?" They called the college on the telephone, and an American medical student picked up the phone. She was asked to identify herself and when she asked who was calling, she was told "The US Navy". They then asked her what she saw around her, and she provided numbers and locations of the enemy soldiers. Our Rangers went in and secured the kids.

Our Rangers did have some guys wounded. I received a casualty message about a Lieutenant in the battalion late one afternoon and immediately let Linda know. The message told me that he had been evacuated to Roosevelt Rhodes Hospital in Puerto Rico. Comms had been established with the Caribbean during the operation. Linda told me that officer's wife wanted to go be with her husband and she was going no matter what, so I got on the phone with the hospital. I worked my way telephonically to the Commander's office and talked to a senior petty officer. He couldn't tell me anything about the Ranger's status. I told him the wife was coming and that I would appreciate it if she had a place to stay. He said no problem, they had guest houses. I ended the conversation by asking for the hospital commander to call me. About all I knew at this point was the Lieutenant was alive.

Several hours later, the hospital commander, a Navy Captain called me back. I identified who I was and informed him that the wife was on the way the next day. He seemed willing to talk, so I asked him how the Lieutenant was. The Captain told me he was fine. He had been in a L shaped ambush of an enemy force of 5 Soviet BTRs-armored personnel carriers. The Rangers had fired an anti-tank weapon to stop the first vehicle. When the vehicles stopped, the Lieutenant who was positioned at the bottom of the ambush stuck his head up to see what was happening. A Cuban soldier had exited the rear of the last vehicle to provide security. He saw the Lieutenant and sprayed him with his AK47. The Lieutenant was hit in the lower abdomen and took a glancing round off his neck. He had already had surgery to repair his abdomen and was scheduled for an operation on his neck the next morning. The Doc was convinced he would be fine. Good news, which I passed on.

Roosevelt Rhodes is in the center of the island and the airport was in the capitol city of San Juan, on the west coast. I had to get the wife from San Juan to the middle of the island. By now it was 10 o'clock at night and I called the post headquarters at Fort Buchanan, Puerto Rico. A private answered the phone and I asked for the senior person on duty. I heard "Master Sergeant Lugo, sir". I said: "Lugo are you in the Army or the Guard"? I was fried at this point and was ready to do almost anything to get that wife to the hospital. He replied proudly: "Puerto Rico National Guard sir". I told him what was happening and threatened to find him if he did not coordinate for transportation like I needed. In retrospect he handled it very well. I did not have any flight information so I told him I would call him back.

I finally got the flight information, but before I could call Puerto Rico, Lugo called me. I passed on what he needed.

The next day, the wife's flight arrived in San Juan. The passengers on the plane were held while she and her luggage were removed from the plane and a Navy Lieutenant with sedan escorted her to the hospital. I called Lugo back and told him he was a hero.

The operation was over almost as fast as it started and the Ranger S-1, who was their rear party Officer in Charge came to my office with a list of requirements for their arrival. They wanted hangars so they could conduct their AARs, tape recorders to record the AARs and finally a location to meet their families for a brief minute.

The day before the Rangers were to get home, I got a call that informed me that Good Morning America was going to cover the arrival of the Rangers which was supposed to happen around 1700 one Friday afternoon. I immediately called Linda and she passed the word because the families were encouraged to be at the event. Shortly after that, I got a call that the Chief of Staff of the Army, General Rogers, and his wife would be attending also. The problem I had was that the Rangers in the air to Hunter didn't know this, and we needed to tell them what to do in the little arrival ceremony. So, I called the Ranger S-1 and he agreed to take on that mission.

The great day came. General Rogers arrived and I escorted he and his wife to the lounge they had in the flight ops building. I told him the situation with the Rangers and advised him to wait comfortably until the boys were about to exit the aircraft. He said fine.

The aircraft landed and taxied to in front of the airfield ops building. The Ranger Battalion S-1 and a few other rear party Rangers ran out to brief the boys. I could see them talking and talking. General Rogers appeared beside me. The families were cheering like crazy, and GMA was filming it all. Finally, the Rangers started filing off the aircraft. Many did not have their hats, there were holes in many of the uniforms and a few wore slings. There was a nice little ceremony, the Chief made some nice remarks and then it was over. Then the truth came out.

I had learned mid - afternoon the day of the arrival, that the first Rangers back were from the 2d Battalion, not our 1st Battalion. We were told not to tell the wives and potentially spoil the GMA production. When she realized that the soldiers were not from the 1st Battalion, I think Linda would have killed me if she could of, with good cause.

Our boys arrived early the next morning and per their request we had hangars and tape recorders ready for them to conduct their AAR which took more than 2 hours. They then marched to a field in the middle of post where we had been instructed to construct a barricade to keep the families back. The Rangers were in formation on one side and their families were 30 yards away facing each other. The battalion had been given the command of rest and they stood there several minutes more. Finally, the CSM of the battalion started slowly walking towards the families and pandemonium broke out. There was hugging, rejoicing and pure joy. God was there. I was so happy I almost cried; the tension of the past 3 weeks just evaporated. Suddenly, the Rangers got back in formation. I turned to the Ranger S-1 and asked him "What are they doing?" He replied: "Sir they have to clean their weapons before they are released." My admiration for the Rangers was at an all - time high, to have the discipline to say goodbye to their families for another hour or so before rejoining them was super impressive to me. Rangers are the finest soldiers I ever knew.

General Schwarzkopf came to our headquarters to do the post operation press conference. All the major networks were there, and it went well. Then all the commanders went to the Officer's club for a lunch and to my surprise, the old man gave me a medal. Grenada was over.

I had been selected for battalion command about 6 months after I arrived at Hunter. They asked where I wanted to go and I said "Ft Stewart, of course!" Van had called me and said he was staying for another year. At that time, battalion commanders stayed a minimum of 2 years but could stay a third. That policy was changed when my year group went into command- we were only given 2 years. Van had done well under General Galvin, they had similar personalities, quiet and scholarly. Schwarzkopf was a huah guy who was intense, forceful, and direct. Van was good to me, allowing me to attend training briefings the battalion gave to the new CG so I could learn. But I do not think he enjoyed his last year of command.

BATTALION COMMAND, 1984-86

Van and I changed command on a beautiful, though hot morning. The new chapter of my life had begun. I felt I was ready. Three of the serving battery commanders in the battalion had been Assistant S-3s for me. I had served with the CSM and knew most of the key leaders. I had written my command philosophy which I called Flak Panzer the last few months I was at Hunter and had asked Van and the CSM to review it in advance. The afternoon I took command, I spent 3 hours with the officers and the CSM reviewing the document giving them a chance to comment and make suggestions. We were off. We were going to try to be the best Air Defenders in the world and beat the Infantry, the standard in any Infantry Division, in any competition assigned.

Our first chance to go up against the Infantry was during a division parade that would happen shortly after I took command. We marched the soldier's butts off during every free minute we had during the day. The post instructions for the event which told us what order we would line up in etc. and stated the only the infantry could march with fixed bayonets. I was trying to make warriors out of my men and to me the bayonet represented the final mental hurdle that anyone needed to cross to become a killer on the battlefield. So, I went up to post headquarters and argued with the DPT to no avail. So, I went back to the battalion and in addition to our marching, we started practicing fixing bayonets, or mounting the bayonets on the end of the rifles. When a bayonet is secured on a rifle, it makes a distinctive clicking sound so the objective was when we had 850 soldiers do it, we wanted to make one big click.

The day of the review came, we marched on the parade field. All the soldiers were wearing their bayonets. I brought the battalion to attention and ordered "Fix Bayonets". I was rewarded with one huge click. I looked over to the DPM Sergeant Major who was the chief evaluator, and he was writing like crazy. After the parade, General Schwarzkopf asked me what had happened, and I told him. He roared and told the DPT that anyone who wanted to march with fixed bayonets in his division could do so. We won the competition.

It was a wonderful advantage taking command of a battalion whose mission, people and the climate of the division was so well known to me. Van was tremendously gracious, even letting me attend two of his quarterly training briefs (QTB) that were the real center of gravity at that time. General Schwarzkopf had served under General Vuono who was making training the center of the Army's mission. QTBs were really an exercise in how the training program was integrated from battalion down to the platoon level. I briefed, the CSM briefed, all the battery commander's briefed and a platoon leader and one platoon sergeant from the battalion briefed. Everybody briefed from their own easel that had a large pad of paper attached. We spent hours going through everybody's chart side by side trying to ensure we were connected.

My first QTB started out ok until the B Battery Commander briefed. He was preparing for an NTC rotation with the 2d Brigade and had a lot going on. Schwarzkopf had a rule if a unit trained on a weekend, the soldiers were given a compensatory day off. Well Tommy Trumps didn't have one for a weekend exercise and the CG caught it. But instead of simply admitting the mistake and promising to fix it, Trumps started this long dialogue that there was no way that he could do everything he needed to do and give soldiers time off. The old man started getting fired up and I finally had to step in and make peace, promising that those soldiers would get their day off.

I was miserable. I had had two chances to get this right due to Van's generosity and it was NOT going well. We finally got to D Battery, and I had selected one of the Chaparral Platoons going to Ft Campbell to support West Point Summer Camp. The C/V battalion in the 101st Airborne Division had all Vulcans, but the branch wanted to show the cadets the Chaparral, so we sent a platoon. The Platoon Leader gave a solid brief and then his PSG, SFC Frank Pollard, got up to talk. He started off mentioning a soldier whose wife was going to have a baby and sharing his concern that the husband might be away when the baby was born. Next thing I knew the CG and SFC Pollard were discussing his career when he would be promoted to 1SG. Pollard shared that he was going to retire before that happened because he believed as a 1SG he would be too far from soldiers.

The CG was overwhelmed-the old man cared intensely for soldiers and this was the kind of fair, caring leadership he was looking for. He gave SFC Pollard a medal on the spot.

I walked the old man to his jeep, apologizing for things not going as well as I hoped. Schwarzkopf was not angry, in fact he complimented me for a good first start. He drove away and as he stopped for one of my soldiers to cross the street to our motor pool. The General had a big plate on the front of his jeep with two stars and the soldier didn't salute him! He put the soldier in the back of the jeep and took him to the division headquarters and turned him over to the division CSM. My CSM, who had served with the Division CSM in Germany and who had a mutual respect, went to the division HQ, got the soldier and brought him back to our headquarters building and gave him a "gentle" counseling with his chain of command. The soldier left the CSM's office and when he was crossing the street to go back to the motor pool for a second time, he failed to salute the Assistant Division Commander who was leaving a QTB with the Cav Squadron who shared the building with us which had not gone well. My CSM had to go back to division headquarters to get the soldier a second time. Such was life in the division. And when you have 850 men you are trying to control, one quickly learns the limits of what one can do. In a line Infantry Division, intentions don't matter, results do.

As the S-3, I had set up at least the shell of the battalion training program. The quarterly platoon evaluations continued, the Best Battery evaluation continued quarterly to prepare for the annual IG inspection, and we added a Combat Capabilities evaluation which was a check of miscellaneous tasks that were evaluated quarterly. Between training and me inspecting them, my batteries were super busy. Working on the battalion staff cohesion was always a challenge and they were busy doing their jobs and frequently leaving the office to inspect the batteries. Our program had tasks to train everyone but the battalion staff, but the division did have at least one division level exercise per year and there were 2-3 Command Post Exercises the division ran each year, usually supporting the 18th Airborne Corps. These opportunities allowed us to get better.

Being a battalion commander was the best time of my life. I knew exactly what I was doing most of the time and I had a group of great officers and NCOs who worked with me. From a group of about 30 officers that battalion produced 14 battalion commanders, 6 Brigade Commanders and two Generals. I know this because one of the future Generals that had been in the battalion told me after doing the math. All the 1SGs who stayed on active duty became Sergeant Majors.

I was especially blessed with two outstanding CSMs, both of whom were very direct with me. CSM Jimmy K Williams, my first CSM, was a little more outgoing that my second CSM Glen Ingram. Ingram came to us from a Nike Hercules battalion that was deactivating in Europe. I did not want a guy with a High-Altitude Air Defense background leading my soldiers and I had told the assignment people that very forcefully. I learned there was a promotable 1SG with divisional experience who was at the Sergeant Major's academy who was on the CSM list and who was going to Ft Stewart. I visited him on a trip to Ft Bliss and he told me he would love to be the CSM. I was at Leavenworth going through the pre-command course when the Sergeant Major personnel people called me and told me Ingram was coming. The other guy would get his chance later. I was furious.

CSM Williams left as he was selected to be the CSM of a brigade in Europe. CSM Ingram reported in. He was a small man, but one could detect power in his persona. We had a nice introductory conversation during which I told him I always wanted him to be absolutely truthful with me. Ingram had been a 1SG in the 8th Infantry Division; the Hercules job had been forced upon him, so my worry about him not being a divisional guy went away.

About a month later, after he had had a chance to look around, the CSM asked if he could see me. He came in and closed the door. "Sir, you and me got to talk". We had many, many conversations and they always began with that phrase. He was concerned I was too hard on the officers. I asked him to keep looking and come back later and tell me what he thought. He came back some time later and shared that he now understood what I was doing. But Glen and I talked often and about everything. He became a good friend and advisor. I lost him about three months before I gave up command. He was selected to be the CSM of our 2d Brigade, unheard of for an Air Defender.

Success for a battalion commander was based on two things in those days-how well your unit was trained (principally proven by your performance at the NTC) and your annual maintenance-administrative inspection.

We seemed to be always sending a battery to the NTC. General Schwarzkopf had kept General Galvin's policy of taking any NTC rotation that another division declined, and he really emphasized the post rotation AAR. We were learning like crazy, changing our procedures and tactical SOP with every rotation. The NCOs took the battalion to the field with no officers once a quarter for three days, so that was my time with the officers. We talked about our potential war time OPLAN in Iraq in detail and I gave the officers a test on the TACSOP. This really worked. The key to being effective when one is busy is to plan's one's time and having the leadership to insist that those events occur.

I went to the NTC for every rotation. It was my chance to train my battery commanders. I would ride in the back of their APCs, and we would discuss the battles that were being fought. After the battle, I would get in my jeep, strap a thermos of coffee to the radio antennae support bracket and drive around the battlefield, offering a cup of coffee to my boys. You have never seen anyone scrambling to find a coffee cup like those guys who had been up most of the night and who had just conducted an operation at dawn.

There were many stories I remember from the NTC. One rotation, I arrived a day or so later than I usually arrived, just before the second battle. We were supporting an armor battalion that was defending a ridge line just to the south of crash hill, a prominent terrain feature there. The OPFOR had Hind helicopters which had flown onto the battlefield and stood off at about 3KM and damaged several tanks. Our Stingers, which were with the tanks, had a range of 2KM, so we were out ranged.

The Battery Commander said one of the Stinger gunners wanted to talk to me. The young soldier came up and recommended that he and his partner take two Stingers and that they go out into the no man's land between the enemy forces and our unit and then under the cover of darkness, dig a hole and when the Hinds showed up, gas 'em. And the next day that is exactly what they did. I gave those two soldiers an Army Achievement Medal when they returned to our lines. No leader should ever underestimate the ingenuity and resourcefulness of the people he works with.

Since we were going to the NTC three times a year, we got good. LTC Tom Grainy who commanded 3/19 Infantry had a rotation where he won every battle he fought, except the first one which the OCs determined was a draw. The Observer Controllers were mentioning privately that no one was better. The NTC was a challenge, accepted by the leadership of our division and every leader in our division worked hard to master. Every new idea was examined, nothing was discarded until it had been vetted. Great effort was put into making as much SOP as we could, so the planning before the battle could focus on what was most important, the enemy.

The incubator for a lot of what we did at the NTC was Captain Chuck Dreissnack, the same Vulcan Platoon Leader whom I had seen destroyed at the whale gap on my first visit to Irwin. I had asked for permission to continue to live in Savannah when I took command, which was 40 miles from Ft Stewart. The division had a policy that all commanders needed to live on post or in Hinesville. Miss Marilyn was not buying any of that, she was very happy in Savannah. It was approved for me to stay in Savannah, and I drove the 40 miles every day with an aviator lap pad on my thigh, thinking of things that we needed to do. The boys suggested that Chuck, who also lived in Savannah, should ride with me. I said ok and it quickly became apparent why they wanted me to have company on my drives. Chuck and I got in the car every night and each time he had a pile of stuff he wanted me to discuss with him. I eventually got on to what they were doing so I started driving the train.

We worked for about a year to standardize the initial positioning for a Vulcan battery in every type of offensive and defensive operation in the manuals. I wasn't getting my lists done, but I was driving the conversation. Chuck was a West Pointer, a brilliant soldier and he was a great athlete, he had run track for Army. His Dad was a retired Air Force LTG, so we got into all kinds of stuff. I would work for Chuck in my retired career. I always considered him a good friend.

General Cooley, who replaced General Schwarzkopf had brought in a new Inspector General, LTC Jim Eisenhower. Jim was a great guy, but he had convinced the old man that we needed to raise the standard with the IG Inspection. We had passed two IG inspections when I was with the battalion earlier only failing one of 38 inspected areas on each one-crew served weapons. Word started filtering in; 10 battalions in a row had failed the new standard. We started talking to everyone; this was going to be a comprehensive inspection and the areas usually excluded, like inspecting the battalion commander's jeep, were all included. Jim had told us if we had questions to ask his guys and my staff pounded the IG office with questions. We wanted to know the standard.

We had worked our butts off to be ready, everything from the in ranks inspection to the condition of our vehicles. I had hired Mike Penhallogen to be my XO. Mike had come from the IG office but he had only showed up a month or so before the inspection so his assignment did not have the full impact of what it might have. Mike had set it up that every vehicle called up for inspection would go through a five-point inspection process insuring they were as right as we could make them before the IG boys inspected them.

The day of the inspection, the soldiers marched into the motor pool with Eye of the Tiger playing on a PA system I had borrowed from my buddy, Bill Culley who was the Commander of our Signal Battalion. Sure enough, the first vehicle called was Headquarters 6, my jeep. I had lubed every vehicle in the battalion trying to lead by example, so I put on the coveralls and old hat I kept in the motor pool and went under my jeep with the inspector. He was a little surprised. No faults noted. We were off to a great start.

I checked throughout the day on how things were going. One time, I went down to the motor pool and the boys were changing a transmission on one of our Stinger Jeeps. These vehicles had been returned to us when the Stinger sections were consolidated back in the ADA battalions and my Infantry and Armor friends had not treated the vehicles well.

Jim came to see me at the end of the day. He was very surprised; we had passed every area. He commented on my soldiers and their knowledge (we had made a little pamphlet called the IG Assault Book that every soldier had carried around for a few months before the inspection -we assaulted everything), the care of our weapons and vehicles, and we had a lot of vehicles-almost 100 tracks and over 250 wheeled vehicles.

I was not a popular guy. At the next division commander's call, I sat across the table from Colonel Dennis Malcore, the commander of the 1st Brigade. He was a funny guy, always joking and he said to me "Ok Semmens, perfect score huh, you really screwed it up for the rest of us." General Cooley mentioned our IG and sort of embarrassed the rest of the commanders. Suddenly, everybody was calling us for advice on how to pass the IG, which we happily shared.

While we were preparing for the IG, we were concurrently planning a deployment to Honduras for a small portion of the battalion-a Vulcan platoon, several Stinger Gunners and assorted comm and support folks. Forces Command had a program where they sent people all over the world to collect intel and other tasks. Our job was to teach members of the Honduran Army how to shoot the Redeye, the predecessor of the Stinger, and I had finagled bringing a Vulcan Platoon for "security". All my battery commanders also went as we had the mission of surveying several Air Defense fire unit sites for potential later use.

Part of our support team was our Chaplain, Captain Ben Richardson and our Physician's Assistant or PA. We got all kinds of messages out of Southern Command telling us there was a potential threat from large groups of well-armed bandits to guidance on how to deal with civilians. The Honduran economy was in the toilet and an American dollar was worth a lot. They wanted us to help keep the economy stable, so we were not to share American money with the locals, though they pleaded for it.

Ben had found out that there were people in the vicinity of El Cajon, where we were going to do our Vulcan firing and Redeye training, that were in desperate need of clothing and medicine. He asked if we could dedicate a 463L pallet on the C5 that was going to fly us south, for clothing. A 463L pallet was 8 feet long and 4 feet wide; if the Chaplain needed a whole pallet, that was a lot of clothes. The PA had started collecting additional medical supplies. I said sure it there was room, but mission requirements took precedence.

We flew into Tegucigalpa, the capitol of Honduras. Captain Harry Bloomer, my S-3 had been in country for several weeks coordinating for sites to fire the Vulcans. Honduras then was divided into 9 regions corresponding to the 9 battalions in the Honduran army. Harry had some funny stories. He visited one battalion and after explaining the capabilities to the commander, the commander pointed to a nearby hill and suggested that as the target for our firing. Harry got his binoculars out and the hill was almost totally populated. "Sir there are people on the hill", Harry commented. "Si they are banditos" replied the commander. He wanted us to solve his problems for him. Boy would USA Today have had fun with that one.

We decided that the shoot would take place at El Cajon dam, which was about 50KM north of T-town. We coordinated with JTF-6 which was the American presence in Honduras and the commander dedicated a helicopter to me for the duration of our visit. We were checking in with Stewart every day as XVIII Airborne Corps had assigned a Satellite Radio team to our mission.

Honduras was hot and very humid. We lived in a tent city and since it rained a lot there, the streets were all mud. I was glad to get to my chopper to fly up to El Cajon. The staff was super busy arranging for transportation for the soldiers and the Vulcans north.

Honduras is a beautiful country. Our pilot who had been in country for a couple of months acted as our tourist guide, pointing out things of interest. We flew over miles and miles of banana fields run by the Dole company. It doesn't sound like much, but it was breath taking.

The Honduran battalion at El Cajon was the Honduran Special Forces battalion, commanded by a Major Piedra. His headquarters was built on the side of a hill with the battalion street, a dirt road with rocks sticking up in it all over the place, dropped off the top of the hill steeply. There were barracks on either side of the street. All northern Honduras is rugged, jungled terrain. The El Cajon dam is the only source of electricity for the entire country, so its security was important. We drove out to the potential firing site which was a dirt road just wide enough for a track. The Vulcans had to park sideways to fit, but Harry and I decided it would work. We would be firing across the dammed river into a high hill with steep hills all along the river that made it look like a Norwegian fiord. The dam was to left of the firing line. We had only brought High Explosive ammunition instead of the Target Practice Tracer (TPT) rounds that we normally fired in case we had to engage some of the banditos.

I flew back to our base camp late that afternoon. The takeoff was a bit dicey. We had landed on a large ledge just outside of the battalion headquarters. It was almost a straight drop off from that ledge. So, we had to take off, gain a little altitude and then drop into the abyss to gain air speed to get going. I had my heart in my hands each time we did it but I sure as hell wasn't going to show anyone that I was nervous. One time we were taking off and we all heard a loud POP. I was on the intercom and the crew chief who was riding back with me started yelling "what was that what was that"? The pilot immediately landed, we shut the bird down and finally concluded that the fuselage must have hit a wind current which caused the sound.

When I got back the equipment and soldiers were ready to leave for El Cajon. Several squad leaders came to me, concerned their tracks were going to fall off the trucks on the road north. The edges of the tracks were halfway off the sides of the rented Heavy Equipment Transports and they had cause for concern. We were committed and off they went. The Battery commanders dispersed to go recon their sites.

We all arrived at El Cajon; it was a miracle but there were no incidents coming up. The soldiers moved into the barracks provided for them and 1SG Rufus Wallace, the Delta Battery 1SG who was my NCO in charge for the mission and I moved into the aide station with the other officers. 1SG Wallace was a great NCO; short and thick, he was always on the move. I woke up several nights and he was up, standing on the porch of the aide station just listening. We had guards posted, the 1SG was just being with his guys.

The Vulcans spent 3 days preparing to fire and during this time, the 6 or so Stinger gunners would train groups of 30 or so Hondurans to fire the Redeye. The boys noticed the 3d day that the same 8-10 guys returned each day for training. I asked Piedra who they were, and he replied, "Contras". An adjacent country had secured Hind helicopters and the Hondurans were preparing to defend themselves. I called Mike Penhallogen one night on the TACSAT which had accompanied us to El Cajon and asked him to inquire with the division headquarters if we could ship a couple of Redeyes to Honduras and put on a dog and pony show. Mike was nervous, everyone was worried about security for the missiles, but he said he would ask. He first met with the Chief of Staff, Colonel Gene Daniels who said not just no, but hell no. Mike agreed with him, but when they asked General Cooley, who was an out of the box thinker, he said ok.

General Cooley came down to see us. We had already fired the Vulcans and since we were using HE ammunition, we put the hill opposite of us, over the river, on fire. We recovered the Vulcans and Redeye boys back to Tegucigalpa; the commanders were done with their survey and all we had left on this mission was this dog and pony Redeye shoot outside the capitol. General Cooley was there along with the commander of JTF-6 and several Honduran dignitaries. One Redeye failed to fire and the other missed. Oh well, those missiles were 15 years old.

We began to pack up to leave and we had a lot less stuff than when we came down. While we were at El Cajon, the Chaplain and the PA put out the word that there would be a doctor and some clothes at a location about 10KM away, in the middle of nowhere, in two days. Remember, we had a heck of a lot of clothes and the PA had stocked up on his medical supplies. I wanted to send an Infantry squad with them, but they went out unescorted. They returned that night empty handed, they had given out all those clothes and the PA had given so many inoculations that they had to turn people away. There is always a time for good in any mission.

Command was coming to an end, I only had about 10 days until the ceremony. Our time in Savannah had been great. We enjoyed Cade and Rita a lot, the boys were growing up and Savannah was a great town to live in. I remember playing catch with the boys on our front lawn with a nerf football. Rob was Mark Duper and Mike was Clayton, the other star receiver on the Dolphins. I was Dan Marino of course and I was good when the maximum throw was 15 yards. Rob had started playing soccer and I volunteered with another guy to help coach. We didn't know anything about soccer, so we were telling the boys to hit someone. We played in Dauphin Park in downtown Savannah in January, I just remember it was colder than a gravedigger's bottom in January. That team was the classic example of a team that needed to ignore their coach. Rob and I would have another similar experience when he was a high school senior.

Nana came and visited her old town several times. I was disappointed that Dad stayed at home. Each time a few weeks before she came, the phone started ringing off the wall. All the conversations went something like this: "Hello, is Mary Kate there?" I'd reply: "No she won't be here for a couple of weeks; can I take your name and number so I can have her call you?" Then I would hear "No sugar, this is Dorthey she has my number." That would end the call so when Nana arrived, we had a list of names and no numbers for Nana to call. These were Mom's high school friends and she managed to get hold of all of them. Nana had all the numbers.

Some might consider the people in Savannah to be outright rude. If you were not a native son or daughter, they were polite to you, but you could tell you weren't really included. When I was at Hunter, the General's secretary was Mrs. Maggie Hartnett who had married a man from Savannah 40 years earlier and had moved to Savannah from South Carolina where she grew up. One day I asked her "Miss Maggie, have they accepted you yet?" She replied: "Oh no sir". I then asked her if she thought they ever would, and she just nodded her head no.

The day for the change of command came. It was a beautiful day. My replacement, LTC Al Whitley was a good guy and we had spent a lot of time together transitioning. I was worried about turning my baby over, but Al turned out to be a super commander and we would work at Bliss together later. I remember, I stood on that field and thanked God for putting me in that place, prepared. General Cooley had some nice things to say, and it was over. My lasting thought from battalion command in a line infantry division, besides all the great people I served with, was the constant mentality of getting it done, NOW. Sure, we planned a lot, but day to day whether it was an administrative task or whatever, you didn't wait. You got it done. It was a time of great personal satisfaction. I always had a notebook with me in which I wrote everything down and a small 3 ring notebook that I carried in the cargo pocket of my BDUs where I assigned tasks to the staff and commanders. The boys hated that notebook.

Our next assignment was in Washington DC at the Pentagon. All the separate battalion commanders failed to get selected for the War College after command because none of us had 2 efficiency reports as a battalion commander. We all received one report from General Schwarzkopf and a "Complete the Record" OER from General Cooley. The CG had been in command for 90 days, insufficient time to really get to know any of us, so all our OERs read the same: "I like what I see so far but I have been command for an insufficient time to evaluate their potential." It was fair and we all saw our non-selection for school coming. MG Schwarzkopf was like the rest of us, he had to take a staff job before he took Corps command. He became the Deputy to the Deputy Chief of Staff for Operations, the #2 operations officer for the Army. So, I wrote him and told him that they were doing the same thing to me that they did to him and asked him for a recommendation for a job. After a period of some months, I got a call from a Colonel from an organization in DCSOPS called the Army Initiatives Group, or AIG. The AIG was the four-man personal staff for the DCSOPS, and they had a chief, the Colonel, a LTC who wrote the DCSOPS' speeches and another LTC who did his presentations. The third LTC was an experienced Pentagon veteran who knew the building. I was going to replace that guy, even though I had never been assigned to the Pentagon. Confusion existed because my record reflected that I was assigned to the Pentagon when I was at the Air Force Academy. Army officers are always assigned to an Army unit, even when they work for another service.

CHAPTER TWELVE

WASHINGTON, DC, 1986-88

We had bought a house from the widow of the third General I had worked for at Hunter. General Dick Sharpe had died at Hunter, and I was assigned as his survivor assistance officer, and I got to know Mrs. Sharp helping her plan her affairs and bury the General. She had brought up the house sale, but it took a long time to negotiate the occupancy date and price. In the middle of all this, the AIG Colonel had called me and told me I had to report into Washington 5 days after the change of command. So, we jumped in the car, drove to Washington stayed in very poor quarters while we were waiting for our house to be ready.

I reported into the Pentagon, got badged up and all that. I went to the AIG office and was told that I had been assigned to the Force Planning Office in DCSOPS. What had happened was General S. had left to take Corps Command the Friday before I showed up and over the weekend, I had been reassigned. My new boss was Colonel Hugh Kelley, who I knew from Stewart. When I reported in, he had me come into his office. He apologized for the confusion, told me why I had been moved and gave me the best advice I ever got about working in the Pentagon "This place has nothing to do with soldiers; it's all about money". The second-best piece of advice I got about life in the Pentagon was to hang out an imaginary sign that said "Expert". It didn't matter in what you were an expert, one just had to be the go-to guy for something in the Pentagon, it made the time pass as you met lots of people throughout the entire Army. I became the "expert" on a major analysis the Army was doing, The Conventional Defense Enhancement study and the Operations Research System Analysis (ORSA) program.

Kelly gave me a week to help Marilyn move in. Our house was in beautiful Mount Vernon, an area about 7 miles due south of the Pentagon, near George Washington's plantation. It was a split level with a detached garage and with drainage problems that we never solved. It was two blocks away from the boy's school and less than a mile from the George Washington Parkway, the road I took to the Pentagon every morning which had a bike trail that paralleled it all the way to the Pentagon and to parts beyond. The house was plenty big for us. Dad came out one summer and we finished a storeroom in the basement. Margie and Andy Smoak, our friends from the Air Force Academy moved into the same area.

Life working in the Pentagon was exciting. One always felt that you were doing something important. About 6 months after I got there, Dr. Herb Fallen who I had gotten to know while working for Colonel Kelly was appointed head an organization in DCSOPS called the Analysis Directorate supposedly putting it on an equal basis with the other directorates, such as Force

Planning which managed all the Army's weapons programs which was led by a Major General.

Life in the Pentagon took some adjustment. The first adjustment was getting to work. Although we only lived 7 miles from work, if I did not leave before 6AM to drive those 7 miles it would take me an hour to get to work. Likewise, if I left before 7PM to go home it would be another hour to get home as both ways I had to drive through old Town Alexandria, Virginia. We didn't usually work on weekends but there were some long days caused by the traffic situation.

The second adjustment was the leveling of rank in the building. I was there about a week when I had to xerox a large document. There were big copiers dispersed throughout the hallways for this purpose. There were always lines, lines for the copiers, lines at coke machines to get a drink. So, I was standing in line to use the copier and standing a few places behind me was a Brigadier General with his papers. I turned to him and said: "Sir if you tell me where you work, I'll do that for you and bring it to your office." He smiled and politely declined. I learned later that waiting in line was one of the few times during a day that a leader in the Pentagon got a break. It certainly was a go, go place.

After working on odd jobs for a few months, I finally got a real job. The DCSOPS finally decided to stand up the Analysis Directorate under Dr. Fallen and I was appointed the Deputy. We were supposedly the oversight for all the analysis going on in the Army, but we had a very small office, so we did our best. The Army was running a big study called the Conventional Defense Enhancement study that was "proving" if the Army received another $30B we could hold the International German Boundary for 30 days without the use of nuclear weapons. All the firepower of our conventional forces were upgraded, unit authorizations were updated and late in the study I inserted an Air Defense Brigade into every division.

The Chief of Force Development, MG Woodmansee, had me go to AUSA one year and brief on the program and when I was asked if they should believe the study, I said "The analysis certainly seems to point in that direction." MG Woodmansee chewed me out when we got back to the Pentagon. He believed we could hold the IGB; but I knew the analysis was only as good as the numbers that went into it. I ran into an Infantry Colonel named Dave Hugus, who became a friend and helped me understand the analysis I was looking at. Dave was Operations Research & Systems Analysis trained, and we were using a software called CORBAN. He and I went to Leavenworth, and he made me sit through a coding meeting for the model for a whole day. Painful, but I got an appreciation for the workings of the model. No pain, no gain. One time, we received an intel report that the accuracy of the Soviet Rocket Systems was greatly improved. We raised the probability of kill for those systems and the next time we ran an analysis and the front just collapsed. I went to Dr Fallen and he told me to deep six the result. This study was tottering on the edge for sure, but that's what one did in the Pentagon; make dreams to get money.

The study came in handy. In the spring of 1988, President Reagan went to Iceland and negotiated an agreement to do away with nuclear weapons. The Joint Chiefs put together a Task Force to assess the impact and I was the Army rep. When the AF Colonel who was the lead of the joint study asked when we could have our analysis ready, I told him the Army could be ready tomorrow. He looked at me unbelievingly and I told him we had been working on this problem for over a year. I thought the Air Force guy was going to have a heart attack.

The Air Force was good in the building, unlike the Army who assigned guys there once, the AF had pros who understood the Program Objective Memorandum (the DOD budget) process and knew what they were doing after serving multiple tours in Washington. I often thought we spent so much time on the Army Staff just trying to figure out what to do. Anyway, the AF ran their big computers out in New Mexico someplace nonstop for a week and we briefed the JCS Colonel less than a week after the first meeting. He seemed happy with me and the AF but when it came to the Navy, the Navy rep said that Admiral So in So, the N3 said 600 ships. The Colonel said where is your analysis? The Navy guy replied that they had none, just the N3's decision. The results of the study went to what was called the tank, a room where the Joint Chiefs of Staffs met. At one heated meeting, the Navy was told very bluntly to do some analysis to support their conclusion. So, they did some and the answer was a 600 ship Navy.

Since we were the "technicians" in DCSOPS we received some cool gear to test, including the first personal computers in the Army. They were all Macintoshes. I learned to use mine easily and when the Generals in FD learned I could make charts; every free minute was expended making and correcting charts for the Generals. One of the FD Generals who used my emerging skills a lot, was BG Jay Garner. I had met General Garner when I was in the pre-command course at Ft Bliss. He had just been selected for Brigade Command. He would become my mentor and we would serve together again many times.

Life in the Pentagon followed the same routine. I would meet Andy Smoak at 5:50 AM at a nearby bus stop where he would park his car. I drove every day in payment for his driving in with me which allowed us to get a parking space in the carpool lot. If I worked later that he did, he would just take the bus home. After arriving in the Pentagon at 6:10AM I would go to the Pentagon Officers Athletic center, which at that time was a not so nice gym facility in the building. We would run every morning up the GW Parkway and occasionally into Washington around the Lincoln Memorial. I would then take a shower, go by the snack bar by our office and buy a cup of coffee and a cinnamon roll (they were awesome) and get to work, ending my day around 1830. I would drive home and do it all over again the next day.

The boys were old enough to get into sports. Mike was about 10 and he decided that he wanted to play soccer. When I filled out his paperwork to join the league there was a line at the bottom that said: "Would you be interested in coaching?" I wrote I would coach only if there wouldn't be a team if I didn't. I ended up coaching the Raiders and since practice was at 1700, I had to fight the traffic I normally missed to get home to coach. We went 0-4-4, tying our last 4 games of the year.

The next fall, I was doing my fellowship, so I happily signed up again. I was allowed to keep some of the boys from the spring team. We lost our first game. Mike played goalie and we just didn't generate a lot of offense. The second game, Shef, who was Mike's buddy from down the street and one of our forwards, was sick and couldn't play. I had another goalie, whom I didn't trust much but I needed a forward, so I put him in the goal and moved Mike up. Mike scored 3 goals and we won big! Everything just flowed. Before our third game, I was penciling in the lineup when the Navy Commander who was helping me coach came up. I shared the lineup with him, and I remember he said: "Are you nuts?" I had put Mike back in goal. So, I played Mike at forward that game and he got 2 goals and almost a third. Mike led that league in scoring that year and we ended up 6-1. During our last game, a guy came up to me and asked if I would be interested in coaching select soccer. After some discussion and the promise that I could pick my players, I said sure.

    I went out and recruited players, mostly kids from my team and the league volunteered me a couple of more. There was a lot of administrative things to do; buying uniforms, patches which were exchanged at tournaments, travel arrangements. We went to our first tournament and got our butts beat. The game was just a little too quick for us. The boys adjusted and we tied our last two games, but our record was 0-7-2. We almost won our last game; it was a windy day and one of our guys blocked a pass from the other team. The ball flew up and started bouncing toward the other team's goal. Its final bounce was right in front of the net and my guy went up with the goalie and knocked it into the goal. The ref said it was no goal but then ran over to me and explained that he thought the goalie had enough control of the ball, which meant the play was dead. Soccer rules state that if the goalie has the ball in his hands, he is off limits. He added that if he made that call 100 times, he probably would call it a goal half the time. I was sad for the boys, but that ref's explanation helped me later when I was a ref. Referees are human, you just need to explain to the coaches what you saw and why you made the call.

    We had a kid from Honduras on our team and his dad came to me at the end of the season suggesting that we have a camp. He was a graduate of Howard University there in Washington, and he knew 3 guys on the team who would come out and give us a camp. So, we did it. One of the Howard players was a goalie named Shaka Hislop. He was 6'3" tall and fast as a cat. One of the dads came by one day and asked if Shaka was any good. So, I told the dad that Shaka and I would run a little demo for him; Shaka would punt the ball at distances of at least 40 yards into a radius formed by my arms being extended from my sides. Shaka was 9 for 10, one try was just a foot outside my outstretched arm. Shaka would go on the play professionally in the English Premiere League for over a decade.

I decided that I had to go get my coaching license if we were to get good. I went all the way out to James Madison University to take a coaching course from a gentleman named Gordon Bradley. Gordon was the coach of the JMU soccer team and was involved in the forming of a new professional league in Washington. He had played at the AAA level in the English professional leagues. He taught me a lot: everything from what to wear as a coach to loving the ball.

Our team went into the next season much better prepared. I had an assignment coming up, so I knew my time with the Raiders was short. We added a tall oriental kid who was good and when I left, we were 5-2.

Rob was playing baseball in a neighborhood league. His coach was a Navy Admiral, who was a great guy. They used a field in the neighborhood and at the start of each season, all the dads and moms would go out and do grounds keeping. I always thought Rob was a good baseball player and watching him and his teammates play was a lot of fun. Rob would play one more season of baseball and then he turned to soccer.

Because we were the directorate that got all the off the wall taskers, one day a tasking asking us to review the Army's fellows program came across my desk. Instead of going to the

War College every year, 65 guys were selected to go off and do a myriad of other assignments for which they received credit for the War College. We had guys with industry, several academic fellowships, including one at the Center of Military History. We recommended that the Army cut about half of them including the one at OCMH.

The War College list came out and I was on it. A short time after I had been notified of that selection Mr. John Rientti, who was Dr Fallen's deputy came and in and told me I had been selected to be the first Fellow to the Center of Military History. He asked me "isn't that one of the fellowships we cut?" I replied yes and he just laughed and walked off.

Later that day I got a call from BG Bill Stoft who was the Director of the Center. We set up an appointment.

CHAPTER THIRTEEN

CENTER OF MILITARY HISTORY 1987-88

The Center of Military History is in downtown Washington D.C. Back then I didn't have the money to take the metro every day so I would have to drive my Plymouth Van up the GW Parkway, across the Memorial Bridge and into downtown Washington to the Center. I met with General Stoft, and he told me my mission was to write a long paper or short book on any subject I wanted. He wanted an outline in 6 months and the first draft in a year. It was a 2-year fellowship that I wanted to finish in a year. I was on blanket TDY orders. I could come to the office, where I had an office with two civilian history fellows or stay home and work. Wow.

I drove to downtown DC every day for about 3 months. The roads were so bad, one day I was blocked in and had to take the van through a huge pothole which broke a shock.

Getting enough data to even start an outline for the book was a struggle. I went to the National Archives and to Ft. Monroe that had a history collection of the Coast Artillery. I also went to Carlyle Barracks that had a military history center as well. At all these stops I got bits and pieces for the book, but I noted that there was a lot of stuff on the Pacific, but not much on the European Campaign. I finally talked to a guy who told me what happened. In the late 1940's the commander of the Air Defense Center at Ft Bliss, MG Von Falkenberg, who was a veteran of the Pacific campaign, was approached by the post librarian who said he didn't have enough room for all the WWII records that had been submitted to the library. Von Falkenberg told him to burn the European records which he did. What a terrible decision, surely there was a warehouse somewhere on Ft Bliss where the records could have been stored. This decision created a real problem for me as I had decided to write my book on the AAA in Europe.

We had a week- long orientation at the War College in late August, where the fellows were told that we part of the class and would never be forgotten, etc., all of which was forgotten after we left. At graduation, we had a little problem getting our diplomas and we had to fight to be included as part of the class to purchase the print the class had commissioned. Guess our idea at Leavenworth almost ten years earlier had had an impact.

One of the interesting things we did was on our first visit, we reported to the gym where we had our body fat checked in a water tank and we were asked to do bench presses on a bench press machine. The guy on the machine next to me was knocking out 180 pounds, I could only do 120. I told the instructor with me that I must be a pansy and he replied: "Sir you did good, the average soldier in the Army can only do 80 pounds." I made a mental note, I would have to work on upper body strength for my soldiers. As a battalion commander our PT sessions always included pull ups and climbing of 20' high ropes, but I decided we needed to do things to push more. I would encourage soldiers to use the gym.

About two months into the project, I was about ready to change topics when I got a call from the Editor of the Retired Officers' Magazine. After confirming I was writing a book on WWII, he said he would give me a free advertisement in the magazine for 6 months. So, I wrote my little ad stating "Ack Ack Veterans of the battles of Kasserine Pass and the Remagen Bridge please contact LTC Paul Semmens, OCMH" and I included my office telephone number.

As I said I had been going downtown every day for months. Us three fellows had a secretary named Terry. Every day I would ask Terry, "Any messages bud?" and I got the usual head nod no. After the first issue of the magazine was published, the phone started ringing off the hook. Many of the calls were not what I was looking for such as: "Colonel this is Harold Smith, I served with the Ack Ack on Iwo Jima." These guys just wanted to be heard and propped up a little so I would ask them about their weapon system and any other generic topic that I could think of.

One day I hit pay dirt. A Colonel Sandy McGrain called me who had been the S-3 of the 49th AAA Brigade, the headquarters that led all the Air Defense units into Europe. The network started. I talked to several staff officers from the 49th, who knew guys and just kept connecting and connecting. I finally found Omar Bradley's Air Defense Officer Colonel Pat Patterson and called him. He invited me down to his house in

Florida for a few days to talk. We talked the first night that I arrived and at least 8 hours a day for the next two days. I filled 16 cassette tapes with information. He gave me the ADA log from Headquarters Supreme Allied Command Headquarters which was super helpful. The National Archives chased me for two years to get those documents which I eventually gave the museum at Ft Bliss.

Colonel Pat was a super guy and McGrain had warned me he was a little bit of a braggard. I was conservative in all my documentation, insuring I had at least two oral sources or a good written source before anything went in the book. But some things in war can never be accurately documented and I believed something Colonel Patterson told me and that would bite me later. The calls kept coming in. I got to have a long talk with an Air Defense Platoon leader at Remagen and another at Kasserine Pass. Things were coming together. The WWII generation is often called the greatest generation. I believe that is true; every person I talked to was proud and confident.

I prepared my first draft and sent it to my Dad for review. Dad had served for four years in the AAA in the Pacific during WWII. He convened a panel of his buddies, all retired Air Defenders; Col John Goettle, Colonel Dave Pryor, Colonel Lon Dickson, and Colonel Lee Lewis. Dad ran the review like a military operation briefing the team on the ground rules up front. They had very few comments and a few questions, but their review gave me the confidence that the book was accurate.

I submitted the book to General Stoft. After a few weeks he told me that the Center was not going to publish it. To use his words, "I think you drank the Kool Aide the old boys told you." There was no appeal. I was disappointed and went back and reviewed my documentation. I was satisfied that I was solid except for one item. Colonel Patterson had told me that he had ordered a 90MM Gun Battalion to suck up to the rear of the advancing divisions as they approached the Remagen Bridge. I thought Colonel Pat's statement was true as there was 90MM gun overwatch of the bridge the second day. I stood by what I had done. It was okay, we were out of there anyway.

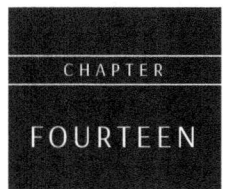

CHAPTER FOURTEEN

FORT BLISS, TEXAS, 1988-90

I had received a call from BG Jay Garner who was the new Assistant Commandant of the Air Defense School. He wanted me to be the Director of Tactics, my dream job. So, I processed out of the OCMH and drove my van to Texas. Marilyn and the boys would work the move. I would fly back to DC and drive our second car down to Texas again. Marilyn and the boys would fly down to eventually meet me.

Being a promotable LTC meant we were eligible for a big house on Sheridan Road, the main drag of Ft Bliss. Unfortunately, the quarters were being renovated so I stayed with my Uncle Skee and his wife, Aunt Liz. When Uncle Skee retired they built a beautiful house on Titanic drive with expansive porches from which they could overlook the lights of the city of El Paso at night. Uncle Skee was a brilliant guy who got throat cancer just when he was coming up for consideration for promotion to General. He didn't get selected, and I think it really bothered him. Aunt Liz was from El Paso. She was a beautiful woman who made the best Mexican food I have ever had in my life. They were very kind and generous with me, and I loved them for it.

I reported to General Garner at the school, and he told me that there was a new program called Project Warrior where Observer-Controllers (OCs) from the NTC would come to the schoolhouse to teach Lieutenants and Captains. It was a great idea; soldiers who had been evaluating combat operations in the most realistic environment we could create would now be assigned to the schoolhouse to teach the new lieutenants everything they knew before their first assignment.

Two days after being assigned to Bliss I flew out to Irwin on a T-41, a four passenger Army aircraft. More on T-41s later. The head ADA OC, Major Roger Mathews met me, and he guided me around the battlefield to meet the four officers I was sent to recruit. It went well with the first three Joel Cowan, Clay Earnest and Jeff Herndon. All were excited and ready to come to Bliss. Two task forces were doing live fire, so the boys were all in the same general location. The fourth OC was on the other side of the installation, near that famous crash hill, the site years before where my Stinger gunners displayed so much initiative. Roger and I drove there. We stopped and I saw my fourth candidate get out of his HUMV. My first impression was he did not have a neck; he was short, thick, he was totally covered in dirt and his body language even from afar indicated he wanted no part of this meeting.

His name was Armando Macias, who ended up serving with me multiple times and who became my best friend in the Army. Mando was not receptive to my sales pitch about Bliss, in fact telling me he wasn't going to come. I said ok and when he left our meeting, he went back to main Fort Irwin and called Colonel Jim Barber at the Personnel Command who had been his battalion commander on his previous assignment and who was now the ADA Colonel's assignment officer.

The rest of the story came out later. Mando was the Adjutant of 3/61 ADA, a job I had previously in the same outfit, and the battalion was facing an IG inspection. Mando was famous in the division. One time the battalion was seriously short of Vulcan Crewmen and after multiple requisitions, the situation wasn't getting any better. So Mando got a 2 ½ truck and drove down to the replacement depot in Frankfurt where all the incoming personnel were staged before being taken to their units. He walked into the big room where the soldiers were waiting and called out "Are there any 16Rs (Vulcan crewmen) in here." Mando then selectively picked most of them and told them to get in the truck. When the Adjutant General of the Division, the personnel officer in charge of assigning enlisted personnel, found out, he was furious. Mando weathered the storm and got to keep his soldiers.

Back to the IG inspection, Barber told Mando that he had orders to Washington where he would be working personnel assignments, and if he stayed for the inspection, he would ensure that Mando went to graduate school, his desire. Mando was supposed to go to Hawaii to be the manager of the Hale Koa, the military hotel there. Dream job. Mando was a CPA, so he was perfect for the job. Reluctantly, Mando said ok and lost a job in Hawaii.

His first call with Barber went well. Jim told him not to worry grad school was his. I went back to Bliss and told Garner what had transpired, and he got on the phone with branch and told me the Macias problem was fixed. A week later Mando got orders to Bliss. He called Jim Barber, whom I know felt terrible, who told him grad school was off.

The boys reported in a few months later, with Mando expecting only God knows what. I welcomed them and a week later he was back in my office saying he had to go on leave. His mother had passed. He wanted a week's leave and I told him to take as much time as he needed. Then, I didn't understand the extraordinary place mothers have in Hispanic families. Mando's father ran the mines in Silver City New Mexico, which was only two hours from El Paso. Mando and his four brothers worked with their Dad, played sports, and enjoyed life. But his mother oversaw their spiritual development. She took them all to mass 3 times on Sundays so they would "get it".

Mando went into the Army after high school and became a paratrooper. He was assigned to the 509th Infantry in Vincenza, Italy, and his unit worked and played very hard. When he was discharged, he returned home and after a welcoming hug, the first thing his mother said to him was "When was the last time you went to confession?" Mando replied "Well 6 years ago Mom when I left for the Army." His mother immediately called the local priest and arranged for Mando to go see him. When the priest asked Mando what his sins were, he replied "All of them Father". Shocked, the priest went and got an examination of conscience card which listed all the sins, and Mando went down the list checking most of them off with a "yep". Mando was a character, full of life, funny and a damn good officer.

We had to train all the incoming Lieutenants, writing all the branch's manuals and overwatching the NCO Education Program which wrote all the lesson plans and prepared the classes for the NCO Academy. I had two retired CSMs, John

Sides and Billy Coleman who did everything for the Academy. They would come in every once and a while and essentially pay me a courtesy call to remind me they were there. They were professionals and when one has pros, you just turn them loose.

The focus of our programs was to make the Lieutenants ready to do their jobs the minute they walked in the door of their new assignments. For the Lieutenants going to divisions that involved creating a new mindset as well as teaching them tactics and maintenance of their equipment. To help with this process we had an NCO assigned to every Basic Course small group who tutored the Lieutenants on the key to their success: working well with their Sergeants. Colonel Jim Smith, my predecessor had instituted the small group policy where students were taught everything in classes no bigger than 16 students with the same instructor for the whole course. It was a great educational advancement and once the OCs had time with the students, Battalion Commanders started calling me all the time telling me how happy they were with their new Lieutenants.

We worked very hard at getting the Lieutenants physically fit and worked on their upper body strength. Everything was a competition including the semi-annual PT test. I had had pullup bars installed and pullups were counted as part of the score for winning the "best section" PT award. An individual couldn't fail the PT test for not doing 6 pullups but including pullups gave an extra incentive to work on their upper body strength. The sections going to divisions had no women, so they did well on the pull ups.

One day a female Lieutenant came in with a convincing story that the Army had decided not to make women do pull ups. I said I would check it out. I called Captain Chuck Anderson, who was an outstanding officer who worked for me at Stewart first as the Assistant Division Air Defense Officer and then as an outstanding Battery Commander. I had worked to get Chuck in my battalion. He had taken the job at West Point over my recommendation to the contrary. I told him it was dead time, but he did it anyway and recovered from it quite well. He would retire as a Major General.

Chuck told me that women DID do pull ups in the Army, that there was no policy against it, and he had women do pull ups at West Point. I informed the Lieutenant and pull ups stayed in the PT competition, but I got the post to buy a Grav-a-tron, a gym machine that assisted with both pull up and dips. You could dial in the amount of help you wanted the machine to give you. I had it installed right in the hallway of the Basic Course wing of Hinman Hall, where we taught. The girls started doing better. My office was right under that of the CG.

My days followed the same routine. Marilyn and the boys arrived, and we finally moved into our quarters. The day we moved in it was hot. The quarters had evaporative cooling, but El Paso was experiencing a rise in the relative humidity, so it didn't help much. I walked out our back door and a neighbor's wife came out wearing a T-shirt that said: "Sherman said war is hell but moving is second." The boys attended St Pius X grade school and Marilyn was very involved with the school.

Our Commanding General was MG Don Infante, one of the finest men I had ever known. When I had my initial interview with him, he asked how the book came out and I told him OCMH wouldn't publish it and why. He said that wasn't a problem as Ft Bliss had a printing plant and he would see that they published it. Additionally, the school historian, a lady named Patty Burke was placed in direct support of me to finish up the details. Patty was a very quiet person, but she really carried the ball getting the book published.

Once the book came out General Infante had me travel to Chicago to give a presentation to a group of WWII Air Defense veterans, about 5 battalions worth. I took about 10 copies of the book with me. The Master of Ceremonies for the event took the books and told me he would give them to the right people. I mentioned during the presentation that I wasn't sure that the 636th Antiaircraft Battalion was at the Remagen bridge, as I had no written sources but did have a map of the operation placed them there. After the presentation, the guys who got a book came up to me and asked if I would sign them. I said of course.

They lined up and came up one by one. I asked each one for their names and what they had done in the great war and when the 5th guy came up, he told me his name. When I asked him what he did in the war, he replied "I commanded the 636th. He then continued "you are right, we were there." Boy it is amazing how God connects the dots. General Infante wanted to build branch pride, so for two commander's conferences in a row, he had me give a pitch to the commanders, the first on Remagen and Kasserine and the second on D-Day. It was great fun.

By 1989 war clouds were on the horizon. Sadam Hussein was threatening to invade Kuwait and our policy was we would defend Saudi Arabia. By then MG Don Leonetti had taken command. I never got along that well with him, but I give him the fact he had guts. He was not afraid to make a decision.

The Colonels on the school staff started meeting weekly and later daily. The Patriot Air Defense System had just been fielded and was equipped with its first version of anti-Tactical Ballistic Missile software. No one had given much consideration to the Tactical Ballistic Missile threat and so the initial software only had the capability to protect the fire unit against missiles. Well good old Sadam had TBMs, and he had proven he was not reluctant to use them.

The Colonels were called for a meeting one day at the CG's conference room where we normally met. The room had a large conference table and stadium seating for almost 100 people. When we walked in the tiered seats in the rear of the room were filled with suits- civilians, and one civilian was sitting at the conference table. The guy at the table was the Patriot project manager for the Raytheon corporation which had built Patriot. General Leonetti started the meeting asking what the probability of kill was for the system outside the self-protect zone. The answer was low, slightly better than 50%; the boss asked what we could do to make it better. The PM said they were working on a new version of the software that would have a much better capability against TBMs, but it would not be fielded for several months. The boss said that was not good enough, we believed an attack was imminent and that we had to do something. That's when all the suits went to work until lunch time. One guy had the first laptop computer I had ever seen.

We returned from lunch and as everyone was getting started, one of the suits in the back row, a real young guy, raised his hand. MG Leonetti acknowledged him, and he asked: "Sir can we shoot two?" The boss looked at me and I said I see no reason why not and the PM flashed a big smile. The other Colonels concurred. After about 30 minutes of analysis, the PK was stated to be 70% plus which the boss said was ok. The problem we didn't understand at the time was we might have the coverage to engage TBMs, but we did not have the accuracy to hit them on the warhead, causing them to explode in the air.

During Desert Storm, with one exception, Patriot batteries pretty much hit all the incoming targets but in the middle or back of the missile, which cause all the debris to come down on what we were defending. This was a real issue in the defense of Tel Aviv late in the war. We were knocking them down, but all the junk was falling into the city and the Israelis were not happy. They would eventually develop their own counter TBM systems. We ended up putting video cameras above the heads of the TCOs in the Patriot vans where real time analysis confirmed that the TBMs were breaking into pieces either due to a Patriot hit or in many cases on their own.

Another problem with Patriot was it didn't have a planner. In the older Air Defense systems like Hawk the system was designed to acquire, track, and engage the target and while there was a lot of operator actions before the decision was made to hit the fire button, the system did everything after.

TBMs were a new problem. Although their trajectory could be predicted they were so fast that an accurate timing of the fire command was not humanly possible. Hawk had introduced an automatic mode when I commanded my Hawk battery in Korea, but that system still required the Tactical Control Officer to hit a button to initiate an engagement. As soon as our Hawk system was upgraded, a Modification Work Order came out which required the welding of a steel cage over the automatic fire button. Our tactical thinking at the time was we absolutely needed the man in the loop, someone to initiate any fire command. TBMs ended that era, all engagements of them in the future would be automatic.

A system planner set the conditions for the engagement of a TBM in Patriot. Eventually TBM types were entered which allowed the system to react much more quickly as it was adjusting off known data, vice trying to predict the impact and intercept point from scratch each time. The Raytheon boys knew what was needed but just hadn't gotten to its development.

One day one of my instructors, Captain Harry Cohen came into my office. Harry was a brilliant guy who had the background to figure this planner thing out. He came into my office and asked if he could brief me on what he had found out. I didn't understand a word he said, but he was confident it would make a difference, so we went up the tape and eventually briefed General Leonetti. The boss got what Harry was saying and sent him to Saudi to brief all the batteries in the 11th Air Defense Brigade which was the senior ADA tactical headquarters in theater. I then lost another instructor to the war.

Captain Pete Loebs, another of my Patriot guys in Tactics, who had served with Patriot before he came to the Department was sent to command F 3/43 ADA and defended against the largest Scud volley during the war. Pete was defending Riyad air base which had three runways that formed a triangle. The battery was right in the middle of the triangle. When the battle started, Pete went into the van with his inexperienced, 2LT Tactical Control Officer and he fought the entire battle with her. Sadam fired double digit TBMs at the airbase that night, and Pete and his boys and girls fought through the clutter on their screens and engaged them all. The air base had no damage. Peter looked up at the missile counter in the firing in the van at the first lull in the battle and realized that he only had 2 missiles left! They had fired 34 missiles. He got his only missile reloader going and called over to airfield ops and told the boys he needed every forklift they had-NOW. A few minutes later Pete looked out the back door of the van and he saw 10 little headlights crossing the airfield and headed his way. A forklift can load a Patriot launcher and the Army-Air Force team reloaded the battery in record time.

In the future, Patriot, THAAD, GMD-would all have very sophisticated planners which the operators needed to understand and that would give me another 20 years of employment later.

Saddam invaded Kuwait and the US declared war. The 11th Brigade prepared to deploy. All the divisions had their organic Chapparal Vulcan battalions. The short-range Air Defense boys were going to do what they always did, suck up on the rear of the mechanized formations as they lacked the range to overwatch the maneuver. After he took Kuwait, Saddam built an impressive tank ditch across southern Kuwait. It was envisioned that breaching that obstacle would be a close combat, tank on tank operation. The enemy had helicopters that could stand off 3KM and engage our forces. So, the problem for the Air Defenders is we had to get our troops way up forward to cover the breach and the thin APC armor which all our Vulcans and APCs had, was not considered survivable in chaos of close ranged tank warfare.

The whole Army was concerned about that breech and TRADOC formed a breach committee which included a full Colonel representative from each branch. I was the ADA guy and this little team talked through all kinds of options. We all went out to Ft Irwin, where they had constructed an exact replica of the tank ditch in southern Kuwait. The idea of the day was to have the Air Force come in with heavy bombers and drop 500-pound bombs; they had a live demo set up. The B-52 flew in and dropped about 30 bombs on the target. We were circling the area in helicopters and the concussion was so intense, we started swaying back and forth. We landed and all those bombs had blown up some concertina wire, but the ditch was intact. We eventually came up with a plan, but nobody, I mean nobody was confident of its success.

I flew out to Ft Riley Kansas to visit LTC Cliff Willis who was the commander of the ADA battalion in the Big Red One, the 1st Infantry Division, who was going to conduct the breach. All my correspondence with the commanders in the field over the readiness of their new Lieutenants had formed a rapport of trust. I flew out to Ft Riley and briefed Cliff and his boys on the plan. I left worried they would have to do something heroic to keep the enemy helicopters off the breaching units.

After a long buildup, the date of the invasion came. We were briefing the students at the end of each day, so they were aware of what was up. Like the tank ditch on my first visit to the NTC, the dreaded obstacle turned out to be no problem as the enemy had pulled back and the boys crossed the obstacle with no problem. I said a prayer of thanks. I watched enviously on CNN while my old division, the 24th, led the hail Mary north. We sent out a Christmas card every year that had a picture of the division patch with the caption "All I want for Christmas is to wear this on my right sleeve" indicating a combat veteran with that unit. Watching my old outfit was sad, but they did well.

In the middle of all the preparations, General Garner came into my office and said General Schwarzkopf wanted an ADA Colonel on his staff. There were two choices: me or Jeff Gault who was a promotable ADA LTC who worked for me. I talked to Jeff, and he went to theater. I have always regretted that decision. I knew General Schwarzkopf and got along with him very well. On the other hand, we were still training Lieutenants and Captains to go into theater. That was the rationale for my staying along with Marilyn's concern. I regret that decision to this day. Had I gone, I might have been a General, but I came close anyway.

With the war over very quickly, the boys came home, and we invited all the commanders to Ft Bliss for an After-Action Review which I coordinated. It was a great time; we learned a lot. We talked a great deal about Patriot performance and the absence of theater level ADA logistics support. We had an Army AD Command in Germany commanded by a two-star General, who had the people to perform the theater logistics mission. But with all deployments, the Army was trying to balance getting enough capability into theater with the transportation requirements. Someone decided that an ADA Brigade was enough command and control for a double-digit number of Patriot Battalions so the 32d AAMDC stayed home. Skip Garret, who commanded the 11th Brigade did a herculean job and was rewarded later with a promotion to Major General. He was a good guy.

Things returned to normal. I got all my guys back and we drove on at work. I coached Mike and Rob on a little league baseball team. The field we played on was just across the parade ground from our house. Rob played catcher and Mike, first base. I always thought Rob was a good catcher. He could hit and he was good at throwing guys out trying to steal, especially at third base. Mike was good at first and just hit. It was great fun.

I'm sure due to Marilyn's influence I got a call one day from the principal of St Pius X. She asked me if I could coach the flag football team in their last game of the season. They were going to play the best team in the league and for some reason the coach had quit. So, I asked a couple of guys from the Department if they could help and we went out and installed a very, very simple offense. Mike was the tight end on the team. We played the big game and lost 7-6, but the boys gave it their all and I think they were proud of what they did.

A couple of months later I got a call from the principal again asking if I would coach the 8th grade basketball team. I said sure and I again recruited 5 guys from the Department who wanted to "help". I'm sure they didn't have anything else to do on Saturday mornings. We got in a few practices, and I installed a couple of things that I had learned coaching Bball with Rob earlier including a good full court press and break the press play.

We had our first couple of games and won easily. The officials would only let one coach beside me sit on the bench, so Harry Cohen, the planner wizard who I designated as the Assistant Head Coach sat with me and the other three coaches sat on the second row. The parents had bought us all polo shirts and jackets, so we looked good.

The third game of the season, the officiating was terrible. We played at St Joe's in a gym near downtown El Paso that held about 200 people. It was packed every game almost exclusively with moms. It was loud which created a good deal of enthusiasm. Toward the end of the 1st half, Rob, who was my point guard, went up to get a loose ball and an opposing player slammed into him late. The ref called the foul on Rob. We were all furious. There were games scheduled back-to-back all day and apparently later that day another coach got so mad at the same officials, he punched one.

The principal called me and asked what happened. I told her the officials were terrible and assured her that no matter how bad the officials were, we would not resort to fisticuffs. She told me, the league had decided to create the correct climate before the game, was going to have both teams and the coaches say a Hail Mary before each game together. Game day came, both teams and coaches huddled and said the Hail Mary. I looked over at Harry and he was mumbling. I was pumped, ready for the game and I told Harry "We do everything 100% including praying on this team, don't you know the Hail Mary?" Harry replied "Sir, I'm Jewish". I told him to learn it anyway and a week later, Harry said the Hail Mary like a lifelong Catholic. He was an exceptional guy.

We were going along great, like 7-0 when I discovered that our leading scorer, Jose, who averaged about 20 points a game had been declared academically ineligible as he had "cheated" on a math test. I asked Jose what happened, and he told me another student had asked a question which he answered, and the teacher thought he was cheating. I appealed to the principal to no avail. We won our next game, but when we entered the post season tournament, we had to play the Episcopalians who had boys that were bigger, stronger and in general more physically mature than our boys. They all looked like they were 16 years old, but I had the birth certificates checked and they were of age. We battled them twice but lost both times. Most of our boys went to Cathedral High School, and one of the kids asked the basketball coach who was the best team in the league. He answered "St Pius" and that made us all proud. After that season, Rob moved to playing soccer while Mike continued to play soccer, basketball, and baseball.

Rob entered Cathedral High School in downtown El Paso taught by the Jesuits, his freshman year. Cathedral was the subject of a piece on 60 Minutes as they installed strict discipline on all the students from the minute, they entered the building until they left. 99% of their graduates went to college, an amazing statistic since most of the kids came from poor backgrounds. Most of the kids could not afford the tuition so there was a substantial scholarship effort and when we signed up, I was "encouraged" to pay for another student's tuition which we did. Rob played soccer for a Hispanic coach, and they often crossed the border and played Mexican teams. I only got to see Rob play a couple of times, but I could tell he was improving.

When I came into the Army, every division fielded a team in all the major sports. Almost all the players on these teams were former college players. When we were in Germany on our first tour, Steve Lindell, who was the QB for Army the year before was the 3d Armored Division quarterback. In El Paso, we had a big field north of Hinman Hall, so I asked permission to have a post soccer team. I gained approval and we were off.

I got my players mostly from the students in the advanced and basic courses (my wife, Christina, who played for me describes the recruitment of the soccer players at the School as being reminiscent of a press gang recruiting sailors in the 19th Century, no one wanted to offend the principal of the school). The purpose of the team was to represent our country in a semi-annual soccer tournament held each year at Bliss.

The Germans had their ADA school there, plus there was usually another country doing new equipment training, and the allied officers in the school formed a fourth team. I originally tried to recruit guys from the Department but Mando, despite being an All-State Quarterback in high school, wasn't much of a soccer player. He and Clay Earnest laughed too much while they were playing.

I recruited students and we played in the tournament. We won our first two games but lost to the Germans. I kept recruiting and finally fielded a team with 10 guys who had played college soccer. My 11th starter was a permanent party sergeant who was trying out for the All Army soccer team. We played in a city league and dominated it, winning all our games and only being tied 4 times so went into the tournament in really good shape. Just before the tournament, we played Santos, the El Paso all-star team and we beat them 3-0.

In the tournament, we beat the Germans the 2d game and went on to be tournament champs. The Germans reassigned several of their players after the loss and replaced them with much better ones for the next tournament which never came.

Mike and Rob, when Cathedral didn't have a practice, would practice with the post team. They even got into a couple of scrimmages. Mike had signed up to play for a "house" team, but his coach was German, and I told him that Mike was going to practice with the post team but that he would play games for him. The coach naturally refused that suggestion. Late in the season, the coach called and told me out of his 14 players, he only had 11 available. He asked if Mike could play in the upcoming tournament. Mike said sure. The big game came.

Mike's team was facing a team that had not been scored on all year. It was a great game and Mike scored 3 goals (Mike claims it was 2, but I'm telling things as I remember). I walked off the field with Mike congratulating him and he told me he was done with soccer. Indeed, he did take a year off, but his sophomore year in High School he tried out for the Heidelberg soccer team that would go on to win the European High School Championship and was the last cut. He had a great season with the JV team.

The observer controllers at the NTC were an incredibly cohesive team. There was a hierarchy like in all military organizations, a chain of command, but they communicated very effectively. There was a leveling and unifying factor in their organizations that I believed came from their use of belt buckles and call signs. Every OC had a belt buckle which indicated they were part of the unit. They were chosen, it was a physical symbol that they were part of the team. Because being part of the team was something to be honored and coveted, if any member lost his/her belt buckle, it was a serious offense judged by a kangaroo court which dictated punishments, usually purchasing beer for the team. While everyone knew the chain of command, everyone having a call sign was useful not only on the OC radio nets but it was a quick way to tell everybody's position. The commander was call sign 06, the overall commander was 07, the S-1 was 01 etc. To me, call signs somehow seemed to relax everyone while maintaining the chain of command.

We found the guy in Barstow who made belt buckles and ordered them for the Department. We instituted the Rules of Engagement for the belt buckles which included the fact that all members had to be able to produce their belt buckles when 3 or more members were present. If one wasn't in possession of their belt buckle, they owed the others a drink. This meant when we were doing PT or at a social occasion, a "group check" was possible.

Losing one's belt buckle as I said was serious. We had a 3-day FTX for the Lieutenants that was simply a gut check. They marched into desert, marched about 30 miles, and camped in places like Rattle snack gulch. Our goal was to increase their toughness and give them opportunities to overcome their fears.

On one of the FTXs one of the Basic Course Section NCOs lost his belt buckle along a tank trail at night. On the following FTX, the group retraced the same route and one of the former OCs noted something shining in the moonlight. He reached down and discovered the missing belt buckle and knew instantly whose it was, as everyone's call sign was on their belt buckle.

When the boys brought it to me gleefully, I directed that we have a kangaroo court. I appointed the former Rhodes Scholar candidate as the prosecutor, Harry Cohen, and Mando as the defense attorney as I knew he had a sense of humor. The whole department was at the trial including the civilians and we had great fun. After Harry read the charges, which had been embellished quite a bit, Mando opened the defense by stating that his client had his belt buckle. The NCO had ordered another when he realized he had lost his first buckle. Harry cleverly turned this argument around when he showed the first buckle. Many in the audience didn't know exactly what was happening and a loud roar went up. The NCO was guilty and despite Mando's pleas to the contrary, his client was found guilty with the penalty of buying a keg of beer for the Department's next social function which he did gladly.

Outsiders probably wouldn't understand this. It could appear that we were publicly humiliating a good man. But the whole contrived affair was nothing more than reinforcing the importance of being part of the unit which I think resulted in great pride (which of course can be a bad thing). Years after leaving the Department, or any of the other units I commanded where we had belt buckles, if I ran across a former colleague, we would call each other by our call signs. To this day when Mando and I talk, I am 07 and he is 16, the call signs of the OCs at the NTC. I had belt buckles and callsigns as a Brigade Commander and as the commander of Army Space Command. We even had callsigns when I started my company upon my retirement from the Army for selected personnel.

Towards the end of our tour in El Paso, the next big event for us was Brigade Command selection. I was hopeful, but I would not have been disappointed if I were not selected. My goal when I came into the Army had been to command a battalion. We conditioned commanders not to expect to command a brigade. During the pre-command course, we had the ADA personnel people come in and talk to the class and I remember one chart they always used. It was a pyramid of little people with one guy at the top. They explained of 100 Air Defenders who entered the service and stayed, one would be a brigade commander. Pretty slim odds. Sure enough, the command list came out and I was the first alternate.

A few days later, General Garner called me into his office and told me that Glen McCloud, who was a guy I did not know very well but one I highly respected, had declined command. I was the first alternate. I talked to Glen about it later and he told me in so many words that he just didn't want any part of it-too much politics. I was designated to take over the 10th ADA

Brigade in Darmstadt Germany. That brigade was part of the 32d Air Defense Command, commanded by MG Jerry Putman.

DARMSTADT, GERMANY, 1991-92

BRIGADE COMMAND 1991-1992

Marilyn and Mom came over for the change of command. I met General Putman who was trying to be something he wasn't. There was a whole generation of ADA officers who had advanced just by doing exactly what their boss wanted. I was lucky in the 24th because what my bosses wanted was always focused on the mission. "Putter" as he was affectionately called was working very hard to please the CINC US Army Europe in whatever initiative he had. So, we would be the first to install kitchens and TV rooms in the barracks, execute sergeants time to the letter and other things like that. Pleasing the boss is one of the joys of command but preparing to go to war must be the foundation and focus.

The Brigade was located on a different Kaserne or post from the 32d. The name of the post was Ernst Ludwig which had the usual motor pools and barracks and one shared mess hall. I had a big office and the staff worked on the first floor of what at one time had been a barracks, common for Germany.

In addition to commanding the Brigade, I was also appointed the Special Court Martial Convening authority. Because of that I had attended a week-long course at the University of Virginia Law school. The Uniform Code of Military Justice had installed this position so that a senior commander would be the one to order a case to courts martial. I was also the appellate authority for 22 battalions of all types for field grade Article 15's. When I was a Battalion Commander, I did not give a lot of Article 15s that were processed. I thought I knew my guys pretty well, so during the two years of command, I put about 100 Article 15's in my desk drawer only to see the light of day when they were tossed in a burn barrel when I gave up command. But when I gave an Article 15 for something I considered serious, I hammered the guy. I ensured the soldiers being punished fully understood why they were being punished and why the punishment was what it was. But inevitably, at Fort Stewart, a couple appealed their case to Colonel John Ellerson, who was the Division Artillery Commander. On one occasion, he called me up to his office and told me he was going to reduce one of my punishments. We debated, but he told me he was going to do what he said. I remember walking back the battalion mad.

I gained a lot of respect for Colonel Ellerson when I became the appellate authority. When I would conduct an Article 15 appeal, I would have the entire chain of command present to testify to the soldier's potential and character. Time after time, a soldier had been punished for a minor offense with career altering implications. Universally the chain of command from the squad leader through his company commander would testify as to how this was one of the best soldiers they had. It was clear that the commander was just trying to be tough or to project an image. But the bottom line is soldiers, people, support what is fair and just. So, I reduced a lot of punishments, even though I wanted to protect the commander's authority.

There were only two full Colonels assigned to the AAMDC headquarters area, me and the G-3, Pete Pozinger. Since every court martial had to have representation from all the ranks, Pete and I were both summoned for every court martial for if the defense or prosecution wanted a full colonel on the jury and one of us was challenged off, there would be one left. We usually were excused.

But one time, a brand-new JAG lawyer handling his first case excused Pete and kept me. There was a tension in the courtroom amongst the legal community for the judge and the prosecutor both knew I was the SPCM, and the lawyers always wanted to be nice to the SPCM so they could get their cases to court.

The judge made his opening remarks and just as the trial was about to begin, I asked the judge for the elements of proof for rape, as the defendant was accused of rape. The Elements of Proof were a step by step guide to prove a soldier was guilty. I looked over at the defense attorney and I thought he was going to have a heart attack. I made a simple plus-minus matrix and kept notes during the trail substantiating the guilt or innocence of the defendant.

When the trial was over, there was some concern about the amount of penetration, but I thought the dude was plain guilty. We got in the jury room and carefully explained to the boys that their vote counted the same as mine and asked them if they wanted me to share my notes to which they enthusiastically agreed. We discussed everything and in about 10 minutes we arrived at a guilty finding. It took us about 30 minutes to agree on the sentence which was several years for the defendant in the Leavenworth military penitentiary. I walked out to tell the judge that we were done, and I ran into him in the hallway. He was surprised we already had a consensus so quickly and he reconvened court. After the sentence was passed and things were breaking up, I walked over to the Defense Attorney and said one simple thing. "It doesn't pay to mess with the SPCM." He weakly smiled and said he had learned his lesson.

When I reported in General Putman told me that I was going to be assigned the Assistant Commander's house which was a mansion right next to the Commanding General's house. BG Vern Connor was being assigned and since Europe was drawing down, he would not be replaced. General Connor had about a month left, so the Putter asked me if I wanted a BOQ room or a house. I said I preferred a house which turned out to be fortuitous. I moved into a three-bedroom house with Marilyn's two cats, Socks and Shoes.

A lot of units were being inactivated and as a result, good people were available, but they couldn't move for several months as with all the turmoil, the transportation system was overwhelmed. LTC Jeff Pinasco was coming in to be the Deputy Brigade Commander and I asked General Putman to get me Larry Newman to be the S-3. I had known Larry from the NTC and although he knew nothing of Patriot or Hawk, he was a bundle of energy, organized, and it was good for my soul to have another soldier with a divisional background around me.

The work was there to be done and since neither of them could move quickly, I had both guys transferred immediately and they moved into the house I had been assigned, which got to be known as the Prima house after the Brigade's motto. Every couple of weeks we would have a party on a Sunday afternoon and invite all the bachelors-geographical or otherwise to a brunch at the Prima house. Jeff was already impressing me with his organizational abilities, and he would do everything for the parties. All the boys had to bring was beer and we took care of the rest. One-time, Major Bob Lennox who was one of the finest officers I had ever met and who eventually became a LTG, brought Miller natural light beer to one of our parties; in Germany, the capitol of the world when it came to beer. We kidded Bob all the time about that later and threw the natural light in the trash. Darmstadt had its own beer-Darmstatter-which was delivered weekly. They put a case outside the back door and the guy would come each week and replace the empties and you would only be charged for what you used; perfect!

Marilyn timed her arrival with the boys perfectly, just when the General's house became available. I remember good times there, the house butted up on a perfectly manicured German forest and it was spacious and most pleasant. The house was located between the CG's house and the Chief of Staff's house, who was my friend Jack Costello. Jack was a Redskin fan, and he would invite me over some Monday's at 4 AM to watch the Redskins. Jack's great wife Micki would get up with us and make us breakfast. She was a saint and would go on the do great things for Army families later. Jack would become a LTG and had a great career until he died way too early.

We got into the routine of a High-Altitude Air Defense Unit; tactical Tuesdays where the whole brigade would link up our tactical communications nets and fight a common scenario, directed from the Brigade's TSQ-73 which was an amazing piece of equipment. The Brigade had fire direction officers that would assign whole clumps of targets to one battalion or another. Our intel estimated the size of the initial enemy aircraft sorties in the thousands of aircraft. The AAMDC would counter it with 3 belts of defense. The 10th was the first belt and there were two behind us. I would later learn that the directions and system description for the Q-73 was one of the clearest and best written. I would encounter it when I became a contractor later.

We had another device called the Patriot Fire Control Trainer or PCOFT. The AAMDC owned this thing and tracked usage. The problem was the Patriot fire units themselves had a built-in trainer which the units used to produce very challenging tactical situations for the Tactical Control Officers and NCOs. When we were told that the PCOFT was coming to us I protested their scenarios weren't challenging enough, but the G-3 told me to suck it up. So, we brought the brand-new Lieutenants into Darmstadt for a couple of days and ran the socks off the PCOFT.

I tried to visit each of my battalions once per week. I had a Volkswagen van with an assigned driver, Sgt Peterson. Pete was dating a German girl and I asked him if he would have her write 3 simple sentences in German for me each week which I would translate while we were driving around.

I had initially four battalion commanders. Kevin Campbell commanded 2/43 in Hanau, Larry Dodgen commanded 8/43 in Giebelstadt, Harry Cohen had 4/42 in Giessen, and Steve Moeller commanded 3/52, the Hawk Battalion in Fulda

Germany. Campbell and Dodgen would go on to be LTGs and Moeller would become a Brigade commander. To drive the loop connecting the battalions was probably almost 200 miles.

Each had their own set of problems. Moeller was as far east as one could get in West Germany. The climate was unforgiving in the winter and all but one of his batteries were spread out in a line to his south. This battalion had the mission of raking off the low altitude enemy aircraft that would surely initiate the Russian attack.

These Hawkers were tough guys and never backed down from a challenge. Moeller was a devout Catholic and a guy who enjoyed life, taking pleasure in its simple offerings. Every time I went to visit him, he had some activity planned in addition to conducting our business. One of my goals in becoming a Brigade Commander was that every soldier in the Brigade know my name. So, I instructed the battalion commanders that when I came, to reserve part of the time for visiting troops. I would give the guys a little pep talk and tell them how important what they were doing was for us to accomplish our mission. One visit, Steve took me to the Kreuzberg Monastery which had been occupied by monks since the 13th Century. Like many religious orders they developed a trade to pay for their expenses. Well, these monks made beer; good beer that one year was ranked by Playboy Magazine as one to the top ten beers in the world. They made a Christmas beer, and we ordered a keg for our Christmas party in Darmstadt.

Kevin Campbell was in Hanau Germany, where I had lived as a kid. He had a tactical site on Fleigerhorst Kaserne where we had lived in the 1950's and I found our old house. It looked like it hadn't changed a bit. Kevin's big problem was his relations with the locals. The battalion didn't have any place to run except through town and the Germans complained about the jodies being sung so early in the morning. So, the battalion stopped singing and then the Germans complained about the loud noise the feet were making on the pavement. Kevin was an almost stoic New Englander who was brilliant and soaked everything in. Hanau was close enough to Darmstadt so that when I visited, I would not have to stay overnight. Howard Bromberg was Kevin's XO, and he was a great soldier. Dave Farisee replaced Howard and his wife; Gina was an AG officer who would eventually become a general officer. Later, when we deployed to Saudi, US Army Europe would not let Kevin's replacement deploy in an effort to keep our footprint small (crazy-the whole battalion was there without its commander) so Dave commanded the battalion well for 6 months in a combat zone. I never worried about 2/43' readiness. The battalion had a proud history in Desert Storm and a lot of the soldiers in the battalion were veterans of that conflict.

8/43 was in Giebelstadt about 60 KM south of Darmstadt. The town was out in the country and a very pleasant place to stay. I always stayed in the same Gast Haus there which was owned by a lady named Lutz for decades. Anyone who served in Giebelstadt knew Frau Lutz. I had asked her, like the lady I stayed with in Giessen, to speak only to me in German, which they both did. One day at breakfast, Frau Lutz walks into the room and said to me in German "Herr Obrest, du Deutsch no ist gut." Colonel, your German isn't good. I happily agreed.

Larry's battalion had supported the Hail Mary into Kuwait during Desert Storm and defended the peace talks at the end of the war. Larry had already turned in his equipment and sent it back to the States. So, he was looking for things for the soldiers to do. So, he had events-all kinds of things to keep the soldiers busy. One of the proudest moments of my life was I was privileged to be invited to give the bronze star medals to the soldiers in the battalion who had earned one.

As one might suspect, most of the officers and some high-ranking NCOs received a medal but at the end there was a buck sergeant named Siferheld. He had driven a truck through an identified mine field to retrieve a launcher that one of the batteries had stumbled upon in their haste to follow the advance of the maneuver units. After the ceremony, he asked if he could have his picture taken with me. I told him "I want to have my picture taken with you."

Larry was a generous guy and was always trying to give General Putman and me gifts. One time, he gave us each a AK47 on a plaque, still operational. Remembering my experience with the Rangers in Grenada, I declined the gift, telling him that I really appreciated the gesture. Not deterred, he had the weapon de-militarized by having it chopped up into pieces. The Putter and I were both still uncomfortable, so we referred it to the lawyers who said the weapons needed to be destroyed.

Harry Kremcowitz commanded 4/43 in Giessen. Bob Lennox was his XO and Fred Chronis was his S-3, a super soldier who should have been a brigade commander. Harry had a solid battalion, well run with no serious disciplinary problems. Harry was not an impressive guy to look at, sort dumpy looking and balding. But he was decisive, if something needed to be done, he got it done with no fanfare. Problem was the Putter hated him, so I spent a lot of time sending the CG notes complementing Harry's battalion on this or that. Harry should have been promoted to full Colonel, maybe not selected for Brigade command, but certainly he had, and deserved, to be a full

Colonel. One of my great regrets was General Putman killed Harry on his OER, essentially ending his career unfairly; my efforts at consolation had little impact.

One of the problems we had in Air Defense back then was SHORAD guys, guys whose experience was in divisions, if they did well, they ended up commanding high altitude air defense units. Dave Heebner, the guy I replaced had a lot of divisional experience like I did, and General Putman was a divisional guy as well. Sometimes, this led to a clash of cultures. High altitude air defense units in the past had to work very hard just to keep the equipment operational. I remember when I took over the battery in Korea, the basic Hawk guys were petrified to turn the system off once the improved system was on site, the old Hawk system had been that fragile. God knows what would have happened if we tried to move it. HIMAD guys were focused on getting the job done and their operational readiness was the center of their lives. They had little time for flashy demonstrations of enthusiasm. They were businessmen, getting the job done. Harry had always been a HIMAD guy, and he was good, but I guess General Putman never understood him despite my efforts. Harry's situation was one of my real regrets as a Brigade Commander.

I devoted myself to trying to make sure that the units were as combat ready as possible. In high altitude units this was done through an evaluation called a Tactical Evaluation or TACEVAL. Units took a TACEVAL from Brigade once a quarter. My team originally consisted of a Warrant Officer, and several NCOs. Units were practicing for this evaluation almost every day. Battalions had their team, and they would give the batteries an evaluation in advance of Brigade coming. Smart. Observing a TACEVAL is kind of like watching a Triathlon, you know a lot is going on, but you can't see much. TACEVALS checked out system readiness as well as the crew's ability to perform a ready for action crew drill. Important stuff.

I went to my first Brigade TACEVAL, watched grass grow for a while, but when my warrant came out, I asked how it went and he replied "OK". The Chief sat down with his laptop and started typing up a report for the unit on things that went well, and those areas that needed a little work. I asked him, "You are going to do an AAR, talk to the soldiers, right?' He replied, "Sir I don't know what an AAR is." I was dumbfounded.

I got back to Darmstadt and talked to Larry Newman who was the Brigade S-3. Larry was a former OC at Irwin, so he understood AARs. I told him we needed to implement them ASAP. The problem we had is that very few people in the Brigade knew how to do one. The ADA branch had instituted a Table system like the maneuver units had done for years to measure a unit's combat readiness. Table VIII was combat ready. Table XII, the goal, had the same tasks as Table VIII, but it was performed under NBC conditions. The soldiers had to do everything while wearing their chemical protective gear.

The first scheduled Table XII evaluation was for a unit in 4/43. We went to Giessen and ran the evaluation. Larry did the AAR; he talked to the Chief and the other team members and came up with his plan very quickly. Larry started and the first thing he wanted to talk about was the Antennae Mast Group (AMG) which was the microwave communications receptacle for the tactical control net. He kept calling it an OMG, an Operational Maneuver Group-the term applied to a large Russian tank formation. The members of the unit kept looking at each other until I finally corrected Larry gently, but he kept calling the AMG an OMG but at least everyone knew what he was talking about.

The unit failed because they did not achieve the minimum time to be ready for action. This kind of surprised me as the unit seemed to set up efficiently but the issue was the launchers had not been remoted into the Engagement Control Station in time. The launcher evaluator said the launchers were ready in plenty of time. The TCO has to initiate the process to receive the launchers, and during the AAR, which is a give and take event for all the participants, the TCO asked the Launcher PSG why he hadn't remoted the launchers. The NCO simply replied "Ma'am, because you didn't ask me to." The value of an AAR was proven to all present. The Chief's report probably would have said the launchers were not remoted in time, but the AAR determined why.

General Putman had told me around early October that the Brigade was going to deploy to Saudi Arabia to cover the final withdrawal of our logistics personnel from theater. We would deploy in early January. So, the Brigade's Christmas party was special. We had had a formal dining in a little earlier and had invited the CG. The colors of each of the battalions was marched in and the honors for each was given: 8/43 which followed the Hail Mary, 2/43 which moved north and defended King Kalid Military City and 4/43 which had defended Tel Aviv in Israel. The 3/52's colors were marched in. They had not been part of the war, but they had been the point of the Air Defense spear in Germany for decades, the first unit that would have been involved in any Russian air attack. I was so proud to be the leader of this unit. All assembled then did "Honors to the Regiment". I warned General Putman in advance, but one side started "Who's your Mama? The other side repeated that line and then side one said: "If she ain't Prima" to which the other side replied: "Then she's a dog". General P uttered a curse and then started laughing.

We had the Brigade Christmas party a couple of weeks later, a much more private affair, which was highlighted by having a keg of Christmas beer from the monastery. When the boys tried to tap the keg, the cork blew out of the top and the beer which had been jostled around trying to get it to open, exploded and drenched the roof of the ornate room in the officer's club that we were using. It was a mess, but we cleaned things up and proceeded with the party. Fortunately, there was enough beer left for us to all have a couple. That was good beer.

While Rob was honing his soccer skills, Mike was playing basketball for the Darmstadt team. We had a gym on our post and me being the garrison commander meant that we could get it any time we wanted. I was the coach and my TSQ-73 warrant, Terry Tate, was my assistant. We had a few discipline problems on the team and had to have at least one player miss a few games to get our point over. When I deployed, we were in the playoffs to win the USAREUR championship. I left and Chief Tate did a great job and the boys won it all. Mike was a tall gangly kid, but he was already showing his athletic talent.

3/52 was inactivating but before they did, it was decided that they would have their Annual Service Practice at Crete in the Mediterranean Sea where NATO had a range. We fired the last American Hawk missile fired in Europe, the last of many thousands. Tradition was the battery had a dinner after the shoot and we did it up brown. After dinner, a soldier came up to me and asked if he could have a Brigade coin to use as the prize at a pool tournament that was about to start. I said sure and the soldiers played for hours for that coin. After the banquet was over Steve took me and a few other boys to a very small bar in downtown Nampfi that had welcomed American Air Defenders for years. They had all kinds of memorabilia on their walls and the owner could tell stories about each unit. We had had a little to drink at the dinner, but we all really lived it up at this little bar with its warm and welcoming atmosphere.

Steve Moeller was a great commander and leader. As we prepared to deploy, he was left on his own to inactivate his battalion and turn in all his equipment, which had to be in perfect shape of course. We talked all the time when I was in Saudi, and I managed to get him in theater for a couple of weeks. He would later be the Garrison Commander of Redstone Arsenal in Huntsville Alabama, a well-deserved job equivalent to a Brigade Command.

I really believed in the professional development of my officers and being an historian, I wanted them to understand the roots of their branch. So, I told Jeff Pinasco in November to organize a trip to Remagen for the Brigade staff. I don't know why, but I never visited Remagen while I was writing my book. We showed up the night before and pounded a few beers and the next day we headed out to the battlefield which of course was in the middle of town. I now know it was the Holy Spirit but when we ascertained where Lt Karl Timmerman first saw the bridge, I knew exactly where I was and we started the tour from there, ending up at the bridge at the end of the day. As night drew on, we all went under the bridge and got a chunk of the bridge; stones had fallen off and were just lying on the ground under the bridge. The Remagen museum was selling little part of the bridge for 50 marks, about $35 so I thought we were getting a real steal.

When I got back in my VW bus to go home, I noticed the rear end was sagging and when I threw my helmet bag into the back instead of it going down, it stayed level with the top of the rear seat. The back of the van was filled with a 4-foot-long, 3-foot-wide piece of the bridge which Jeff Pinasco and the boys had commandeered after I went to bed. When we got back to Darmstadt, we put it in our backyard. It was later moved to Ft Bliss, then Ft Sill when the branch moved there.

For our deployment we would not be taking our equipment or tools, falling in on equipment left by the 94th Brigade who we were replacing. We flew down on leased commercial aircraft. Our plane was an old 737 that had the first-class section in a bump in the top and I had the Brigade Staff and commanders ride up there. We were all a little worried about the maintenance on the aircraft and when we landed in Dharan a panel fell off the wall of the aircraft, but we were safe.

We walked off the plane in full battle rattle and a Colonel from ARCENT met us, surprised at our attire. I remember walking off the plane at midnight and it was so hot, it felt like the air was being sucked out of my lungs. We were bused to our little garrison called Dragon Base because it had been the home of the XVIII Airborne Corps during Desert Storm which had a dragon on its patch. The 10th Brigade headquarters was on Dragon Base and the battalions had their own buildings in Dharan and Riyad. We were all tired, but we checked out the headquarters building which was formed in a square with a long-neglected courtyard in the middle. I had an office about one-third the size of my office in Darmstadt but the outer wall behind me was all glass. We soon discovered that the Saudis would not let us fly the American flag outdoors even on US compounds, so I had American flags put all over the place indoors. I still have the one from my office. You don't appreciate things until you cannot have them.

I reported to BG Ed Brown, who was the commander, a logistician, who was shutting the theater down. He understood what Patriot could do as 2/43 had shot down a Scud while he was taking command of the TAMMC, the theater logistics command. He would leave about a month before I did and for his farewell gift, we gave him a piece of the scud that had been shot down that day (the units kept scud parts; they were all over after the war) and we had it presented by the Tactical Control Officer, Lt Karen O'Conner, who shot it down. Karen, and many others that were with me, really transformed my opinion of women in Air Defense. She was the best TCO in the Brigade and I am proud that it was not hard for me to admit it.

Brown wanted me to come to his daily staff call every day. I sort of pushed back a little saying I would send a senior member of the Brigade, but he was insistent. They did business with 3x5 cards. All actions, requests-anything that you wanted the command to do was requested on a 3x5 card. The meetings were uninteresting and only occasionally of value, but I went every day. The Brigade motors people had fixed up an abandoned HUMMV which had no canvas. We put a big Prima 6 on it, and I would drive it to the staff calls instead of taking my driver and our Non-Tactical Vehicles or NTVs which was a Toyota 4 Runner. The Japanese had provided these NTVs during Desert Storm as their contribution to the war effort. We had a VIP NTV, a Chevrolet Suburban and think most of the officers had some type of NTV.

One of the ARCENT meetings that was useful was the planning session for General Brown's change of command. I wanted to wear the light weight BDUs which had been issued to us and our helmets, weapons, and Load Bearing Equipment. Instead, we wore the chocolate chip BDUs with those ugly floppy hats which were heavier that our issued BDUs. It was 125 degrees at the change of command. My future wife, Christina, stood that formation and fainted. We had medics in the back of the formation and just before we moved out, I saw her marching back into formation with a determination that would have knocked down a wall. Before I dismissed the troops, we did Honors to the Regiment which none of those logisticians around us understood.

2/43 was in Dharan and 4/43 was in Riyad. 2/43 was primarily defending the coalition airfield in Dharan while 4/43 was defending the same airfield that Pete Loebs defended in Desert Storm along with an oil refinery on the outskirts of the city.

I drove the 400KM to Riyad at least once per week. Very occasionally I would get a ride in a T-41 and once I got a ride in the leer jet that belonged to an Air Force BG who was heading a task force to integrate all the Air Defense activities of the Army, Navy and Air Force in theater. We were in direct support to the Task Force, but more on that later. Usually, it was just me and Sergeant Draper "6Y". In fact, I owe a debt of gratitude to all my drivers; PFC Hunter who was my APC driver in Germany; SP4 Curry who was my jeep driver at Fort Stewart, PFC Hudgins who drove my HUMMV in Germany and Sergeant Peterson in Germany and Sergeant Draper who drove for me in Saudi. All great kids and they really took care of me. The purpose of these visits was just to see soldiers and talk to my commanders to see if there was anything that I could help them with. Usually, boring.

When we went to Riyad, we usually went shopping in the gold market, or zuk, in downtown Riyad. The shopping was right next to "head chopping square" where the Saudis carried out their sentences for serious offenses. If one was convicted of stealing, they cut off the right hand; if one was convicted of murder they were beheaded. If Americans were in the area at the time of a sentencing, the Saudis would push them to the front so they would be assured of seeing the carnage. Justice in the Kingdom was executed in less than 48 hours.

We all bought some gold, they had great rugs, I think from Iran, and just about anything else you could think of. It was fun walking around and haggling with the merchants. Major Andre Smith was my adjutant. He was a 6'7", a very black man who looked like a Moor and was incredibly patient and kind person but had a very frightening demeanor. If I wanted to buy something, I had Andre do my negotiating for me and he was good. Anything we bought we sent back to Germany on the weekly ash and trash run between Germany and Saudi. I wondered how the stuff was going to get from Frankfurt to Darmstadt, but it did, Marilyn got everything.

One of the real delights in visiting Riyad, was we had the occasional pleasure of seeing General Victor Hugo who was a former commander of the ADCOM. General Hugo had the best motto for a unit I had ever run across: Think War and Give a Damn. General Hugo was working for the local oil company in some capacity and always seemed happy to see us and talk with us. He and his wife had a beautiful, large apartment in Riyad, and every room had a gorgeous Persian carpet. The General and I talked about everything, and he had many good insights. We need to seek advice from good people until we die for if we do not, our vision will be restricted by what our own little world can see.

I always felt a little guilty about it, but the Brigade staff was on a schedule. Long days for sure, but we took Sunday's off. Sunday was the day I cleaned my little apartment. There were a group of BOQ buildings on Dragon Base and I moved our Field Grades in there. Sunday mornings, I would sleep in and then clean my little apartment which included hosing down the outside windows which were an inch deep in dust. About 10AM I would go to the mess hall for brunch. We had a great mess hall, so good that General Brown asked if his guys could eat there occasionally. I said sure, it would drive up the head count, the number of people eating which in the military is the key to having a successful mess hall. After breakfast, we would have "forced fun". I didn't want anyone moping around because they had too much time on their hands, so we all went out to the Prima Sports Complex on post where we had outdoor basketball courts, a volleyball net, and a soccer field complete with sandbags marking the touch and end lines and camouflage nets for the goals. This soccer field would get great use later. After an hour of two of volleyball, the troops were dismissed, and they usually went to a swimming pool on Dharan airbase. War is hell, but we were trying to take advantage of the situation.

We also built a gym on post. Units of all types were getting ready to leave the theater and many of them had Nautilus weight equipment and all kinds of exercise equipment they really wanted to get rid of. We put the word out and when someone had something, they wanted to get rid of they called us, and I would send Christina, who was the Assistant Brigade

Adjutant, and a 2 ½ truck to get it. She was very selective but 90 days after we got there, we had almost every machine that Nautilus made. General Brown came to visit one time and I convinced him to buy carpet for the building which made it super nice.

I had pullup bars installed of course and we did PT three times a week. We would do our push-ups and sit-ups and then we would run around the post a little, out the front gate and up a road to the main highway where we would turn around and then run back to the gate-exactly two miles. After PT most of us would go to the Dragon Base Gym and work out. I made the gym available to ARCENT and some guys used it, but they weren't into PT like we were. One of the two individual training goals was to get everyone in the Brigade to score at least a 250 out of 300 points on the PT test and we wanted 75% of the brigade to be expert marksmen.

One time on a run, we had turned around at the highway and were on our way back. I was calling jodies for the group on the left side of the formation. Someone grabbed me and pushed me into the formation. At the same time a Saudi vehicle passed us, half on the road and half off, and proceeded to a Trailer Transfer Point; a fenced in area where the Saudis parked vehicles and trailers until they were needed. We got back to the gate, I called out our ready reaction force which was an Infantry squad that had been attached to us and told Yankee to go get the HUMMV. We drove the ½ mile to the TTP and I stopped the Hummer before the gate. I told Yankee to get out of the vehicle and I then drove the vehicle through the gate, which was light wood and barbed wire. I was mad; these dudes could have killed someone. My infantrymen policed up the Saudis who had almost killed us and I took them to

Colonel Kalid whose job in life was to spy on us. He had a building right outside Dragon Base. He was not happy that we had not turned the situation over to him, but I had made my point. He told me later that the soldiers had received non-judicial punishment which included being flogged. I felt bad about that, I thought it was a little over reaction.

We found there was a rifle range in Riyad that we could use. General Brown gave me 1,000,000 rounds of M16 ammo when we arrived, he wanted to give me more, but I wanted to use what we drew. The theater had boxes and boxes of ammunition that had been opened and couldn't therefore be turned in. We had Quarterly training briefings which we did every two months and Dave Farisee and Dave Neely who had taken over 4/43 from Harry Kremcowitz, would brief on their marksmanship and PT stats among other things. By the second QTB, 4/43 had achieved the 75% goal, but 2/43 had not. The reason why was obvious, the rifle range was just down the road from 4/43 so they had used it a lot more than 2/43 which was 400KM away. We set up a date for all Dave's soldiers who had not met the standard to meet me in Riyad.

We all arrived in Riyad, and I had a surprise for the soldiers. I stressed to them how important it was to be good with their weapon. I genuinely believed that good marksmanship comes from practice. Understanding that ammunition is expensive, the Army was cutting back on the number of times we could qualify. Here was a great time to practice. I always tried to create a competitive atmosphere among my units when it came to marksmanship.

Before we got the word that the Brigade and 3/52 would inactivate when we returned home, I had coordinated with the French Artillery School to use the machinegun range in

Draguignan France after the deployment. General Garner and I had visited the artillery school there and I had asked if it were a possibility that we could use the range and the French gave me an enthusiastic yes. So, the idea was we would fly the machinegun crews down on a CH-47, a big cargo helicopter, have the machinegun competition and I would turn the boys loose on French Rivera for the weekend, which was only about 20 miles south of the school.

Dave assembled his soldiers, I told them that being a good marksman took practice and not to worry. Immediately a semi-trailer carrying probably 500,000 rounds of M16 ammunition rolled out behind me; I told them we had plenty of ammo. The first time the unit fired, their percentage of experts went from 53% to 81%; its great what a little realistic motivation can do.

We had one battery in Riyad that was defending an oil refinery outside of the city. To get there, one had to take several dirt roads. Just before one came to the battery there was a "T" in the road where you had to make a hard left. The road from there to the battery was a series of what we called rollers, small steep hills spaced such that you were going up and down constantly until you almost got to the battery. On those hills, you could not see what was coming until you were on top of the hill.

One day, the battery had an accident with the Nomad tribe who was camped just to right of the road after you had made the left turn to go to the battery. The accident was a fender bender, but the Chief of the tribe had declared war on us. I sort of blew that threat off until one day, Yankee and I were travelling to the battery and had just made the left turn when right in front of us, there was automatic weapons fire tearing up the road in front of us. Fortunately, there was a ditch to our left and Yankee put us in the ditch. We piled out of the vehicle, grabbed our weapons and LBE and hit the bank of the ditch. We could see the Bedouin camp and it was quickly apparent that they were celebrating something. People were dancing around, and they all were firing their AK-47's in the air. Apparently, one of the boys had fired in our direction. I will never know if was intentional or not. Nobody seemed to be paying attention to us, so we quietly got back in the vehicle and proceeded onto the battery.

Once we got there, I told the Battery Commander what had happened and for the boys to be careful. I then did what I always did as a Brigade Commander; I started walking around talking to the boys and girls. The Battery systems warrant asked if he could show me something. We walked down the site to the Battery radar where the Chief opened a small door on the lower backside of the radar and sand started to pour out and it continued to pour out in volume for over a minute. These radars and all the equipment had been in the desert for several years and the wear and tear of the desert climate was taking its toll. I commented to the Chief that we had to do something about this. If that radar was full of sand, then all my radars were full of sand.

I got back to Dragon Base and called General Jack Costello, who had taken command of the AAMDC after General Putman. I told him that we needed some depot maintenance personnel to come to us and clean out all the radars. It was not a clear-cut decision. We were not experiencing any down time with our radars, they all seemed to be working ok and when we took a battery offline, then we were taking it out of the defense. And even though Patriot was much easier to maintain, there was no guarantee that once all the circuit cards had been taken out of the radar and cleaned that the radar would turn back on.

Patriot's improved reliability was a dual edged sword. On the one side, the systems were much more reliable but on the other, the maintenance people were authorized to do less maintenance and were trained to a lower standard. In my Hawk battery, Jim Coots and Roland Motta could fix anything, short of replacing a major assembly. My Patriot warrants 20 years later could not, and they were frustrated by it as was I.

General Costello reluctantly agreed, and we obtained a large tent on Dharan AFB to do the work. I admired Jack a lot and was a little puzzled why he seemed so reluctant to give me approval to clean the radars. Commanders and managers have a lot of pressure, but they should always try to meet the common goal, in this case long term mission readiness. But sometimes the measurement of meeting those goals can get lost in the weeds; clearly the old saying that one could not see the forest because of all the trees was true. One of the things I've learned in my life is doing things right the first time makes things last and avoids a lot of consternation later. We got all the radars blown out, most of them wouldn't start after their cleaning, but we had depot level maintenance dudes that were there to diagnose the problems and they got them going.

Toward the end of the deployment, Central Command established a Task Force to integrate all Air Defense Operations in theater. It was commanded by an Air Force BG who was a good guy and very creative. His first goal was for all of us to understand each other's capabilities. We all assembled for a capability brief. I briefed on Patriot and was followed by an Air Force LTC who was the commander of the Stealth fighter squadron. The guy looked like a fighter pilot, good hair, pressed flight suit with a loud scarf. The guy gave a good brief stating that although the aircraft were painted with radar reflecting paint and other modifications, they were not invisible to radars. The commander asked me if he thought that we could pick up a stealth fighter at a range that gave us time to fire a missile and I said I thought so. Suddenly, he was setting up a demonstration. They would fly in 2 E3 radar jamming aircraft in front of the stealth fighter, and we would see what we could do. The commander's G-3 or DO, Director of Operations, would referee the demo by being in our van. I said fine.

I picked Lt O'Connor to be the TCO and the jammers flew in. Karen acquired the fighter at over 150KM, demo over. The DO walked out of the van and told me "Do not tell this to anyone." I guess they wanted their perception of reality to continue. It really was a senseless operation as a stealth pilot would never fly right at a radar like that one did in the demo.

Being on the TF gave me a chance to broaden my Air Defense knowledge as the other services were making a lot of strides in this area, the Navy in particular. The TF commander arranged for me to go out to meet the Commander of the 6th Fleet on his headquarters ship, which was docked at Bahrain, a small island off the coast of Saudi. I arrived at the ship, was piped aboard-which was quite a thrill and then had lunch with Admiral and his staff. Man, those Navy guys lived right, great food, white tablecloths, all first class. I toured the ship, and we started a process to share the Air Defense picture; that is coming up with communications interfaces where I could see the Navy's air picture and they could see mine. With the advent of Link 16 that is the standard now, but in 1990, it was a big experiment. We had some success, and I enjoyed my time with the Navy.

Colonel Kalid came down to my office one day shortly after we had arrived in theater and asked me if I might be interested in a soccer game. I had about 15 officers who had played for me at Bliss and my S-2 clerk, Specialist George, was a super goalie, so I said sure. I guess the word of the upcoming game got around and I got a call from the Director of Morale and Welfare. Like everyone else, he was trying to get rid of stuff. He had about 20 Umbro soccer uniforms-jerseys, short and socks. He asked if I wanted them, and I said sure. We sewed the AADCOM patch on them and I knew before the game that we would look good if nothing else.

Playing on our dirt field with the camouflage nets for goals, we won the first game easily, like 6-0. Kalid said we would play again in two weeks which we did for four more iterations. The Saudi teams got better and better. The last game we won was on a lucky goal, but we were 5-0. I could sense Kalid's frustration. He finally told me that we would play in two weeks not on our home field but at a Saudi Air Force base about 30KM north of Dragon Base.

When the date of the match arrived, we drove up to the gate of the base which was in a bowl below us. And to our great surprise, there was a small soccer stadium! We drove up to the stadium and had to make arrangement for my female players, Christina, and Kathy Moses to get dressed. I walked out on the field which was grass and there were about 2000 spectators in the stands. It turns out we were playing the Saudi Army team which is the AAA team for the Saudi National team. Things did not go well. Christina had to play goalie as Specialist George's enlistment was up and he had left the service. The game started and their coach, an Egyptian who was the ref, kicked me out of the game, so I ended up watching the game from the stands. They killed us, we lost like 7-0. Christina played goalie because she had hurt her foot in forced fun and couldn't jump. So, the Saudis kept chipping the ball into the upper corners of the net. I learned a lot about myself as a coach that game. Sitting in the stands, I saw the big picture much better rather than trying to direct players on the field as I had done before. Kalid was happy. The whole process was great fun.

About the 4th month we were there, we got an alert order that we might have to deploy a battery to Kuwait as a "Show of Force". We made the coordination; we were to meet the Kuwaiti Air Defense Brigade Commander and his staff. We first studied the potential sites for a Patriot Battery to get the maximum coverage of the city, not knowing exactly what we were going to defend.

The drive north was very interesting. The further north we went, the flatter the desert became until it got as flat as a billiard table for as far as one could see. After driving for a few hours, we could see something in the distance and as we got closer, we could see it was a city seemingly rising out of the desert. It was King Kalid Military City or KKMC which had been built to stage equipment and soldiers in northern Saudi Arabia to counter any future Iraqi incursions. We passed through the checkpoint going into Kuwait with no problems.

When we arrived at Kuwaiti Brigade headquarters, the first thing that attracted your eye was the building looked brand new, fresh paint, but it seemed like it was empty somehow. The Deputy Brigade Commander met us as he spoke English and I asked him about the building. He told me when the

Iraqis came through, they stripped the building, right down to the electrical sockets. They had to replace everything, and the process was still ongoing.

We sat down after meeting the Brigade Commander in sort of a conference room. I will never forget the Deputy's intro which went something like this: "We welcome our American brothers and sisters who spilled their blood to make us free." I got chills up my spine. We then discussed possible sites, but the Brigade CO had been directed to put the battery in a certain spot, a little further south than the one we had planned.

The Kuwaitis had a couple of locations they wanted us to see. We went to a house where about 30 Kuwaitis hung on way after Kuwait City had been taken; it was a national shrine. We then went to the war memorial that had a sign "We will never forget." I'm sure that they won't, and we shouldn't either.

The site that we had been directed to use was right next to a large amusement park that was frequented heavily by the Kuwaiti populace, particularly on the weekends. From a coverage perspective we could have repositioned the battery to do better but the battery was there so the people could see it. Kuwait was considering buying Patriot, but they had not yet. We would have a role in that decision later.

We returned to Dharan. The battery had been alerted and was ready to go when the order came. They deployed and I accompanied them with a good portion of the staff. We occupied the site near the amusement park. We installed concertina wire around the perimeter so visitors to the amusement park would stay on their side of the wire. I had my infantry squad who augmented the defense.

A few days later, an Infantry Captain came in and reported to me. He was the commander of a Bradley company which had 12 Bradley fighting vehicles. He and his men had been shooting up north at Udari range. They needed something to do for a few weeks until they redeployed to home station. He asked if his guys could defend the battery. I said sure. I had the commanders meet to coordinate and the next thing I knew the entire perimeter was surrounded with Bradley fight vehicles.

We got the word through ARCENT that the Kuwaiti crown prince wanted to come and visit the site and get a briefing on Patriot. We had a double wide trailer on site, so we had space to get the briefing set up. The Prince would receive the briefing and then tour the site.

The day of the briefing came. As we were getting dressed and headed to breakfast, Jeff Pinasco came running in with a newspaper. The front-page story in the English newspaper that served the Middle East was "Patriot did not work in the Gulf War." People always want to attack what is good, and the criticism of an emerging system I guess might have been fair, but that was history in my mind.

A few minutes before the Prince arrived, some Arabs showed up and literally rolled out the red carpet from the gate of the site to where the Prince would get out of his car. He was accompanied by a gaggle of people including the Boeing Patriot rep to Kuwait. We had been told the Prince's background was such that he didn't always make sense, but during the briefing he asked several insightful questions.

We walked through the site, and I pointed out the items of equipment and I then took him to the Engagement Control Station where, who else, but Lt Karen O'Connor was going to run a simulation of an air battle and let the Prince kill some TBMs. We had debated using Lt O'Connor because she was a woman and the Arabs consider women lesser citizens; an issue which our women faced all the time in theater, but she was my best Tactical Control Officer, had combat experience, was good briefer and she was cool under pressure. So, we went with her.

The Prince came out of the van smiling, thanked me for the visit and left. I asked Karen what happened inside, and she told me that had run a couple of simulated air battles which the Prince seemed to enjoy and then he had asked her "Lieutenant, do you think Patriot works?" The moment of truth had come. She replied: "Yes sir". And he said "Why?" And Karen told him that she had shot down a scud during Desert Storm. The Prince nodded and left the van.

The next day we found out that Kuwait had signed the deal to buy Patriot. I found the Patriot rep from Boeing and told him he owed me and my soldiers. So, for our contribution to getting the Kuwait Patriot sale over the line, every soldier in the Brigade got a coffee cup with the Brigade or Battalion name on it. Not much at all, but a gesture I was happy to do for the soldiers. I still have mine.

The night before we left, the commander of the Kuwaiti Air Force had a big banquet for us. We had packed up the equipment and had had a party for the soldiers that afternoon which was organized by the Assistant S-1, Christina. At the banquet, I was told there would be an exchange of gifts. I regret to this day that we did not put enough effort into getting something more thoughtful. When we exchanged gifts, I gave the General the cheap little thing we had gotten from Boeing, and he gave me a replica of a Phoenician trading ship. The Kuwaitis were the ancient Phoenicians and they traded all over the region. I had to have the ship appraised by JAG before I kept it as anything valued over $1000 could not be kept. The ship was appraised at $800 so I was good to go. It's on my bookshelf right now.

We finally went back to Germany. When we arrived at Darmstadt having driven up from Rhein Main AFB in Frankfurt, everyone was happy to see us. I went into my office which had had all the furniture removed from it replaced by a fest table and a folding chair. It was sad. We had no inactivation ceremony or anything it was just puff; the most forward Air Defense Brigade in Europe which had spit in the enemy's eye for decades had seemingly evaporated. Real sad.

HEIDELBERG, GERMANY, 1992-94

US ARMY EUROPE 1992-1994

General Putman had proudly told me that he had gotten me a job after command as the Chief of Current Operations at Headquarters US Army Europe (USAREUR) in Heidelberg Germany about 30 Km south of Darmstadt. The job had always been occupied by an Infantryman or Armor officer, so selling an Air Defender in the job was something.

I reported in and met my boss, MG Dick Davis, a Tennessean who was the finest staff officer I had ever known. General Davis was an introspective quiet man with an intensity burning under the surface which was not hard to notice. The conduct of operations for the second largest theater in the world combined with the drawdown, which was in full swing, added up to a 24 hour a day, 7 day a week job 365 days a year. I would work both Christmas days we were in Heidelberg for a couple of hours unlike the 8 hours a day I worked every weekend.

I got the message that the new job was a 24 hour a day operation right away. While we were still living in Darmstadt waiting for our quarters in Heidelberg to free up, the secure telephone in the entry way in my quarters rang early one morning about a week after I had started at USAREUR. We had pulled all the Patriots out of Saudi Arabia after the war and Sadam was saber rattling once again. The phone call was General Davis telling me that I needed to alert General Costello, who lived next door, to get a battalion moving. So, I walked next door in the middle of the night, woke the General and Micki up and gave him a verbal warning order. I went back to the house, put on my uniform, and drove to Heidelberg. The order was issued early the next day and thus started the rotation of Patriot units to Saudi which as far as I know is stilling going on today.

We finally got moved into our quarters in Patrick Henry village. The DCSOPs house was 4 or 5 houses down the street which came in real handy at times. Our backyard butted up on a German field that ran all the way to a road at the north side of the compound that connected with a little German farming town. We would go into that town all the time to eat at the Gasthaus and to buy bread for special occasions. The sale of fresh food in the mornings in Europe was first come, first serve. Marilyn was great at getting there early enough to get what we wanted.

My main job was to coordinate deployments. The DCSOPS staff was in the H building, so called because of its shape. The Deputy Chief of Staff, Intelligence or DCSINT, occupied the other half of the building. My office was on the second story of the building, overlooking the large War Room where the CINC held his weekly staff and commander updates and where we briefed him on deployments. The management of the US-AREUR command center which maintained 24/7 situational awareness for the CINC was part of my responsibilities as well.

It was not long before we had the second deployment under my watch. I will always be grateful to the men and women who were on my Crisis Action Team or CAT. We met right after I arrived, I got to know them a little and what they could do, and I told them to always shoot straight with me. Anyway, we got a deployment order in the middle of one night to send Mobile Army Surgical Hospital to Georgia, which was just north of Turkey and south of the USSR. The wall had come down just before I had taken Brigade Command and USAEUR and European Command was making a real effort to be good buddies to the former Warsaw Pact countries.

I called the CAT around midnight. They were all there by 0200, the transporters, the medics, the logisticians, the intel guys, and the operators. The medical people had to first brief us on how much stuff a MASH had so the transporters could start planning the transportation requirements. The intel rep gave a brief on the political situation in Georgia, specifically the situation in Tbilisi, the capitol where the MASH was going to conduct operations. I would love to tell you that I played a key role in this second deployment that I was a part of, but like the Patriot deployment, I was mainly listening, asking questions, and putting together decision briefs for the CINC. We briefed General Dave Maddox who was the new CINC, and he approved the deployment. The CAT was an iterative process, for we would brief the DCSOPS and DCSINT who would put their spin on the op, and I would have to go and negotiate with EUCOM or other staff sections to get things the way my boss wanted. The DCSINT was BG Chuck Thomas who was the finest intel guy I have ever known. Many times, in the future when I convened the CAT, he was there. I will always be thankful for him because the first step in planning anything is knowing the situation you are going into, and General Thomas always set us straight on those things. We had 18 deployments during the 2 years I was the Chief of the USAREUR CAT team. We sent soldiers all over the world often into hot spots like Somalia. Soldiers we had sent to Somalia were present when the famous Battle was fought that was captured in the film Blackhawk Down.

About 6 months after I arrived in Heidelberg, the ADCOPS left and General Davis told me that I was now the ADCSOPS and the Chief of Current Operations. The responsibilities of the ADCSOPS included interfacing with V Corps, managing all the majors in theater to make sure they all got S-3 jobs, political-military coordination for a new program that was sending U.S. reps to the Warsaw Pact countries more than once per month and anything else that came up. After a month, everyone seemed pleased with the setup, but I was working 15-hour days and every weekend. But somehow it was the most rewarding job I had ever had. People would come to me asking for things because I had access to the DCSOPS and CINC. There was a trust factor here that I built up with Generals Davis and Hendricks. If I came in with something, they knew it was an actionable item. Eventually, I started having breakfast with members of the staff and garrison commander which I hope helped them but provided me with great situational awareness. It got to the point if you wanted to know what was happening in USAREUR you called Paul. It was nuts, but I was alive like I had never been before.

Shortly before he was reassigned, General Davis came into my office and closed the door. He told me it was his primary chance for selection to be a division commander. He told me he didn't think he was going to make it but if he was selected, he wanted me to be his Chief of Staff. I was blown away-a duck hunter as the senior Colonel in an Infantry Division. I told him I would be honored. He didn't get selected, but it remains one of the proudest moments of my life.

The watch officers changed out at 0600 each morning and I had to be there to receive their out brief. So, I would get up at 0430, go do my PT in the neighborhood and drive to work. We usually received about 70 actions per day that were meticulously organized by our admin section, headed by SFC Dilly. The actions, once formatted and placed in folders, were passed to my XO who proofed them and made sure they made sense. General Davis approved most actions but 2 or so a day had to go to the CINC for approval. When General Davis was the boss, actions flowed beautifully. When General Jay Hendricks came in to replace General Davis, we all noticed after a week or so that nothing was coming out of the boss' office. It was funny, it just was a feeling that my XO and several of the division chiefs and I had.

Catherine, who was a transportation officer (and my XO) and I went into the Boss' office. The top of his desk was clean, but when we walked around behind the desk, we discovered the boss had pulled his lower right desk drawer out and all our actions were there, stacked almost to desk level. Actions were Catherine's life. We sometimes got documents that were several hundred pages long which I had no time to read but as I leafed through them, I would notice that Catherine had marked a spelling error in the middle of the document. She had read the whole thing!

We gathered all the actions and took them into my office. I approved most of the recommendations and sent a couple into the boss accompanied by a summary sheet detailing all the 65 or so actions that Catherine and I had taken care of. The boss stuck his head in my door that afternoon and shared with me he wasn't a big reader. I asked him if he wanted us to continue with the summary sheets and he said he would appreciate it.

When I was in Europe, the DCSOPS managed the planning of the budget since 80%+ of the money coming into theater was allocated for training. The CINC had the authority to spend the entire budget as he wanted, but no one wanted to sacrifice training. I had an office that worked for me with a finance LTC, Jerry Pinson, and 8 lady government employees who worked for him. The event we planned for was an all-day budget summit every year where every expense in the budget was given a line item and prioritized into categories. An A priority was something that had to be done like paying utility bills or the absolute minimum amount of training. B priorities were things we should and wanted to do and C priorities were hopes, but the goal each year was to fund a couple of "C's". Jerry and his ladies would come up with a rough list and co-ordinate it with the USAREUR staff and the units. This early priority list caused a lot of consternation, and more than one General came into my office to talk to me about raising the priority of various items. Jerry was super busy as the budget allocation meeting approached and his guys worked miracles to reduce the cost of several line items a little so more money could be added to another priority. By the time the meeting arrived, we had gotten to the point that just about everyone was pretty much satisfied and every issue had been discussed in advance.

The CINC only had minimal exposure to the priorities and numbers before the meeting and so the first part of the meeting was reviewing the priorities for him. He would have a give and take with the staff and LTG Jerry Rutherford who was the V Corps commander. Both times I coordinated the meeting, at the end of the A and B priority discussion, everyone was happy. Then the CINC would get to select the C priorities that he wanted to fund.

General Dave Maddox, the CINC, was a Cavalry officer who had a tremendous attention to detail. His gift was when he read something or received a briefing on something, he took it to the core. One time we had a briefing for him in the war room on a new software package that was being issued to the theater. The meeting turned out to be 6 hours long as General Maddox had the briefers take him down to the code for the software while 50 people sat around and mostly twiddled their thumbs.

I respected General Maddox. I was part of the briefing the day he disbanded the Armored Cavalry Regiments which I know broke his heart as he had commanded a Cavalry squadron and regiment. In retrospect we should have retained the Armored Cavalry Regiments for they were a combined arms team with their own infantry, armor, artillery, and logistical elements organic to the unit. Later, we would have a lot of taskers calling for a little bit of this and that and we always had to organize some sort of command and control for the operation. In several instances we could have sent an ACR or one of their battalions with their support slice and been done with it.

One Friday night I was still in the office and the phone that connected the DCSOPS and the CINC rang. General Hendricks had gone home a little while earlier and I was cleaning out my in box. I picked up the phone and General Maddox asked if Major Meg Ardnor was there. Meg was one of our action officers and had written a letter over a week earlier advising a German Mayor that we would be closing the Kaserne in their city. I said no she wasn't here (thinking don't you know its 8PM on a Friday night) could I help? The CINC mentioned he was rewriting Meg's letter and asked me for a little information. We got 70 actions a day and that action was over a week old, but thanks be to God, I remembered it a little and was able to help the old man out a little. We talked for a little while and General Maddox said: "how about coming over to my office?" I replied sure and walked the 5 minutes between the H building where I worked and the Keys building where the boss' office was.

General Maddox had a 12-foot conference table in his office and when I reported in, I was shocked. Sitting on this conference table piled 10 high were our actions. There were over 200 of them, the table was completely full. The CINC was cutting sentences out of Meg's letter and pasting them on a piece of paper and writing in between the pasted lines. Soon the Staff Judge Advocate had been called along with the political-military officer for the theater and we sat around until the General's clerk, who was still on duty, now at 10PM, had retyped the letter several times.

The next day I told the DCSOPS about the actions piled up in the CINCs office and he went to see the Chief of Staff MG Hagan. They ended up adopting the practice that General

Hendricks and I used. The Chief worked almost all the actions and sent a note to the CINC telling him what he had done. I loved Maddox but you needed patience to work for him. There was a popular story about him floating around Europe. A few years earlier, units were encouraged to have briefings on their war plans on site, the location where they were going to conduct operations. Maddox was the Commander of the 11th ACR and when his first squadron commander got up to brief, Maddox asked him for the bumper number of the first of his vehicle that would move. In the mountain of information that a commander had to absorb and process, that was an incredibly small detail that was really the responsibility of the platoon leader of that vehicle. The squadron commander knew the troop or company from which the vehicle came from and after a little fumbling, they got the track number. I learned attention to detail from General Maddox and I also learned you can take it a little too far. Proving you are smarter than a subordinate is not always good leadership.

We were having trouble about 6 months after I got there getting the majors on the USAREUR staff into staff positions in the battalions which they needed to advance their careers. I suggested a plan where I would meet with the Division and the V Corps Chiefs of Staffs quarterly and we would come up with a plan to get the staff guys into battalions and the battalion guys some high-level staff time if they still had time on their tour in Europe. There wasn't a lot of negotiating; the guys on the staff with the most seniority went first and so forth. I had some good guys on our staff, so selling them was not hard. It worked well; we were able to get the majors the experience they needed. I used this process to get Catherine an S-3 job in a logistical battalion, but I heard she had some problems and

I lost touch with her. She was a fierce subordinate who really tried to get inside my head and anticipate what I wanted. I wish her all the best, but I could see how she might get in a scuffle with her commander.

The job was go, go, go from early in the morning until way after dark every day, 7 days a week. We did go to mass on Sunday mornings but after breakfast I would go into the office and work at least until 6PM. We did have some fun though. The thing that made our last tour in Germany so interesting is the Berlin wall had gone down in 1989 and the former Warsaw Pact countries were joining the west. Marilyn loved dishes and Czechoslovakia and Poland were world famous for their dishes and pottery. I was going to Hungary, Czech and Poland as part of my duties so I kind of had the lay of the land.

Our first trip to was to a pottery factory about 60 miles outside of Krakow Poland. Marilyn planned the trip and she, Jim Willet, one of my action officers I was fond of, Catherine and I would drive to Krakow, spend 2 nights in the "foreigners" hotel and then retrace our route back toward Germany in the morning to a famous pottery factory and buy up the seconds or extras they made the previous day. We had a Subaru station wagon and Marilyn had figured the gas mileage very precisely as we wanted to buy gas using our EXON coupons that we purchased from the military exchange. Gas was over $4 a gallon on the economy and with the coupons, we could get it for less than $2. She found an Exon station right at the border with Poland, so if we topped off there, we had enough gas to drive to Krakow and back-barely. I was always nervous when we did this, but we never had a problem.

We arrived in Krakow and checked into the hotel. The clerk almost insisted that I park my car in the hotel parking lot and leave it there, suggesting that we walk or take public transportation wherever we went. I got with the parking attendant and backed the Subaru into the slot and the guy put a U-shaped bar in front of the car and locked it down. People in Poland were starving, the benefits of being free were not there yet and thievery was a real issue.

The next morning after breakfast we walked around town. There were several department stores that we wandered through, and they were all seemingly the same. They all had a grocery store on the first floor and the next 4 or 5 stories had areas that sold the same kind of merchandise but unlike America where all the men's clothes are in one place, the Polish stores might have men's clothes on every floor. Interestingly we saw the same merchandise over and over.

We stopped in a Catholic Church which was made of stone and had no pews. Mass was going ongoing, so we exited very quickly after just a glimpse. The women as advertised were beautiful, but all the people seemed so very, very sad. We would smile and they would just keep on going. We ran across several former Soviet Army soldiers who were selling their uniform items.

I was looking at something in one of the outside concessions when Marilyn called me. She had met an elderly man who spoke some English. He was hungry so we took him to lunch. He told us his story while we were eating. When the Nazis invaded Poland, the Poles who escaped and went to England were formed into Polish units. He had been a paratrooper and had several combat jumps against the Germans. After the war, these Poles were offered British citizenship, or they could go back to Poland. He decided to return home and less than a week after he returned the Soviets rolled in to occupy Poland for over 40 years. I jokingly said to the guy "Bad decision, huh?' and he sadly nodded his head yes. Marilyn gave him some money and we never saw him again.

I went on an official visit later to overwatch a team that was visiting the Polish Air Defense Brigade. The visit was so surreal for me. First, the unit was equipped with the ZSU 23-4 which was an Air Defense Gun which we had studied in the early 70's when I was at Bliss with General LeVan trying to procure a replacement gun for the Vulcan. The Egyptians used the "Zoo" as it was nicknamed effectively in the 1973 Arab-Israeli war, and it was still in service in the early 1990's. The United States would never buy a Soviet weapon but I guess I secretly wished that some other country had it so we could buy it.

The highlight of the visit was a crew drill demonstration and a visit to their gunnery training facility. The gunnery training area had a Zoo turret that was powered, and a guy would take a pocket laser like we used for briefings and would move it around the ceiling while the gunner tracked the laser. They were so proud of it, but there was no feedback mechanism to tell the gunner how he did.

We then were escorted into a large garage area where three crews performed a preparation to fire crew drill. I had very funny feelings. The soldiers wore Russian uniforms, and all the commands were given in Russian. I thought here were the guys that I have spent my life preparing to fight and now they are our friends. I suddenly remember the Blessed Mother's admonition at Fatima to pray the rosary for the conversion of Russia. The Soviet Union had just collapsed it was so sudden; it was starling. And here we were trying to make our former enemies better. The only thing certain in life is change. We just need to own that fact.

Poland is one of the most Catholic countries in the world, but that was not on my personal radar at the time so visiting places like where Saint John Paul II lived when he was a Bishop and opposed the Communists didn't happen or a visit to St Faustina's convent. I regret that to this day.

My first trip to Czech was a big time visit to brief the Chief of the Czech armed forces on the lessons from Desert Storm. I was selected as the senior officer on the trip because I was an Air Defender, and their Chief was an Air Defender. The briefing was given by Major Bill Curry who was a SAMS graduate. The Army had a program where a handpicked few were given an extra year of school after Leavenworth where they studied strategy and political-military stuff. Bill was a quiet, brilliant guy and he micromanaged that brief and did a great job when he gave it.

We stayed at a hotel on the outskirts of the city that we could easily tell was built by the Russians, it had a cold concrete exterior that had the same appeal as a warehouse. The rooms were nice, and we were comfortable. When we reported in for the briefing, we were escorted into a conference room. We had studied Czech rank insignia and it looked like Captains were telling Colonels what to do. I later asked the Chief about that, and he said I was right. The way he explained it, the older officers who had grown up in the Soviet system were inflexible to new ideas and procedures that were welcome to the junior guys. So, the Czech military had bitten the bullet and just put the Captains in charge. If the colonels didn't like it, they could retire.

The brief went well, and the Chief invited us into his office to chat. He served us Cognac, very civilized, and I invited him to visit USAREUR which he did some months later. I wish I could remember his name, but he was a caring, innovative leader that I greatly admired.

That afternoon, we wandered around what they called old town. I stood on the banks of the Danube river at a bridge called the old bridge and looked across the river to the Hapsburg palaces that had been there since the 11th Century. Here I was the historian, and we had skipped this important time of history in every world history class I took, going from the Greeks and Romans straight to the Renaissance. That night we went to a little bistro for a light dinner, and they served Budwar beer, a Czech beer that was the original Budweiser. It was the best beer I have ever had. I fell in love with Prague and when I told Marilyn of the visit, we would visit it several times in the future. The dishes were awesome!

In addition to the trips to Czech and Poland, I also got a trip to Hungary. Our hotel was right on the Danube river again and on the opposite side were another group of magnificent buildings, the home of the Hapsburg monarchs. I chided myself for my historical ignorance again. The owner of the hotel where we were staying came us to us one night and asked if we were Americans. He told me they were trying to add American cuisine to their menu and asked if I would try their newly created hamburger. I said sure and ate it. It was ok, but something just wasn't right. I really didn't know what to tell the guy, I think the beef was just different.

Mike Penhallogen, my old battalion XO, was the G-3 of SETAF in Vincenza Italy. We had talked from time occasionally; he was having a bicycle built for me by a man who did it in his garage. The bike was a little heavy and served me well as in the spring of that last year in Germany, I often rode it to work. Rob would take that bike when he went to Stanford for his doctorate and get more service out of it later.

Mike was having some financial trouble in his unit, and he asked if we could help. I agreed and Jerry Pinson and two of his lady analysts flew down to Italy with us in a T-41. The girls had never flown in a small airplane before, and they were both real nervous. The pilot had told us before we took off that when we flew over the Alps, the oxygen masks would drop, as the T-41 cabin was not pressurized. Sure enough, as we climbed up to cross the mountains, the masks dropped, and I thought the girls were going to jump out of their seats. We got over ok, we were really at the decision line between needing the masks or not, but we got through it, and we landed safely in Vincenza. Mike met us at the airport, and I met him the next morning to shoot the bull after hooking Jerry and the girls up with Mike's people. MG Jack Nix was the new CG of SETAF whom I had known from my time at Hunter with the 1st Ranger Battalion and I said hi to him and asked if we could help in any way. Jerry and the girls got the financial problem straightened out and we flew home.

Late that second year, problems were developing in Bosnia Herzegovina; the Serbs and Croats were killing each other like they had been doing for a thousand years and NATO had decided to help. Admiral Borda in Italy was going to be the commander of the operation, but since it would primarily be a ground campaign, General Maddox offered USAREUR's planning help, which he happily accepted. The boss told me that our plans shop would spearhead the planning for the operation, but he wanted me real involved.

Sarajevo, the capital, looked like a war zone; people were starving. Like any military operation in modern times, the objective was important, and it needed to be measurable so we could keep the support of the American people. I suggested that we provide aid to Sarajevo and report the number of short tons of food delivered each day as our metric. General Hendricks and I flew to Italy and briefed Admiral Borda and he thought it was a good objective. The plans boys went to work and soon we were working through a myriad of problems.

The first was finding a port on the Adriatic Sea where we could come ashore. The Navy helped us with this one and we decided on the port of Split. The transporters and engineers then looked at the road connecting Split and Sarajevo which had a few sections that were so bad, they could not be navigated by a heavy transporter. We had to get 18 wheelers through with the supplies so the engineers came up with a plan to improve the roads to the point we could use them. We didn't know what the reaction of the warring factions would be, so we had to plan for a relatively heavy security element as well.

As we briefed the Admiral (and CINC first) the Marines in Italy who had been assigned the mission of securing the route up to 50KM from the beach, the limit established by joint doctrine at the time, keep wanting to go further and further inland. We resisted, but their insistence was the beginning of a whole new way of using the Marines. By the time of Operation Iraqi Freedom, the Marines went wherever they wanted. I learned from my Dad how important it was to protect service roles and missions. With the advent of a desire in the DOD to become more "joint" much of that went away and the thinking became who could get there first was best. I guess it was good, but I could see an old-world fading.

The plan became mature, but we learned the English were lobbying in Washington to change the objective of the plan to a new objective, separating the warring factions. We resisted, arguing how could that objective be measured? We lost; the objective changed, and we passed the plan to SETAF. Rob would later serve in Bosnia Herzegovina where he was the S-5, or POLMIL officer for his battalion.

It was weird, but I never worried much about Rob or Mike when they were in combat. I trusted in their skills and training, especially for Mike who participated in some heavy action. But when I learned that Rob got in his vehicle with only a driver and rode around in their sector talking to military and civilian leaders, it scared the hell of me. And for some reason it really bothered me when they were in Ranger school. They both did well there, Mike had to retake the last third because some Ranger Instructor was being a dick, but he came out well. I always wanted to go to Ranger School, but slots were limited, and no one saw a need for Air Defenders to be rangers in the 1960's and 70's. That policy changed a little later and the branch started getting a few slots but by then, I was way too old.

One of the biggest exercises in Europe every year was Reforger which was an event used to update plans for the reinforcement of Europe in the event of a Russian invasion. DC-SOPS had an exercise division headed by a full colonel, which planned our participation in this exercise and many others. This was my first Reforger at USAREUR which was obviously a different experience from my first Reforger as a battery commander where my Vulcan battery just drove around the countryside chasing the armored Brigade we were supporting.

As I said earlier, General Maddox was a stickler for detail so a great deal of effort for this exercise went into planning the headquarters facility for the exercise which was the biggest tent I have ever seen which was well lighted and heated. In the center of the tent was the operations section which had a huge map we used to keep the tactical situation current.

We were still using paper maps back then, but I had helped General Davis with the development of what was supposed to be the Army's first digital TOC. BG Rick Shinseki who would later be the Chief of Staff of the Army, was then the Assistant Division Commander (Maneuver) for the 3d Infantry Division was brought in as a Subject Matter Expert (SME). We went through several iterations of the technical layout of the TOC with the objective of General S using it in an exercise. Right before we were to roll it out, at the final coordination session, General S asked me a favor. "Paul can you put a map here on this blank wall?" He had everything he needed to track the battle in the computer without the map, but old habits die hard. By the time Mike and Rob were in the Army paper maps were out and everything was done on digital maps that were also in the situational awareness technology.

Back to Reforger, we had a big briefing with all the commanders. The Russians were expected to create a large penetration of our lines and we wanted to allow them to get about 30KM inside the original line of contact before we counterattacked. Our German units were to be the first to move but not until the enemy had reached the designated phase line. All the commanders were briefed, the plan was in place.

I came in early to the TOC the next morning, and my watch officer was waiting with his head hung down. I asked what was up and he told me the Germans had already started moving, hours before the CINC wanted them to go. Suddenly I felt a presence by me, and it was General Maddox who stood there silently. I told him the Germans had moved and he just nodded and left, I presume to go see the Germans. Many leaders would have been upset that their carefully crafted plans had gone in the gutter and taken their frustration out on those around them. Maddox didn't and I learned that lesson from him although I don't think I put it into practice as much as I would have liked.

A couple of months before we left, we got in a new full colonel who had been a Corps G-3. Division and Corps G-3s are very special guys who are bright, incredibly hard working and talented. When General Hendricks told him he was going to be the Chief of Current Ops, my old job, he wasn't very happy. And when he found out I was going to be his rater; he was really upset. Right after General Hendricks arrived, word had come down revising the OER scheme. The CINC was senior rating for way too many Colonels and the real issue was he really didn't know a lot of them at all. So, for the headquarters staff sections, the Deputy became the rater, and the staff principal became the senior rater. The new Colonel went to see General Hendricks about this, worried his career would take a bump due to the situation. The boss explained the situation to him but when he came back to debate the situation a 2d time, the boss called me in and he told the new guy that he had two choices, go with the system in place or get the hell out of Europe. He stayed and I wrote him what I thought was a good OER when I left. It took a little adjustment to give the guy his space after doing a job for almost 18 months.

General Hendricks was one of the nicest guys I had ever met, humble, hardworking and from what I have been told a brilliant tactician. He would later become a 4 Star General.

I had worked hard right from my arrival in Heidelberg to help V Corps any way I could. There was some tension between the Corps and USAREUR. V Corps had 90% of the ground forces in theater and they really thought they could handle most things by themselves. Early in my tour I went to an AAR for an exercise the Corps had been involved in and I met LTG Rutherford who was the Corps Commander. I developed a relationship of trust with him, and he knew I would try to make things happen for him if it wasn't contrary to what the CINC wanted.

By the middle of my second year at USAREUR I guess I had a proven track record and I used to get calls from BG Montgomery Miegs, who was General Rutherford's Chief of Staff. At first there were things that I could do but as things progressed, Miegs started asking me to go talk to the DCSOPS and get him to go up the tape to change things that we knew the CINC wanted to do. This went on and on until, frustrated, I went into see the boss and I explained to him what was happening. Furious, General Hendricks picked up the phone and called General Miegs and proceeded to call him every so in so concluding with "Do not call us again".

Years later when I was going up for promotion to BG, General Miegs, by now a 4 Star, was on the board. General Garner and General Jack Costello, who was now the CG of Ft Bliss were working to get me promoted. Costello was on the board. I made the next to final cut. The board had gone from 2500 fully, and I mean fully, qualified guys and had eliminated all but 50. The next cut was the final cut to 33, the number that were to be promoted. The board was looking for any excuse at all to remove guys from the list and Miegs told Costello that he couldn't vote for me. Jack asked if it were something about me and he replied no, he just hated General Hendricks and that he associated me and Hendricks together.

Had I gone to Desert Storm and helped General Schwarzkopf; I think this hurdle could have been overcome. So, I would retire as an old Colonel. I had given my best and although I was bitterly disappointed, I was not angry like my Uncle had been when he was a non-select because of his cancer. All you can do is your best and leave the rest to God.

It's hard to describe how varied and intense life was in DCSOPS. We were operating over an area that comprised 20 or so countries, we were deploying people all over the place regularly, running exercises, working a big budget every day, trying to stay on top of a mountain of actions daily, planning and executing deployments and the grind of knowing everything that was going on, which was impossible, but we did a pretty good job of tracking at least the big stuff. When I had to go on a POLMIL trip or anywhere out of the office, it was a big decision. We all understood why I went on those trips to the former Warsaw pact countries, they required a former Brigade Commander and the only other guys in theater that generally met that requirement were the Chiefs of Staff of the divisions, and we sure didn't want those guys out of pocket. Despite the cost that being away took on me when I got back, my trips to the former Warsaw Pact countries were fun. I did get one opportunity to take a trip to the west, and it was special because I got to take Marilyn with me.

I had about 6 months left on my tour, and we got a tasker to start planning the 50th commemoration of the D Day landing.

The event would not occur until 1994, a couple of years later. I assigned Jim Willet in Current Ops to work the tasker. Jim was a very good action officer, but he came to me a few weeks after he got the tasker and told me that he had to lay eyes on the ground to do it right. I went in and saw the DCSOPS who asked me if I had ever been to Normandy, to which I replied no, and the boss said I was to go along.

Additionally, we were to take our Liaison to the French Army, Colonel Marcel Letre with us. In the early 1990's we still had a couple of positions that were vital when tensions were high during the peak of the Cold War. We still had two incumbents in these now unnecessary positions; our liaison to the 1st French Army, Marcel, and the second was our liaison with the British Army on the Rhine which would have been to our north. Our British LNO was a hoot, telling jokes constantly. He really didn't have anything to do but he always kept me informed of his whereabouts.

His name was George Smyth, and he came in one day and told me he was going on leave for a week to visit his sons in Scotland who ran restaurants there. When he came back, he "reported" in, and I asked him how it went. He told me a story that would serve me well later.

When he got on the train, he picked a compartment and there were 3 other guys already seated there. Two were dressed in sport coat and tie like George and the third had on a scruffy sweater and dirty khaki pants. After the train took off George suggested that they introduce themselves as they would be together for a long time. George led off: "Smythe, Colonel, married, 2 sons, both prominent restaurateurs in Scotland." The second, dressed like George then said "Wilcox, Colonel, 2 sons, one is a member of the Coldstream Guards and the second is a member of Parliament." The third nicely dressed man said "Curtis, Colonel, married, 1 son, 1 daughter, my son is a brain surgeon, and my daughter is married to the CEO of a very successful company." The three colonels turned to the unkept man in the khakis, and he finally said "Jones, Sergeant Major, never married, 2 sons, both Colonels." I roared with laughter.

To this day I am not sure if that was a true story but years later when we were teaching the pilot GMD course I noticed after my introduction that the students seemed tight. Our faculty consisted of retired full and half colonels. There was one LTC in the course, but the rest of the students were Majors and below with a lot of mid ranking enlisted. My team was fighting like cats and dogs until I hired a retired CSM whose job was to teach but also straighten out our egos. At the break I called him into my office and asked him what he thought. "He replied "Sir they are scared to death of all the rank". I replied we were all retired, and he said it didn't make a difference. So, I went in and told George's story at the start of the 2d period, got a big laugh, and things loosened up. I thank God for the NCOs that worked for me when I was in the Army and later in my business career. They always provided sound, reasonable, advice.

Back to Marcel and Normandy. I called him and asked him if he could come see me and gave him the mission. He shared with me that he had planned the 45th commemoration. Marcel had attended the French artillery school as a Captain and had studied French in college. He could talk the talk and he knew his way around, so his help was invaluable.

We drove in in late January and stayed at a hotel not far from Omaha Beach. The hotel was shaped like a "U" and the middle, which was obviously a courtyard in the summer, had a plexiglass cover. Marcel seemed to know the bartender and they chatted for a minute when we came in, and we sat down. We were all having drinks when the phone rang, and the bartender called for Marcel. He talked on the phone in English and when he returned to the table, he told us we were going to have a visitor.

About 10 minutes later I was sitting with my back to the street, almost in the street as there was almost no sidewalk, I noticed movement to my left. Something was strange. I looked again and a Lincoln Continental was pulling into the curb to park. An older guy came in and embraced Marcel who introduced him as "Howard". We sat across the table from each other, and I asked him when he first came to Normandy. "5 June 1944" he replied. Howard had been a member of the 82d Airborne Division and had jumped in the night before the invasion. He left the Army after the war and became a policeman in New Jersey. He and his wife often returned to Normandy for vacations and after a while, they bought a house. When he retired, they moved to France for good, returning to the States a couple of times a year. His car had New Jersey license plates, which was odd in France, and I asked him about that. He said, everyone knew he was not only a veteran of the 82d, but he was also a retired cop, so the French Police let him get away with it. Howard had a harder time getting them to agree when he brought over a 2d Lincoln for his wife but they did. The dinner ended and Howard promised to meet us the next morning at St Mere d' Eglise. I told Howard I was looking to buy some French wine and he said he could help me out. When I watched the 50th commemoration years later, Howard was a prominent personality, representing those great men he had served with.

The following day was fantastic. We met Howard at St Mere d' Eglise. He showed us where he landed, the wall he jumped over to provide him with some cover and described the uncertainty and fear that the paratroopers initially faced with the tactical situation being so fluid. He showed me the famous church that John Steele hung from when his parachute caught on the church steeple, and we had a nice lunch at the John Steele café. We visited the beautiful American cemetery and I have never been so proud to be an American.

Mando told me later that the 82d Airborne jumps about a hundred guys into Normandy each year. This is a privilege reserved for the most senior parachutists in the division, that is those with the most jumps. Mando was a platoon leader in the 82d's Air Defense Battalion and because of his time in the 509th and more jumping with the 82d, he had over 300 jumps, so he got to jump into France. He said the people were so appreciative almost 50 years after D-Day that it really made him proud. It made me reflect that none of us are in anything alone and we need to give thanks always to those who served with us, who taught us, who helped us. Gratitude overcomes many sins, and despite our many faults, I always have been grateful to those who helped me and my family.

Rob and Mike were playing soccer for Heidelberg High and at first, it was one of the finest soccer programs I have ever been a part of. The boys on the varsity would play for a German club in the fall and then play other American teams in the spring. Rob played for SGK Kircheim in the fall whose stadium I passed every day going to work. In Germany all practices and scrimmages were played on clay playing fields, saving the game field for games. This local club had a small stadium complete with a gasthaus.

I went to one of Rob's scrimmages and the coach played him at fullback. Rob did not understand a word of German except here (Hier) but somehow, he understood he was to mark his guy and go everywhere with him. One time a ball popped loose, Rob left his man and passed it to a teammate who started a counterattack. Rob immediately went back to his man, but the coach chewed Rob out for leaving his man. Oh well, I guess the lesson learned is you gain initiative only after you master the fundamentals.

Mike tried out for the varsity soccer team in Heidelberg and was the last cut from a team that would win the European High School Championship. Mike wanted to play baseball his freshman year in high school; Heidelberg had a team and a field but no coach. I talked to the boss, and he said sure, coach 'em. We started with a clinic presented by some college baseball coaches from the states. I learned a lot from then and would learn as much from as the boys as we started the season.

We played mostly German teams and they had some interesting field configurations. One place had a U-shaped backstop like a batting cage that was lowered down for games. Soccer was king in Germany and the field was used for soccer when we were not playing baseball. Mike and our catcher were the two best kids on the team. Mike was a singles-doubles hitter who hit over .400. Our catcher hit for a good average and had pop in his bat, hitting a couple of big home runs for us. We were the Heidelberg Yankees of course and I designed a logo for our uniforms. The boys were constantly giving me advice on the lineups and how the players were feeling.

Heidelberg was selected to send a team to the European championship which would be played at a Cavalry Regiment's

Kaserne which had been shut down. All the coaches met, and we picked the team, and I was asked if I would help another coach and I said sure. The field we played on there was a converted soft ball field, not as good as I thought it should have been for a championship. We advanced to the finals and in the championship game, the other team had a great pitcher. Late in the game, we were down 2-1 and Mike was up. He had struck out two times previously and the count was 2-2 on his current at bat. The other team called time and I walked down from third base where I was coaching to chat with Mike. He was very tense, so I started telling him a joke. About halfway through, Mike stopped me and asked: "Dad, what are you doing?" I told him I was trying to loosen him up and he told me he was fine. He then struck out. We lost 2-1 but we gave it a hell of a run.

Rob's soccer team was having problems. They were off to a good start but about halfway through the season a teacher was reassigned who had been the soccer coach at another American High School that closed. He insisted on being the coach as our German coach's position was very unofficial. The kids loved Klaus and they were not too happy when the new guy started asserting his authority despite the fact it became really apparent quickly that he knew nothing of soccer. Klaus was very gracious but eventually left with about a third of the season left. The kids were flat the last few games of the season but qualified for the European Championships which would be held in Berlin.

Right before the team left for Berlin, the coach called me and asked if I could help him coach in the championship. He understood I had a lot of coaching experience. I told him I would under the condition that my advice would be followed.

We had a great tournament. My major contribution was getting the boys to relax. We would talk before, during and after the game and I sought their input and then we did what they wanted. We went 5-0 and didn't allow a goal and won it all. I guess it was another lesson for me in communicating. The guys one is leading are always full of good ideas and you just need to listen sometimes and turn them loose. I played Rob at center midfielder as much as I could; he always had a gift for seeing the field and distributing the ball.

It was nearing the time for our transfer back to the States. Rob graduated 3d in his class and had several scholarship offers, many of which were ROTC scholarships. He had been accepted to West Point, making the very competitive final cut. Despite being a bright scholar his whole life he didn't do particularly well on the SAT exams which limited his options some. He was intrigued by an offer from American University in Washington DC where he would have studied International Relations. He kept putting off deciding about West Point. I finally told him he could go where he wanted, but he was going to visit West Point first. I told him West Point was always a good place to have been from.

We flew him back for an official visit. I told him to talk to the soccer coach about playing for him. He came home and told us to leave him alone, he had to think. Three days later at the dinner table he shared his impressions of his visit. "I went to three classes; I was ahead of them in two of them but followed the instruction in the third. I don't think academics will be a problem. I talked to the soccer coach, and he told me to come try out, but was not particularly enthusiastic. I stayed with a Plebe who had graduated from my high school the year before (smart West Point) and he said the biggest challenge was the discipline; people were yelling at you all the time." Rob then said: "Dad I'm your son and I'm used to being yelled at-I am sure I can handle the discipline." He then told us he was going to the Military Academy. I have never been so proud; my Mom had arranged for me to get a political appointment to the Military Academy when I was in High School, and I turned it down because I was afraid of the math. Years later at Air Force I saw how the Academies saw their students as an investment and worked hard to help them. I'm sure I would have worked hard at my books, but I took satisfaction at least one Semmens was going to Army. Mike was ready to begin his junior year wherever we were headed.

Marilyn and the boys flew back to the States and the Colonels in DCSOPS gave me a farewell dinner. We met at a gasthaus, and the boys gave me a Civil War painting entitled "Silent Tribute", a picture of General Lee reviewing the troops before the battle of Gettysburg. I still have that painting; all those guys worked their tails off and to honor me like they did was special.

My replacement was identified at USAREUR, Colonel Jimmy Banks, who had just given up command of the Berlin Brigade, which was the trip wire that the Russians would have run over quickly but would have started WWIII. Jim was a good guy, and we had a smooth transition. The day before I left the CINC called to say thanks, a gesture that I really appreciated. My last day I took the watch officer's brief at 0600, said adios to General Hendricks and I was off. Branch had offered me the typical list of old Colonel jobs-serving on a military records correction board and various assignments advising this or that National Guard unit. I didn't think I was quite done, so I called General Garner who was taking over the Army's Space and

Missile Defense Command (SMDC). Note: one of the things that made it so difficult for outsiders to understand the military is we used acronyms a lot. It was part of who we were, how we talked, and I guess over 20 years after retiring, it still is.

CHAPTER SEVENTEEN

COLORADO SPRINGS, COLORADO 1994-96

ARMY SPACE COMMAND 1994-1996

General Garner had me assigned as the Commander of Army Space Command in Colorado Springs. I reported into Washington first and went to see the old man. I was ushered into his office and told the General was running late to sit tight. I looked around at the boss' memorabilia and noticed a new autographed picture of the Florida State football coach for so many years, Bobby Bowden. The boss was an FSU grad and a huge fan; in El Paso he had another autographed picture of Bowden in his office. When he came in, we exchanged pleasantries and I commented on the new Bowden picture. The General replied: "You're right it is new; and he really signed that one." That was General Garner. Everyone really liked him or hated him, but he could get the devil to buy charcoal.

Army Space Command (ARSPACE) was a TDA brigade equivalent. There were line units and TDA units. Generally, TDA units were organized to support the combat operations of the Army, the line units. To document that fact that ARSPACE was a brigade, I lobbied with the boss for UCMJ authority which he reluctantly gave me. I never came close to giving an article 15 there but having that authority soothed my ego, I guess.

The command was about 1/3 military and the rest were DA civilians with a large group of supporting contractors. We had one battalion, a Defense Satellite Communications System unit, that manned the ground stations that communicated with the DSCS satellites in orbit which gave early warning of enemy missile attacks. We also had four or so Army Space Support Teams which provided satellite communications, global positioning equipment, satellite mapping and a few other space goodies to deployed commanders. Everybody today has satellite comms and maps, but then we were the only source. The command had earned its stripes during Desert Storm when the Hail Mary offensive, led by my old Division, the 24th, plunged north across terrain with absolutely no recognition features that were traditionally used for determining where one was. ARSPACE deployed the first Global Positioning devices used for navigation during that war.

The first six months I was there, I travelled a lot to Washington, Germany, and the Middle East mostly. I knew what USAREUR needed, and I made several trips to insure they understood what we could bring. We also had space advisors at all the Joint Commands and my guy in PACOM kept asking me to visit, but I never did which I now regret. Hawaii is GREAT. But I would have several opportunities later.

We rented a house just outside the Broadmoor area in Colorado Springs. It was just down the street from Cheyenne Mountain High School, our old rivals. They had a registration for fall soccer in the school gymnasium and Mike and I were the first to arrive. They had pictures of all the sports teams on the walls and Mike went around looking at each picture. He came back to where I was sitting and said "Dad, I'm going to be ok here". Mike would go on to play 2 seasons of soccer under a great coach who it turned out was married to the sister of my first girlfriend, Nancy Cook. Small world. The second year Mike played they won the state championship. Mike was still playing fullback, I always thought he should have been a stopper, the center fullback as he had great anticipation for where the ball was going.

Mike also played basketball and baseball. Basketball was tough; one year he had a coach who some called abusive (I think he was eventually fired for that). Mike was a little under 6'2" tall and he was the second tallest guy on the team. Unfortunately, the tallest guy on the team got hurt the first game of the year, so Mike ended up playing center amongst the much taller opposing centers that all the teams seemed to have. There was a lot of drama with that CM basketball team, but Mike just did his job as well as he could.

Mike made the baseball team easily, but the issue was where he would play. Most of the kids on the team had been long time proteges of the head coach and they had a first baseman, Mike's position, that was pretty good. It was a good program. The pitching coach was a former major leaguer who had a cup of coffee in the majors. He taught study hall. Mike and I would go to the field on Sundays trying to improve his throwing accuracy from 3d base, where the team needed his bat. That didn't work out so well, so the usual game scenario was Mike would pinch hit in the 5th inning or so and then go play left field. He continued to be a special hitter and when he was getting ready for college, I told him I thought that he should go to West Point and play baseball. Mike wasn't interested in Army, and I originally thought it was because of the same reason that made it unappealing to so many: the discipline.

As Mike has grown, I admired him more and more. God gave him a beautiful humility from the start, maybe caused by his dyslexia. He always has been slow to judge others, always tried to build unity and cohesion and has a caring heart. All those traits would serve him well later.

The pace at Army Space was slow compared to USAREUR. One of the problems I identified almost immediately was the outfit had a strange organization-they had a Colonel in charge of operations and another in charge of support. The two Colonels Jim Kulbacki and Bill Hoyman advised me on the climate of the command. They were happy with the command's organization, and they were most reluctant to change anything. I saw an expanded role for the command and my goal was to make space a tool, rather than a place. The space terminology was a challenge, but I eventually caught on. I went ahead and organized the command into a standard S Staff model, but I felt that every single person in the command was against me. It was hard but when you feel you are right, and you have no support; you must persevere.

Another problem with the command is it seemed like every time someone had a complaint, they submitted a formal complaint. Most of the time they were just BS. Suddenly, for the first time in 26 years I was getting investigated. The first time occurred when I asked my S-4 to go to Europe with me. She refused and I tried to entice her by saying we would have a good time. She submitted a formal complaint of sexual harassment to higher headquarters, and I think she got a monetary recompense. Even if one smelled a formal complaint, nobody was talking to anybody; everyone was afraid to try to solve the problem. I tried to help a woman who had an issue with the federal woman's program by having her talk to the Equal Opportunity Representative. I got investigated for mixing programs. I got investigated for buying T-shirts for the soldiers from the Army's safety program. That investigation was finally put to bed when the inspector saw we did indeed have "Safety First" embroidered on the shirt tail of each shirt. The soldiers did have to look at the shirt tails-and think safety- when they were putting on their T-Shirts! The last accusation was I had in inappropriate relationship with just about every woman in the command. That gained a little traction, more on that later.

I had been at ARSPACE about 4 months and General Garner came to visit on a very snowy night. I wanted to have a 4-wheel drive vehicle for just such occasions, but the Petersen AFB motor pool didn't have one to issue us. So, I rented one, and barely avoided another investigation. It seemed like every decision I made was a target. Mando and his wife Heather had been assigned to the command and we would go for a beer across the street from the Headquarters on Friday nights. One night, Mando got pulled over by a policeman immediately after leaving the bar. The policeman confided that someone had called from the command and said we would be driving drunk, and the police should stop us when we left. This cop didn't appreciate the situation and drove with Mando home. I am sure glad that Mando came to the command with me, I wouldn't have had anyone else to talk to.

The annual budget review came around and I asked my money guy how the review was held. I was told everyone sat around a U-shaped conference table and we went through it line by line. We tried this, but it quickly became apparent that the Staff had a good idea, but not a complete idea, of what they were spending the command's money on. So, after a short time, I told them I wanted every action officer who was working an action to do the briefing. That way, I got some pride of ownership and briefers who knew what they were talking about. We came up with a quad chart that described the program, gave the deliverables from the program and the impacts if it was not funded.

About a week later we had the review and I thought it was great. The action officers fought for their programs, and I could see exactly what we were paying for. It seemed like every contract we let had a deliverable called the weekly report. When this was briefed, I asked the leadership of the command who was sitting around the table with me if anyone had read so and so company's report. The answer was universally no, and I eliminated the report as a deliverable. By the end of the review, we had trimmed enough waste, so the command saved over $5M and eliminated 40 contractors. There was sort of a quid pro quo going on and I was not a popular guy. I got to talk to the SMDC, our higher headquarters, finance guy about that.

General Garner would come to visit about every 2 months. He was fighting off the wolves as well, with folks in Washington having instigated a new investigation into his decisions every month he was in command. We gave him his normal situation briefing and then walked into my office which had a spectacular view of Pike's Peak. He asked me what I knew about Tactical Operations Centers. I told him I knew what the requirements were, but I had never bent metal or had anything to do with making a TOC. He told me not to worry about that because the Program Manager for TOCs in Huntsville was Colonel Dan Montgomery who was an Air Defender. He said Dan would build the TOC. I asked what the TOC would do, and he replied: "Kill Scuds".

Everyone had tried to find and kill Scuds during the Gulf war with very limited success. The problem was Scuds would move rapidly after they fired so if you found one, you had to shoot almost right away. I put together a selected group of guys from the staff and we came up with a list of requirements for what would eventually be called the Army Tactical Missile Defense Element, the ATMDE. We had polos made, so I guess we were official.

Dan Montgomery who was a prince of a guy, got the requirements and we held several coordination meetings selecting the processors and equipment for the TOC. We identified the programs that would help us find the missile launchers, have situational awareness of the friendly forces and we had a Field Artillery program that would allow us to calculate a fire mission for a MLRS battery, which in theory we would have in Direct Support all the time.

I remember when MLRS was fielded. The Field Artillery battalion commander at Stewart who received the first battery, was friend of mine and he had invited every commander at Fort Stewart to a big demonstration of the first MLRS fired in Savannah. It was a real dog and pony but when it came time for the system to fire, nothing happened. The boys worked to find out the problem, but we all went home without seeing a missile fired. My friend was super embarrassed, I felt sorry for him. Michael Mac would use a MLRS battery to get him out of a tough spot in Iraq one day during his 2d deployment to Iraq. The system by then, over 10 years later was reliable and incredibly accurate.

General Garner had us develop a crew drill for acquiring and engaging scuds. We practiced it over and over until the boss was happy and we introduced sufficient drama into each scenario to keep the visitor's interest.

The TOC was built in 2 months. The integration of all the systems was crude. We had a TV cable box with push buttons on the top and we would push a button to see the intel picture, then another to see the friendly force layout etc. The boss wanted to get some validation of the concept, so he arranged for us to take it down to Tampa, Florida, and give a demo to General Peay who was the Commander of Central Command. The demo went well and afterwards I noticed that the boss and General Peay were standing off to the side talking. I walked up cautiously, not wanting to disrupt their conversation and as I was walking up, General Peay waved for me to join them. The CINC was thinking, so I asked him: "Sir what's bothering you? Is it the absence of maps?" He replied no, he was thinking about the person who ran this TOC was like God, that is he could do whatever he wanted throughout a large portion of a theater of war due to the range of the MLRS. General Peay saw the world changing. He was like all the other 4 stars I would meet later, thoughtful, highly intelligent, and caring. Every time I met a 4 star, I always was reminded that there was good in the Army promotion system and the Air Force and Navy as well.

It was now late December and the boss called me and told me that we would be deploying the TOC to the Pentagon in mid-January. Garner had a brilliant marketing strategy. We set the TOC up on the east lawn of the Pentagon. The east side of the building is where all the General's offices were on the Army staff. They all could look out their window and see this TOC which resurrected good memories from their tactical days. We made no announcement in the building about why we were there. Slowly, they started drifting out to see what we were about.

When our visitors came in, I would sit them down on a camp stool and give them a capability briefing. We would then run a crew drill and include the visitors in the decision to "fire" the MLRS against the scud. While I was giving the intro, every uniformed officer that came into the TOC kept looking around while I was talking. I would universally say "Sir is something bothering you?" After almost all of them replied yes, I would say "No maps?" And they enthusiastically replied yes. Garner finally got the Army Acquisition Executive, the guy who funded all the acquisition programs in the Army, to come visit and it was a great success. We had him "advise" us on when to fire to engage a scud and as we were getting close to executing the shot, he suddenly started saying "Kill the SOB, Kill the SOB". General Garner was very pleased with how things went.

In the spring of 1996, we participated in a Joint Exercise at Ft Bliss. We were part of 3d Army, and we briefed the CG on the TOC's capabilities. We were using drones to find the live scuds which were provided by an organization in New Mexico that had the mission of collecting Soviet equipment so we could study its capabilities. The scuds would drive around the Ft Bliss maneuver area and we would find them and engage them, virtually. We had developed an Intelligence Process for the Battlefield (IPB) for locating areas where scuds might fire from. The desert north of Ft Bliss was a challenge as it was flat and there were a lot of tank trails for the scuds to use to move around. We nevertheless narrowed down our search area and had pretty good luck. The exercise directors had time outs where we would turn off our acquisition and the scuds would move around. One time when we were hot, we looked and looked for the scud without success. Frustrated, I was walking out of the TOC to take a quick mental break and one of the boys called out that he had found the scud. It was at the MacDonald's in Alamogordo, New Mexico, off the reservation, getting lunch. I'm sure the restaurant employees were surprised with a scud driving through the drive through, but I was happy we found it.

When I was the City Manager at Hunter, the Rangers deployed to Panama for their annual jungle training. They left behind a rear party consisting of soldiers who were about to be reassigned and those who were injured; the Rangers always had a lot of injured soldiers due to the severity of their training. This rear detachment officer in charge was Major Steve Pullen. Pullen came over to my office one day and told me that their commander had told him to keep me informed of what they were doing. He then told me the next day they were going to run to a dock area we had at Hunter, jump off the bridge going over the river; swim ½ mile and then run back to post-a total of 5 miles. I was concerned about the soldiers jumping off the bridge, but Steve assured me the correct safety procedures were in place.

Steve was in the rear detachment as he was going to command a British Airborne company. The Brits were big in ruck walks and not so much in running, so Steve was carrying his rucksack all over Hunter to get ready. Steve was a fine guy. He was quietly sure of himself and very capable. I liked him and we got along well.

For the exercise in El Paso, Steve, who was now a Full Colonel, was the commander of all the Army Rangers who were scouting for us and minimizing the enemy's ability to acquire information about 3d Army. I remember thinking that this was a weird mission for the Rangers who were the Army's shock troops, the infantry that drew the toughest jobs. Steve had come to the TOC as the exercise was beginning and I gave him a little brief. As he left, he put his big hand on my shoulder and said "Brother, don't you shoot nothing unless you coordinate with us first". I told the boys to do so, and if we weren't simulating tactical comms, we could have walked almost next door to the SOCOM TOC and coordinated with us face to face.

The Third Army Commander came into the TOC late one night and told me that his intel boys had discovered an enemy ammunition dump that was packing up and he almost sheepishly asked if we could shoot the target. Excited to support the big boss, we fired the mission, "destroyed" the ammo dump, and the boss left pleased. Next thing I know, Pullen had his arm around my shoulders, and I thought he was going to squeeze me to death because we hadn't coordinated with him before shooting. I explained about the General and it didn't matter to him. We had to coordinate, which was a real-world lesson. When the exercise ended, we had a firing out party in the courtyard of our hotel. The manager came out and asked me to hold it down as we were disturbing the other guests. It turned out that there were only 2 other guests in the hotel, we occupied almost all of it, and when we invited them to the party, all was well.

Garner and his beautiful wife, Connie, had come to Colorado Springs around Christmastime of 1995 and we went to the Golden Bee in the Broadmoor Hotel for dinner. We had a nice dinner and when we finished the boss told me "We are going to make you a General". My former boss, Jack Costello, was now the CG of Ft Bliss and he wanted me to come and be the Assistant Commandant. Jack was on the promotion board, so they thought they had a pretty good chance of success.

I had mixed feelings when General Garner relayed the story to me that I was not selected. Surely, I was disappointed at not being promoted, but I had already exceeded my goals when joining the Army. My main goal was to command a battalion and I had commanded one 2 Brigades. I should have been satisfied and to an extent I was. But I went into a funk. I had commanded a line brigade and then worked at USAREUR for 2 years which was like being in a Division all over again. We respected our bosses, we tried to help them succeed.

But here I was at Army Space where 4 or 5 what I considered to be troublemakers were making my life hell. I was under a microscope; they hated the new organization, they were always bringing up roles and missions to me despite the fact we were being paid for our initiatives, they were all looking to get offended so they could file some sort of complaint. The complaints kept coming in. I felt I was being squeezed on all sides. General Garner came out and he recommended that I retire. It was time. Like an old soldier had told me years earlier, you will know when it is time. It was time.

I filed all the separation paperwork, and a farewell was arranged, a joyous occasion for some. I received many lovely gifts from the elements of the command, even the Army Astronauts gave me a memento. General Garner gave me some Jefferson cups which I still have. On the way to the dinner, someone asked me to give a speech to a group of young officers at a local hotel. I told them I would, but I was short of time, and they agreed to let me talk whenever I showed up. I gave an impromptu speech, that was one of the best speeches I every gave in my life. I got a big round of applause and as I was walking out of the room, a civilian stopped me and told me that was one of the finest speeches he had ever heard, and he handed me divorce papers. So, two big parts of my life were over: The Army and my marriage.

The divorce proceedings would go on for almost a year with Marilyn being extremely focused on getting all she wanted. My lawyer told me to argue for a 50-50 split of our assets; I came up with a proposal that gave her all my retirement if she did not work and half if she did. My expectation was that she would work. I was frustrated at the slow pace at which the divorce was proceeding but in retrospect I don't blame Marilyn at all. We never were close, mostly my fault, not hers. She would find another man years later and one of the happiest days of my life was the day my oldest son told me it was good I divorced her as we were both much happier apart. I never talked badly about their mother to the boys as I really didn't have anything to criticize her for except maybe when she stopped work after about 5 years after the divorce which meant I had to pay her my half of my retirement per the agreement. I once calculated that I paid her about $250,000 that I would not have paid had

I followed my lawyer's advice; but that was ok. It was awkward being around her at family events for a while and for a period she didn't want to have anything to do with me, understandably. But we mutually found out that there were two reasons that we would never be totally separated, our boys.

I dated many women when I was separated from Marilyn for that 18-month period before the divorce was finalized. I met Christina when I was in Washington on a trip, and we hung out for about a week and agreed to stay in touch. It is hard sometimes to figure out what attracts two people. She was smart, athletic, had a burning desire to succeed and something else that I would discover later-a love of God. She was not the prettiest, though I thought she was beautiful, she wasn't an interior decorator or gourmet cook like Marilyn instead satisfied with plain food and a clean, neat house. But she never gave up on our relationship. I guess she was convinced she had found her man, even before I had decided she was the girl for me. She was 22 years younger than me, and I realized that having friends my age was going to be the exception, rather than the rule.

TRANSITION TO HUNTSVILLE | COLSA CORPORATION 1996

I had been offered a job by COLSA corporation in Huntsville while I was still on active duty and my last TDY there I had breakfast with the President of the Company, and he firmed up the offer. I would be the Vice President of Strategic Operations. I learned a lot about company operations in the next 20 years and one thing that I learned was titles were not too important. I once ran across a company that had thirty or so employees and 27 of them were Vice Presidents. When Mike and I started Imprimis, he wanted to be the President and I became the Executive Vice President. I eventually had cards made that just said "Founder" and that seemed to suffice.

I took a month's leave after I retired which was the first time that I had ever done that and then settled into the big office they had redesigned for me in the COLSA building. The first day I went to work at COLSA, it had snowed a little, just a dusting but with patchy ice underneath. As I was crossing a bridge, I saw a snowplow plowing the snow off the ice. I slowed down and hailed the driver and told him please not to do as he was eliminating the only traction on the ice. I arrived at the office and let myself in, there was nobody else there. The whole building which normally housed I guess about 100 people was empty other than the security guards.

The following day, the ice was gone, and business was back to usual. Frank Collazo, the owner of the company came in and we had a nice chat. Frank was a retired warrant officer who had grown the company from scratch. Even after the company got on firm ground, Frank would drive an old pickup truck he had to all the meetings. This lesson learned I struggled with my whole career in business: do you show the customer that you are still hungry by giving the impression of poverty or do you have a nicer establishment where you portray competence and success. I think I finally realized that the answer was in the middle somewhere as with most things and when we got Imprimis on the ground, my offices in Huntsville were nice but not ostentatious. Mike liked nicer digs and when I would travel out to visit him, I was never comfortable with what we were paying for his space; it was taking a bite out of the profit line. But it was his company too, and that was his choice.

Mike is as fine an engineer as I have ever met, super creative and innovative. I guess our conflict here was our disagreement of whether your personal credibility or the trappings is what you needed to obtain work. Mike believed you needed both, I sort of thought the personal credibility was enough, but I could see his point. Maybe the real issue was Mike was in it for the long run while I was ready to pursue the challenge if it was there and if it went away, then I was ready to quit. He was building for the long term; I was building for the intermediate.

Back to COLSA. After Mr. Collazo came in another colleague came in whom I had never met and we made small talk, family stuff. As he was leaving, he asked me "Paul are you for Alabama or Auburn"? I really had no idea what Auburn was, so I told him "I'm new here and I really don't have an opinion", an answer that I thought was noncommittal. He then said: "Let me ask it another way, are you for Auburn or Alabama?" I had seen Alabama play in the Sugar Bowl years earlier under Coach Bear Bryant, so I said "Alabama". In Alabama, you must choose sides in college football. If your choice isn't Alabama or Auburn, then another SEC school is marginally ok; but a school from the Big Ten or PAC 12 would be frowned upon. There definitely was a regional bias. Since that day I picked Alabama, I have rooted for them ever since.

I originally rented a two-bedroom apartment in Huntsville near a lake. They had a small gym, but I joined a gym that was about 5 miles away. It was less than 10 minutes from work. One of the blessings of living in that apartment complex there was path on which you could run around the pretty large lake next to the apartments. Across the lake, there were some nice houses and less nicer ones behind those. I was very comfortable. Christina eventually joined me, and we were happy.

In late August 1996 Dad was really struggling with his second bout with cancer. The cancer had returned 15 years earlier and I wish I had the eyes to see the valiant struggle that he carried on against this terrible disease. He had been put in hospice care and the nurse told Nana that he didn't have much time. I had a big conference that week and told Nana to tell Dad that I would be out there in 5 days and to by God hang on until I got there. Christina and I flew out, Mike was already there. Dad looked bad. Mama was making dinner and Dad wanted to have a drink with us. I made him a drink and we had to help him sip just a little of it. It was the first and only time that Christina every met him.

The next morning, Mom called us all in, Dad was going to the Lord. We all sat there trying to comfort him; Mama was holding his hand; Mike was touching his arm and Chris and I were holding his feet. My father who had pushed me all my life and who was the toughest human being I had ever known was gone. I prayed for his soul, but I have often reflected why then I wasn't more broken up. Dad and I did not have a great relationship; I never thought I measured up. We learn wisdom with old age, and I know now that he was doing all he could to make me a success. Today, I really love him, and I know he is in Heaven.

Christina and I were married in a civil ceremony on September 14, 1996, less than 2 weeks later in a nice little chapel out in the woods somewhere. Christina was a beautiful bride, and I hired a limo to take her to the wedding and to drive us back to the house after the wedding. We went to Nashville overnight and had a great time walking around the downtown after a nice meal and sticking our heads into one of the many bars which featured emerging country singers. For some reason I really remember the great breakfast we had the next morning in the hotel dining room. We then drove back to Huntsville as I had to go to work on Monday.

One of the guys that "worked" for me was a guy named Mike Marazo. Mike was an engineer who had been with the company for quite a while and was well connected in town. He got Christina a job at a communications company across the street from COLSA. She was doing well there until the bosses put out the word that they wanted the female sales representatives to dress a little more suggestively and we jointly decided it was time to quit. Mike remained a good friend before, during and after the drama that led to my leaving COLSA. He died a few years ago unexpectedly which was a personal loss and a loss to his lovely family.

My division at COLSA was new so I spent a lot of my time just looking for things to do and trying to understand what the people that worked for me did. In companies, the VPs come and go, but at the worker level, I always found the direct supervisors had much more longevity and really were the ones that knew what was happening. I had a couple of employee sensing sessions, and we were able to realize some good from them, but I was counselled not to give out too much information about company operations as typically employees have loose lips when talking with friends from other companies and some of them could even be classified as spies for bigger companies. Man was I in a different world. The only loyalty seemed to be to the bottom line. Frank had gotten the contract a decade earlier to build and then run, the Advance Research Lab which experimented with all kinds of space initiatives. He lobbied Congress every year to keep that contract and he did. Having a steady revenue that was enough to keep the company operating should be a real goal of every company which Mike did at Imprimis years later.

Life at COLSA was interesting. I spent a lot of time talking to my managers seeing if there was anything I could do to help. I had to make these visits quick though as most of them were charging their time directly to the contract. In my mind, if I was charging my time by talking to my boss to help the customer, that was time well spent. Some guys were much more literal, and I had to respect their beliefs.

One of the things a leader must do when he comes into an organization is flame the fire of creativity wherever it exists. I had an employee who was working on a contract, but his love was installing security systems. I talked to Clarence Tidwell, our President, and he said it was ok if we pursued this if it didn't interfere with his direct charge work. He was able to balance the two challenges and his security work became a solid new line of business.

We had a fair-sized contract to provide IT support to the Space and Missile Defense Command. We bought the equipment for the contract and ran a help desk to help the employees if they had a problem. The manager of this contract was a good guy and when I asked him how it was going, he told me that he had a disaster on his hands. The customer was unhappy because the equipment was old and it broke frequently and when the employees complained, the boss was unhappy. We looked at the budget and saw that the monies were available to start a replacement program for the equipment which we could finish in two years if the SMDC boss bought into it. I went to see the IT guy at SMDC along with my Program Manager and got his buy in. We started replacing equipment, people gradually got happier because their stuff worked, and the boss was happy. All I did was added a little company influence with the customer and my leader. In other words, I helped implement what was right. That is always the task of a leader.

Mando and Otis Ferguson, who had replaced me at ARSPACE came to Huntsville and came by the apartment late one night to say hello to Christina and me. Otis commanded my old battalion in Desert Storm and had supported the 24th Division beautifully during the operation. He had been with me at ARSPACE for several months transitioning into this strange new world. It was smart of General Garner to do so. It's always good to watch something you are going to replace beforehand when you are detached. The problem is the incumbent sometimes resents having the new guy around. I thought it was a good thing.

Otis travelled with me everywhere I went seeing what I did and meeting people. It was interesting watching a guy who was 6"7" negotiate with the airlines for an aisle, exit row, seat so he could have a little more leg room. One time we had to go see a lawyer at SMDC about one of the investigations that was going on and after we had done our business, the lawyer said "Colonel Semmens, I have a daughter and if she ever went into the Army and went into combat, I would want you to lead her. But we don't need guys like you in peacetime." I had to restrain Otis, he was coming out of his chair, and I thought he was going to hit the guy. But I guess in some ways that summed it up. I always wanted my soldiers to have a hell raising attitude, disciplined in what mattered, but supremely confident that they could do anything they set their minds to. I think one of the things I did above average was continually creating opportunities for my soldiers to get out of their current mindset and do things that were challenging. My units were tight, somewhat arrogant because we were better than the other units we were with, and collectively we thought we could play Notre Dame and win. There is a fine line between confidence and pride, and I know I stepped over that line at times.

Frank was having a party and invited them both. Otis had a commitment, but Mando said he would be happy to come. Frank came from Puerto Rico, and he hit it off with Mando right away. That was one of Frank's gifts, he could talk to anyone and treat them as his equal. Frank came from very humble beginnings and eventually built one of the largest defense contracting companies in Huntsville. He was a multi-millionaire, but he could talk to anyone.

We had a few drinks at the party and Mando asked me what I wanted to do in the company. I told him that I wanted to be president when Clarence retired. Mando said let's go talk to Frank about that. We did and Frank told me he thought that was a great idea.

Frank told Clarence of our conversation which wasn't received too well. I was an unknown and while I had done well at the company bringing in $9M in unexpected revenues, I was not part of the long-term establishment and thus not to be fully trusted.

We had a party a few weeks later and Gary Riggs, the company lawyer attended. He asked to talk to me and when we did, he started asking questions about Christina and I. Feeling I had nothing to hide I truthfully answered all his questions. I would talk to Gary years later when we shared an office building and he told me he rode for the brand. He supported what his boss wanted right or wrong. Collecting what he considered dirt on me he knew was shady, but he did it anyway.

Next thing I knew the Defense Investigative Services was in talking to me about some trumped-up security issue. It was total BS, but I had lost credibility in the company because of this smear campaign. I talked to General Garner, and he was unable to help. Mike Marrazo who was a long-time friend of Frank's set up a telephone conversation between me and the owner, where he told me he was all for my being the President, but the establishment that had made him rich would have none of it. Another lesson learned; an owner of a company really needs to be in real control of his company. I resigned from COLSA, and I am happy with that decision to this day.

CHAPTER EIGHTEEN

HUNTSVILLE, ALABAMA, 1996-1997

Christina came in one day and told me she was pregnant. To be honest, I was shocked initially but after some reflection I was glad. It meant that Christina would always have someone to look after her when I was dead and at the time neither Mike nor Rob had kids or the prospect for having any, so the baby would be my surrogate grandson. I was 50 years old.

We went through all the doctor appointments and ultrasounds and the big day finally came. I rushed Christina to Huntsville Hospital. We had done LeMas and after having that experience twice previously, I thought I was ready. Christina's Mom was there as well. Christina labored and labored. As we entered the 12th hour, I went and got a nurse and told her I thought something was wrong. There was an issue, and the next thing I knew they were handing me surgical clothes and we went into an operating room. Sean was born with no complications there via a C-Section and I was amazed that what seemed like a gaping hole in Christina's stomach healed so well, and the scar was so little, you could not tell it had happened. The date was January 28th, 1997.

Sean was a beautiful, big baby. He was full of curiosity, laughed a lot and was always looking for something to get into. Christina was a beautiful Mom who was the one who got up almost all the time at night to feed him. He started sleeping through the night very early, so all was good. Nana came to visit several times as did Roberta, Christina's mother, and he fell in love with both.

Christina and I had become season ticket holders for the University of Alabama at Huntsville's hockey team. After Sean was born, we used to take him to the games with us. One game, when he was 2 ½, he got up during the game and walked the 6 or 8 rows down to the glass. I walked down to him and asked "Bud, what's up?" He looked at me and very sternly said "Sean play hockey". I replied "Well, you need to learn to skate first". He replied: "Sean skate". The next day his mother took him to the recreational skating at the Von Braun Center and he took to it like a duck takes to water.

We bought him a hockey uniform with all the pads, and we talked to Coach Doug Ross, who was the UAH coach, and asked him if Sean could go to his hockey camp that summer. Doug was a great guy and he said sure. The first day of camp, after letting the boys skate around and warm up, Doug had all the boys move to the end line. He was going to do a standard hockey drill: skate to the blue line and back, then skate to the red line and back. Sean's turn came and when the whistle blew, he was off. All the other 15 or so boys stopped at the blue line and started back, but Sean just kept going. Doug yelled at him, and he came back. I walked next to the glass and tapped on it to get Doug's attention. I said "Coach, he doesn't know his colors yet, he's only two." Doug nodded and started giving Sean more specific instructions. Sean would continue to play hockey until he was 6 or 7 and because he started skating so early, he could skate circles around boys his own age and even those a couple of years older. But he played hockey with an unbridled joy. He sensed he was better and just loved scoring goals.

SY TECHNOLOGY, HUNTSVILLE 1997-98

I started looking around for another job and Chuck Dreissnack called and asked me to come see him. The platoon leader who I had watched die at the Whale Gap 16 years earlier was now a major and was running several programs at SMDC. Looking back, God always provides. My contractual arrangement was I would be a consultant to SY Technologies, the company that General Garner went to work for when he retired. The President of SY in Huntsville was my old friend, Jim Starkey, my brother battery commander in Budingen 25 years earlier. I worked on various tasks as assigned including when Mando brought the ATMDE to Huntsville for a mission. God puts people in your life and while you can offer that up as coincidence, I really think it is His providence that is the source of all good.

Eventually, SY got the contract to provide personnel for the emerging National Missile Defense Program, the legacy of President Reagan's Star Wars Program. The government had established an office to integrate all the government agencies that had been working to build the pieces or components of the system. It was time to integrate all the parts into a cohesive program. Chuck was the Defense Satellite Communications System (DSCS) program lead which had the mission of sending secure messages to the missile in flight even in the aftermath of a nuclear explosion.

Chuck had a little government team that included 4 or 5 contractors. We worked in a long skinny building next to University Drive and everybody was crammed into this building that was a block long. Space was at a premium. I made charts for Chuck who was constantly briefing the bosses. A lot of them were schedule charts where I had to reflect the whole program schedule and our part in it. Chuck had a meticulous attention to detail, so I made many of those charts over and over. Nana came to visit us, and I showed her my "office" which was a place on an eight-foot table that I shared with two other people. She was not impressed and told me I had to do better.

Chuck was an up and comer in SMDC and he was appointed as the Program Manager of a new Army Program called Sword. Sword was the first attempt by the Army to build a system to shoot down small rocket and artillery projectiles up to 240MM in diameter. I had an intermediate boss at SMDC named Ron Smith and he and I became good friends. Ron was a manager who got involved only when he needed to; he hired the best and he just let them go.

The foundation for the new system was an interferometric radar developed by a company in Ontario California named Technovative Applications. The owner, chief engineer and administrator was a gentleman named Jim Williams. Jim had worked at Hughes Aircraft for a long time until it was purchased by another company. The Hughes management model was every program had a Chief Engineer and a Program Manager who were sort of co-leads. At Chuck's recommendation, Jim hired me to be the Program Manager.

The radar development would be done in California and the rest in Huntsville. The first step was to develop a very detailed and technical concept briefing and brief the leadership in Washington. We went to DC and briefed the Army Acquisition Executive. We got a lot of positive head nods, but the AAE wasn't sure. Additionally, there was no operational needs statement, that is a requirements document from a warfighter, which is necessary to start the development of any system. Chuck and Bill Reeves, Chuck's boss argued for a chance to prove the system. The AAE said ok and told us we had to eventually brief IDA which was an organization in Washington whose mission was to validate technical programs.

I called around and finally with a lot of help, got to present our needs analysis to the Eighth Army G-3 in Korea. They had a real growing threat from the North Korean development and fielding of the 240MM rocket. The Israelis had an emerging system that used a laser that could defeat the threat, but the atmospherics in Korea, frequent clouds, and rain, plus the fact their prototype system had to dwell on each rocket to destroy it meant that it couldn't handle the volume attack that was expected. The G-3 liked it and set us up for a briefing with the CINC, General Telelli. I had met the General years earlier at a conference where we chatted briefly, but when he walked into my office at USAREUR in Germany, he called me by name. What a gift to remember names.

When Bill Reeves, Ron Smith, Jeff Holder, an engineer from Georgia Tech that was helping us with system integration, and I met the CINC, he remembered me again. We briefed him and he signed the needs statement with some enthusiasm. It was finalized and sent to Department of the Army; we had documented the need.

After the briefing Bill, Ron, Jeff, and I went shopping in a suburb of Seoul called Etewon. This area was famous for its shopping. The Koreans were masterful at duplicating any existing product so they featured knock off Rolex watches, Gucci handbags and just about anything else you could think of. You had to watch yourself as some of the stuff was junk, but some of it was good. I was walking down the street and this guy grabbed me and hauled me into his shop. He had sports clothing, including a beautiful Yankees jacket, complete with the Starter logo and everything. We negotiated for a while, and I got it for less than 25% of the price it would have cost me in the States. I had purchased a Gortex camouflaged jacket from Korea years earlier that had a ¾ length Gortex lining but the shell of the coat was not authentic. I never wore it in public, but during nights at the NTC I gleefully put it on in the dark. It kept me warm. I still have those two jackets today and they are the warmest jackets I own.

Bill had a long list from his wife, and we spent most of the time ensuring that the boss went home successfully. His wife must have been picky because we spent a long, long time picking out the handbags she wanted. All in all, it turned out to be a successful trip.

We got back to Huntsville and the effort to prepare the briefing and documentation for IDA drove on. Most of the discussions were technical, so I contributed very little. My main input was following up with the team members reminding them of things that had promised to deliver. Jim Williams gave me free access to all his people, and I remember coordinating with the fellow who was writing the software for the radar. He lived near Los Angeles, and I had to wait to mid- morning there to call him, as he surfed every morning.

We finally went to IDA and briefed a panel of scientists for two days. They called us in for their brief to the Army Acquisition Executive and they told him the system would work and was a cost-efficient solution to the problem. We never fully developed the missile technology, which was important because the major reason the Army hadn't developed a system previously was the cost per kill. Killing a rocket or mortar round that cost hundreds of dollars with a missile that cost tens of thousands of dollars, didn't make sense. We tried to reuse everything to drive costs down. We originally tried to mount the missiles on a stinger launcher, but to defeat the 240's we needed more propellent and thus a longer missile. I recommended to the boys that we use a MLRS launcher, which was longer, and they agreed. Jim was right, having a former user that understood the tactical environment helped very focused engineers from time to time.

We got word that Jack Costello, the new Commanding General of Ft Bliss was travelling to Korea. Jack supported the Israeli system and we got word that he was going to sell that idea to General T. Bill Reeves called me and asked if I could go to Korea and brief MG Lennox, the brother of the XO of 4/43 ADA whom I had served with years earlier. Jim thought it was a great idea, so I called Bob Lennox and asked if he could set it up for me. He agreed and I got word from Korea that I had an appointment on a Saturday morning. Jim got my tickets and told me he had a surprise for me. I would be flying out on a Thursday, arriving Friday night, briefing on Saturday, and flying home on Sunday.

I stayed in a real nice hotel, but that Friday night, I did not sleep at well. The next morning, I briefed General Lennox on why the Israeli system would not work and he got it. I then went to Etewon and shopped my butt off, buying gifts primarily for Christina and the family. Sunday morning when I was boarding the airplane, I gave the flight attendant my ticket and after she took it, I headed to business class, which was how I had flown over. She stopped me and said "No, no sir, you are in first class". Surprised, I walked up to first class which on a 737 is a bubble on the front top of the aircraft. As I was locating my seat, I noticed a large group of flight attendants in the back of the cabin. A young girl came over to my seat and in typical Korean fashion knelt down and told me "Sir, I am Miss Kim. I am YOUR flight attendant." She brought me something to drink and about halfway home, she made my seat into a bed upon which I slept like a baby arriving at LAX fully rested.

Jack found out I had been to Korea ahead of him and I guess it really made him mad. He got back to the States and really reduced the funding of the program and told his chief scientist, Daryl Collier that there was no way that he would look favorably upon me being involved with the program. I said goodbye to Bill, Ron, and Jim. They were all sorry and thought the dismissal was not only unfair but was hurting the Army because we were developing something it really needed.

Jack had turned on me for some reason and just hated my guts. I was sorry because he put a personal grudge over the needs of the Army. God gave me the grace to forgive and forget, but I was out of work. Jack died way too early, and I pray for his soul every day of my life.

Sword had been a great challenge and working with a team to achieve a common objective was great fun. I made several good, good friends from that experience and I would work with any of them happily again, today.

CHAPTER TWENTY

COLORADO SPRINGS, COLORADO 2000-06

Well, I was out of work, and I decided that continuing to work in the defense industry was not what I wanted. Defense contracting and weapons procurement is so eaten up with politics that doing what's right is not always done. Just before I retired, the Israelis had developed a system with the French and the US to replace Patriot called MEADS and every indication was that it would work and improve our capability significantly, especially the mobility of the system. Raytheon went into the Pentagon and lobbied for more improvements to Patriot and despite MEADS' impressive test results, the program was cancelled, and Patriot kept getting modified and modified. After the bitter cancelation of SWORD, I was fed up with the whole process.

I decided that I wanted to become a school principal. I needed references so I called North Texas University where

Colonel, now General Hurley, had become the chancellor. I talked to his secretary and about 2 hours later he called me back. We chatted and caught up and I told him what I was trying to do. He told me with no experience, that would be tough, but he would write me a letter anyway. It came about a week later; it was beautiful, I still have it. What a great man.

I had two interviews. I flew to Houston to interview to be the Principal of a High School that was held in a prison. I interviewed with about 5 guys and was told at the end that I had not been selected. The 4th guy I talked to said I was too "military", and he didn't think I could relate to the students. My thought was a little military discipline was what they probably needed. Houston is a great city, but it didn't appeal to me at all. I'm glad in retrospect I didn't get that job.

I had also applied for an educational position in an organization in Milwaukee Wisconsin. We flew up there and after talking to the lady for 10 minutes, she asked me why I had applied for the job, and I told her I thought I could do anything. We didn't get that one as well. I also applied to be the President of the Rose Bowl Committee, the organization that makes all the arrangements for the game and parade each year. I thought that would really be neat to manage the events around the game that Dad had played in years earlier. I had some traction in the interview process, but that opportunity went by the wayside as well. Christina and I always saved money, I have always tried to live below my means, so we were ok financially. I had seen so many people either spend every penny they had or start charging things, essentially spending more than they made.

Christina and I threw a party one night and during that evening, General Garner walked in, unannounced or invited. It was great to see him and after I got him a drink, he asked if we could talk privately. Both levels of the house were full of people, so we went down to the garage, and he asked me if I was committed to staying in Huntsville and if I would be interested in moving back to Colorado Springs. SY had the contract for the new National Missile Defense Training program and my mentor wanted me to run the program. We cut a deal, I would remain a consultant with my own company, Prima Inc., and SY would provide the people that would work with me. I insisted on at least having a say in the hiring of at least the senior guys and they agreed.

I called Nana and told her the good news. She proposed the idea of the family trust buying a house for us to live in and when we left, the trust would get the profits from the sale of the house. The trust eventually bought a big place, over 5000 square feet in the shadow of Cheyenne Mountain. We moved in under Nana's direct supervision and were happy there. My closet was as big as a normal bedroom and Christina had one just as big. It was a beautiful house.

I checked in at the NMD training facility which was on Academy Boulevard. It had one big classroom, a few offices, and cubicles everywhere, and a "lab" where the NMD command and control consoles were located where we would run air battles and learn about the system. Mando was my right-hand man, and he would be the lead training developer.

Our first discussion amongst the team was tasks-what were we going to teach. Our on-site government boss was a GS-15 named Richard Yu. Richard's family was originally from Taiwan. His dad was a tank commander who fought the several Red Chinese attempts to take the island right after WWII. The family then moved to Korea for about 10 years and when

Richard was a teenager, and then they moved to Dallas Texas. Richard was fluent in Chinese, Korean and English. He was an interesting guy. He was full of ambition; he had a burning desire to succeed, and he was an engineer, so he felt a little out of place running a training program. One day he sat Mando and me down and he told us when a Chinese guy said yes, it wasn't a firm commitment. We both said how can you say that, and it was clear that Richard was trying to be Teflon, nonstick if something went wrong. He had a Major, Rob Olsen, who was his deputy who was a Mormon and a nice guy. Rob retired and his first job as a government civilian would be to supervise the installation of the GMD system at Ft Greely, Alaska.

Our first job was to determine the tasks for the instruction. We spent a lot of time on the system, and it quickly became apparent that because the window for engaging a target was so small and so much accuracy was required, the system had to operate in automatic. So, the operator's job was to monitor what was happening and identify what we called "off nominal" behavior, when the machine would do something that was not normal, or expected. The instruction therefore had to teach the operators how the system thought, or behaved, and the circumstances when it was not doing what it was supposed to do. The purpose of the system was to hit an object about the size of a car engine flying 15,000 miles per hour in outer space.

We began the process to determine the tasks. Mando was in his glory; we would have internal meetings and once the task was ok'd by the group, we would start doing what are called Task Analysis Reports or TARS which was a 3-5-page document for each task, describing the task and giving a reference for the task. We also decided that our training development process would follow the Army's Training and Doctrine Command's model, even though it was a joint program. Mando was in heaven and was the impetus for all we did. His last job in the Army had been at the Command and General Staff College, where he instructed and developed training using the TRADOC model. We had many discussions on the requirements as any regulation or procedure has parts that are subject to interpretation.

Everything was so new, we knew we had to get the operators or users, involved. The users of this system included Air Force Space Command as they had the early warning satellites, the North American Air Defense Command or NORAD, that Dad had been assigned to in his first job in Colorado Springs and Cheyenne Mountain which housed the command center that had the mission to alert America in the event of an attack to the homeland. And there were many others, and we made a concerted effort to include every one of them.

We decided to get the users buy in for the training, we would have a series of task reviews, then a review for the program of instruction, the timing and sequencing of the tasks. Next, we would have a pilot course where we would teach everything to the users or their representatives.

We were planning our first review, and I asked the SY program lead if they would buy all the participant's lunch. They said sure so we had foot long sandwiches for the first meeting that was a big success. After several of these task reviews which at one point were almost weekly, we started to see the user's buy in of the tasks. Because they had approved them, they were starting to own them and that is exactly what we wanted.

One of the reasons I wanted to own my own company and retain some of my independence was that larger companies sometimes tried a little too hard to shine their products which resulted in useless labor. For example, as we got closer to the time to teach the course, SY told us all the instructors needed to be TRADOC instructor qualified. If we had gone to the week-long instructor certification course when we were in the Army, that would suffice but we had to show our graduation certificate, so the count was accurate. Nobody keeps their certificate from a week-long course. Christina and I looked everywhere without results. One day one of the other instructors who had gone to the TRADOC instructor course while he was serving, mentioned that it was annotated on his form DD212, which was your summary of service. I looked at mine that night and he was right, one of my skill identifiers was instructor. I went to the SY management and asked them if that was good enough and they said sure.

Here we were working 10-12-hour days and we had to send key guys away for a week to Ft Carson to go to course they really did not need. Once they graduated, they came back to the facility and reminded us of what we had been taught 30 years before, like starting each class out with an attention step. So good came out of what I considered bad, which I think is always the case if you look for it.

We had to spend a lot of time in the lab, trying to document the "behavior" or logic, of the system. Our theory was if the operators knew what the system was going to do, then they could identify when it was not behaving as it should or "nominally" as we called it. I remember we were in the lab late one night and we were engaging a simulated Medium Ranged Ballistic Missile going against Hawaii. Everything looked ok, and then the system fired 5 missiles at about $70,000,000 a copy. My colleague and I talked for a long time about what happened and just couldn't understand it. We called Boeing system engineering and the next day, they sent an engineer over, and he took the tapes of the engagement back to his office for analysis. Boeing was good about coming back to us with an explanation of what had happened, but we still didn't fully understand. Finally, we went to Richard and requested a software performance review from Boeing. It was a big event held in our facility and it was the first time I experienced the detail with which the prime contractor building a system went to. The review was Greek to most of us, we had a few guys who understood it better than others and we got copies of all the documents associated with the system's performance.

When we first started, before the GMD Training Center opened, we reviewed Boeing's training proposal, line by line. Boeing had an interesting marketing strategy. They would low bid on their proposal for a contract and then charge for every little thing they did, which in my opinion was unfair to their competitors. For example, we wanted copies of a document for use by the students. They told us it would be a dollar per page for each document.

After we costed the Boeing proposal, SY was asked to make a proposal on how much they would charge to teach the operators and they came in at less than one-half the price. Boeing would later learn the advantage of the low bid, which gave the government an opportunity to select Boeing, even though its technical proposal was weaker than some of its competitors. I would run into this problem years later. Some of the training documentation that Boeing suggested was ridiculous and unnecessary. We ended up writing what was needed ourselves in addition to teaching the course. Mando was hard over on the guys teaching the course should be the ones developing it which made infinite sense to me. In larger operations, the developer and the instructors were sometimes separated.

We xeroxed the behavior documents and gave every guy a copy. We had daily reviews to see if anyone had any insights on understanding the behavior. There were heated arguments amongst the team as we knew that understanding this material was central to what we were trying to teach.

Mando and I always argued about the depth of the material that we taught. He argued that we should teach them what they needed to do their jobs, the essentials. I argued for more depth and a complete understanding of behavior. We compromised to start; we taught a little more behavior than Mando wanted but as upgrades to the system occurred, and we understood the behavior better, we added more and more of it to the instruction.

It took us almost a year to get the users to approve all the tasks and then we started on the development of the course. We finished the Task Analysis Reports, which were painful and then moved on to the development of the instruction, module by module. We had asked for 21/2 years to develop the course, but the users started pushing for a pilot course around the two-year point. At that stage, the course wasn't finished. Mando hated this as he was a purist, but once the classes were assigned to the instructors, many guys, including me developed a rough presentation of the class. We pushed back on the users, but Richard finally caved in and agreed to a pilot course when they wanted it.

We had completed at least two modules of instruction, a module roughly equaling a week of instruction, that had rough presentations, but the TRADOC documentation was not complete. About a year after we started teaching the course, while simultaneously finishing the development, TRADOC did come in and they approved the course which was a big deal-we had credibility.

According to the TRADOC regulations, a pilot course was supposed to be prime time, that is there were no excuses, you couldn't tell the evaluators that you were going to clean something up later. We had murder boards for the instructors during which we followed the TRADOC instructor course guidelines. Mando and I were the evaluators, and we were tough. Several guys had to give their presentations a second time and some three times. All this was taking time and our program had conflicting energy flows-me trying to get the instructors ready and Mando trying to finish the development which all required the same guys.

We had call signs and our team was cohesive. The core-Mando, Clay Earnest (the former OC and Tactics instructor), Joe Falls who had been my XO in Tactics and new guys like Joe Evans. We also had several retired Air Force guys who had served at Cheyenne Mountain, and we even had a guy who had served at Shemya, Alaska where a key early warning radar was located. We had our beer calls on Friday nights which most guys attended. The good thing about beer calls is you can tell if a guy had a drinking problem.

When I was the S-1 of the C/V battalion going to Europe, every Friday morning my job was to reserve a table at the officer's club for happy hour. The battalion commander wanted to know when that task was completed and the times, I forgot to tell him, he came hunting for me. The happy hour was set up in the ballroom of the Fort Bliss Officer's club and there were probably 120 eight-foot tables in the room. Dancing girls would dance, the boys would drink and raise the roof, but it was generally harmless. But you could tell who had a problem with booze and I learned how much I could drink and still safely drive. Today's Army had de-glamorized drinking and that is not bad, but the old beer calls were a real teacher if one approached them with the right perspective.

Part of the development was writing the examinations and determining the passing grade. We talked among ourselves and concluded that our students were going to be defending America and if they made a mistake, we could lose Los Angeles, literally. We concluded that the students had to score 90% on their exams to pass. The TRADOC standard was 70% so there was some discussion in the user community. Finally, we had a Council of Colonels, Chuck's idea, which had a representative from all the interested organizations. We gave a little pitch on why we thought that 90% should be the standard and they agreed. For those who failed, they were given one retest and if they passed, regardless of their score, their recorded grade was 70%. These operators had an important job and they had to be good.

In addition to teaching the operators in the GMD Training and Exercise Center, we also had to train any other operators in the nation's overall Air Defense system, so they were familiar with the timing and procedures that the Ground Based Missile Defense System used (renamed early in the process; changed from the National Missile Defense system, that I liked). The operator's final exam was written and included a hands-on crew drill evaluation. The tasks for this eval were much of the undone work when we started teaching the course. We started including crews from the Cheyenne Mountain Operations

Center as the operators had to get familiar with the CMOC procedures because by doctrine, they were the ones who declared a target hostile. The doctrinal authority for weapons release, the ability to fire a missile was another question.

Normally the Commander in Chief of a theater had the authority to release a weapon as their area was the zone threatened. But the range of GMD and the ability of an attacking missile to transit at least two theaters, put that tried and told procedure into question. MG John Holley was the GMD Program Manager. He was a great guy and was very thoughtful. When the first missiles were flown to Alaska, giving us a minimal capability, he had thousands of little flags carried on the aircraft which he gave to everyone who was working on the program. General Holly was a salesman and he got hold of Richard and told us that he wanted us to put on a road show and brief the CINCs of Pacific Command, Northern Command and CINC Strategic Command, a new organization located in Omaha Nebraska that had the mission of integrating all the joint commands.

I wish I could remember the names of the great men I briefed. Every one of them was humble, eager to learn and asked a lot of questions. Universally, we would brief a conference room full of guys but after General Holly gave the program overview, I would explain how the system worked. In STRATCOM and PACOM which both had Navy CINCs the Commanders wanted me up close to field their questions. We tried to carefully avoid the sticky question of weapons release but CINC PACOM, when I was describing an engagement timeline to him, literally cried out "I will have plenty of time to give weapons release!" The cat was out of the bag, and we waffled an answer and simply stated that had not been determined by the big boys, the

Joint Chiefs of Staff. Thank God he understood. The eventual decision was the National Command Center in the Pentagon would give weapons release, which added another party to the conference calls we would have before an engagement. All our comms equipment was an internal net, but the CMOC only had telephones and land lines for security reasons, so we had to retrofit our consoles with telephones. The Crew Chiefs who were LTCs had one ear on the telephone and one ear on their headsets listening and talking to the crews.

When I had orders in 1976 to go to Safeguard which was America's first NMD program that my Dad had helped to design, I was going to be the junior scope dope on the Perimeter Acquisition Radar, the primary acquisition radar for the system. I was a Major then, my crew chief would have been a full Colonel, and now we had Captains and Sergeants manning the system that performed the same mission. The technology had gotten that much better.

Chuck called me in 2004 and told me he had been appointed as the Program Manager for the Theater High Altitude Missile Defense system or THAAD. He asked me to get some work done for him and I agreed. He gave me a contract for $99,000 which was the maximum amount he could award without a competitive bid. I was working 10 hours a day. I cleared my involvement with THAAD with the GMD brass, but I could tell there was some trepidation on their part. I flew to Huntsville and met Carlos Kingston, a Texas A&M Aggie, who would be our direct supervisor. He was the director of logistics for the program and training fell under his prevue. Carlos was a quiet, slow talking guy, but a wonderful person whom I admired and liked. We would have a relationship for a long time.

I had a year to spend that $99K and if I had an accounting section, they would have been getting on me because I was WAY behind on expenditures. My brother Mike was living in Austin Texas working as the President and CEO of a battery company called Electrosource. Mike had worked for Braddock, Dunn and McDonald, a defense contracting company after he received his master's degree in mechanical engineering at CSU. Originally, he worked in Washington DC and he and his wife Sherry had a beautiful house in the Virginia countryside. He was then transferred to Albuquerque New Mexico where he was placed in charge of the company's skunk works. If anything, technical, needed solving, Mike and his guys did it. He did all sorts of interesting and creative projects for both government and civilian customers. When Mike had well over 10 years in the company, BDM was purchased and the new ownership wanted to put their own guys in charge so Mike and his new wife, Cheryl, moved back to Washington where all the former leading executives of the company were given odd jobs.

One of Mike's tasks under this new arrangement was to fly to Austin Texas to help a company called Electrosource to straighten out their books and operation. The company was owned by two cowboys and after Mike had out briefed the results of his work, they asked if he would come work for the company. Mike almost flippantly said "Only if I'm the President and CEO". The cowboys said sure, and Mike had a new job. Mike and Cheryl and my two nephews Damon and Mathew moved to Texas.

Mike, like everything he does, flew into the job. Electrosource had developed and was continuing to improve a battery that would be awesome in electric cars as it held its charge longer. Mike briefed Ford and others and for a while it looked promising, but in the end, Ford wanted to develop their own battery. Without this major source of revenue, things started getting rocky around the company after a while and Mike was finally asked to resign after 8 years in the job. He and Cheryl decided to move back to Colorado.

We visited Mike and Cheryl and the boys several times while they were in Austin. Matt played some serious hockey and we got to see a few of his games. Damon was more of the scholar and would eventually go to the University of Texas there in Austin and then on to the Notre Dame law school. They were both fine young men and I was and still am very proud of them.

So, Mike moved back home. Chuck had gone to Washington and suggested that THAAD could kill Intercontinental Ballistic Missiles, quite a claim as most folks had questions about the system's ability to kill Medium Ranged Ballistic Missiles. The bigger the missile, the faster it flew and there were people who questioned whether THAAD could even compute a firing solution against these faster targets. Mike was doing a few odd consulting jobs after returning to Colorado so I thought he might have time to help Chuck prove that THAAD could engage any ballistic missile target. I talked to Chuck, and he said great, and Mike did the analysis on several targets going into Hawaii which proved THAAD had a good- to- satisfactory coverage against ICBMs. This capability was never advertised as the Missile Defense Agency used the marketing ploy that they were developing a system for each type of TBM. GMD was for ICBMs, THAAD for MRBMs and Patriot for SRBMs, even though Patriot was being developed by the Army.

We finished the $99K contract and Chuck asked if we would consider teaching the THAAD operators. We were told there was no guarantee that we would get the contract, despite the fact we had done some work on setting up the training program already. I talked to Mike and suggested that we form a company and he agreed. But like at Electrosource, he wanted to be the president. I didn't think about it enough and said yes. Ours was a training company, we did training. But by including Mike in a key role, I was creating a tension in the company as being an engineer, he wanted to take the company in a certain direction, and I wanted to take it in another. At times things that he did frustrated me and at times made me damn mad. I am sure he had the same thoughts about me. He created several opportunities that I thought were bordering on brilliant, but there was no money coming in. We were helping a lot of people for nothing which I now realize is always good but at the time it felt like our effort was being dissipated. When you are starting something, you need to think it through, who is doing what and what your objectives will be. I didn't do this, I just wanted to get to work.

People think of defense contracting companies in big buildings with nice furnishings. Well, they must start somewhere; Mike and I wrote the proposal for the THAAD contract in his kitchen. Cheryl did the cost proposal as she had done that kind of work at BDM. We submitted the proposal and stood by for the result.

Chuck called and said we had won. It was truly a great day. We had already provisionally hired Mando and his wife, Heather. Heather was an incredibly talented person. Not only an accomplished Air Defender, she would also go on to get a master's degree in management. Her thesis was on how businesses could use the Army's After-Action Review methodology to help them be more efficient. So, we had Mike, Cheryl, me, Mando, Heather and Christina-we needed an office.

Mike loved to think about offices. So, we looked around and found inexpensive office space in the Mining Exchange Building in downtown Colorado Springs, a block from the famous Antlers Hotel, a landmark in the Springs. There wasn't a space big enough for all of us, so we rented a couple of spaces, all on the top floor. The Mining Exchange building was famous in Colorado history for it was the location the miners in Cripple Creek took their gold to exchange it for cash. The building was an interesting old lady with nooks and crannies all over. My office was a long, narrow room. I worked off a conference table which was an efficient way to have meetings. Cheryl arranged for all the contractual matters and Christina set up our security. Me, Mando and Heather tackled the THAAD contract. Chuck and Carlos came out from Huntsville to visit, and we proudly showed them our space and discussed Chuck's vision for the program.

Sean was quite the athlete and like Rob and Mike, I coached him in everything that we did until he was a teenager. After Huntsville, his first love was hockey, so I volunteered to coach a traveling team for kids under 10 years old. Sean was 31/2. Our league was under the auspices of USA Hockey, a program that I really respected. One season, the director of youth hockey at USA Hockey had his son on my team. The Dad was a super guy and stayed in his Dad lane but offered many super recommendations that I happily accepted. I hadn't played hockey since high school and all we did then was scrimmage, there were no drills.

We had a great group of parents and we decided in addition to league play, we would play in a few tournaments around the state. We had a tournament in Pueblo Colorado, 40 miles to the south of C-Springs where our first game started at 6AM. We all got the boys up at 4AM and caravanned south. We arrived at the rink, which was probably 40 years old, we were assigned a locker room to get the boys dressed. They were all so young that the parents had to dress them. I watched the parents not only putting on all the pads but trying to wake the boys up. Right before the ice, I said boy this is going to be something.

Well, it was, the boys played the best game of their lives and we won handily. For our league games, the coaches skated on the ice with their kids, but in Pueblo I did not. I hadn't skated since high school, but I protected myself with a knee brace, elbow pads and ultimately a helmet after a boy cut me down from behind one day at practice causing a real rough fall on the ice. We practiced all over as hockey was very popular and ice time for practice and games was at a premium.

One January, we took the boys to Gunnison, Colorado for an outdoor tournament. Gunnison often records the coldest temperatures in the nation as the city is in a bowl and at altitude. We were to play three games in two days. Our first game was in the morning, and it was a balmy 20 degrees and we lost. Our next game was that night at a rink in the middle of a neighborhood. The rink reminded me of when I played for St Mary's. The Antlers hotel had a rink, complete with lights, boards, and glass outdoors behind the hotel that you could use free. To use the lights though, it was 25 cents an hour.

Our game started at 7PM and it was cold, very cold. I skated with the boys and didn't take any of the breaks the boys did at shift changes. One of the parents had brought a propane heater and all the moms had blankets for the boys and I would look over at our bench and all I could see was a mound of blankets. It always took a minute or so after I called for a shift change to see any movement in the mound.

The first period was tight. We were tied or a goal ahead. The second shift of the second period, Sean came in, strutting around like he was Wayne Gretzky, like he always did. When he was on the ice, it was like he was in a different world and there was an inner peace and joy that just radiated off him. He had scored a few goals previously, but that night under the stars, we unveiled a behemoth; he scored 3 goals in one shift! He was everywhere, scooping up loose pucks and just enjoying heck out of himself.

When Sean was about 5, we told him that travel hockey was just too much for us and suggested that he play in a recreational league where all the games would be local, and half the practices. Sean was so much better than the other kids in the league, many of whom were 3 and 4 years older than him, that he would take the puck into the corner, draw two or three defenders to him whom he would beat to the net, where he usually scored a goal. He had 47 goals in 20 games.

That league had an arrangement with Colorado College, which was one of the premier hockey programs in the country, to let the kids scrimmage between periods at the CC games. Our turn came and it was exciting, skating into the World Arena, a much bigger rink than we normally played in. The fans loved watching the little guys play and they roared when a goal was scored. I remember our guys were all business, it was fun to watch. At the end of that season, I think Sean was bored with hockey and told us he wanted to play soccer. My thoughts were "okay", at least I didn't have to skate to coach soccer. More on Sean's soccer career later.

Mike and Rob had both gone into the Army. I had recommended after supporting maneuver guys, infantry, and armor guys all my career, that they become one of those guys. I recommended that they both go into the Infantry, which they both did.

Mike had decided to go to Virginia Tech who had changed their name from the Virginia Polytechnic University so when he called me to tell me, I had to ask him where the place was. He initially was admitted to the college of engineering and Christina, and I attended an information presentation given by the Dean of the department. She told us VT was ranked as the number 14 engineering school in the country. She then continued that one of their big goals was to get engineers to express themselves in English not equations or formulas. Wow, I had met a lot of engineers who couldn't speak in simple terms about what they were doing. They thought in mathematical terms and computer code and explaining what they were doing in common language (English) was tough for most of them.

I remember thanking God for Mike and my son Rob, who eventually would work at our company for several years, because they could explain engineering concepts in terms I could understand. Mike had not taken calculus at Cheyenne Mountain, so after his first semester in which he had some struggles, he changed his major to accounting which he did real well in. Here was the kid that fought dyslexia his whole life having been accepted into a very prestigious engineering program and while it didn't work out, I was still proud of his academic accomplishments. Mike joined the Corps of Cadets at VT, which initially surprised me a little as he had not pursued going to West Point due to the discipline there, I thought. VT's discipline would be equally severe or worse.

Mike's Professor of Military Science had known me casually in Europe and I was glad he was in good hands. VT participated in the Ranger Challenge each year where a squad of cadets competes in five events as a team, the last event being a long march/run with full rucksacks. Mike was a freshman or sophomore when he first made the team and then competed for his school. All was going well until the ruck walk. All the participants had to carry a canteen, but the boys would not fill them to save weight. There was water at the turn. Mike went out, made the turn and then about halfway to the finish passed out. My friend, the PMS was there and took him to a local hospital where he was pronounced very dehydrated. My friend called me and told me what had happened. I called Mike and all he was concerned about was that his team had come in second place as they had finished the ruck walk short a man. One thing I will tell you about my son Mike is he had grit. They went out again the following year and won it.

Rob was doing well at West Point. Every cadet has a sponsor, a member of the faculty or cadre whose job is to give the kids a little taste of a home atmosphere. Mike's sponsor was a Captain named Joe Diantona who was an Air Defender. I had met Joe when I took Rob up to West Point for "R" or registration day. We were divided into groups of about 30 parents and kids and escorted into the cadet gym for our orientation. Some LTC started by congratulating all of us. 1000 cadets had been selected from a list of 2500 "fully qualified" young me and women. That list of 2500 had been the result of narrowing down a much, much bigger list. I was mildly surprised when

Rob had been selected to West Point as his SAT scores did not indicate his potential. After hearing the briefing on the selection criteria, I think the thing that got Rob over the hump was he was an Eagle Scout, which the Academies consider an excellent qualification for future leaders. The Colonel finished his brief and he turned the program over to a cadet wearing a red sash, indicative that he was a leader for R day. The young man didn't say much simply "Class of '98 say goodbye to your parents and assemble at the top of the bleachers, you have 30 seconds." I looked over at Rob and big crocodile tears were pouring down his face. I hugged him as hard as I could, and I told him to go kick butt.

Late that afternoon, we were told that there would be a parade of the new cadets and their swearing in ceremony. I hung around the campus, admiring the beautiful statues, constantly trying to peak into the quadrangles in the cadet areas where there was a lot going on. Finally, the time for the parade arrived, Joe found me and stood with me as the parade was forming up. The Commandant of the Academy administered the oath which he explained "Was the same oath on the same field taken by US Grant, Robert E Lee, George Patton and Douglas MacArthur." Chills went up my spine. The cadets then passed in review, and I was able to pick Rob out as his company went in front of me and Joe. They looked surprisingly good since they didn't have much time to practice.

In 1996, the middle of Rob's second year at West Point, Mando and I went up to West Point to ask the Dean of the Faculty if he had any professors who might be interested in coming to Colorado for the summer and doing some projects for Army Space Command. Joe found me and Mando and he got us into Rob's room in an area that was called the "Lost Forties", the barracks closest to the cadet gym. We chatted with Rob, and I asked if I could meet his plebe. All sophomores have a freshman who they mentor and help. Rob was super reluctant, but Joe encouraged him, and Rob left to tell his plebe that he was about to have company. Shortly after, Rob, me, Mando and Joe walked into this poor freshman's room. I thought the kid was going to pass out; here in his room was more rank than he had probably seen in one place in his entire life! We wished him well, and every time I bring up that trip, Rob makes me feel guilty for scaring the devil out of his plebe.

I had been to West Point years earlier when I was the Director of Tactics. Air Defense was losing cadets who promised to go Air Defense to other branches. So General Garner told me to go up there and pump the boys and girls up. My escort was Rambo, Captain Chuck Anderson who served with me at Fort Stewart. Rambo got the kids together on a Saturday morning and I gave them a hurrah speech. Chuck had asked me to stay over on Sunday which I did. He asked me if I was interested in working out on Sunday morning and I said sure if it was after 0900, I wanted to get some sleep. I was staying at the Thayer hotel, right on campus, and I met Chuck and his wife Tammy in the lobby.

Here was Rambo whose body looked like an inverted triangle, with no waist and massive arms and shoulders. Tammy was thin as a rail, and we discussed her diet as we were working out and I got the impression that drinking water would have been a risk for her. We ran up the hill to the cadet gym which was a little more than a mile from the hotel and we then went into the cadet gym to the class of '62 room. The class of '62 had donated every nautilus machine ever produced by the company. There were about 30 of them. Chuck suggested that we go through each machine doing 10 reptations on each. By about the 20th machine, I was feeling it big time, but I followed a gleeful Chuck and eventually finished up all of them. We then ran back to the hotel and as we were arriving, I suggested to Chuck that we might like to go and buy a cup of coffee and a doughnut. I was nearing exhaustion, so I suggested that I had to stop and get some money out of my room. With a big smile Chuck replied he had money and kept running. Finally, I told him I had to walk, which we did. Chuck eventually was promoted to Major General and played a huge role in Operation Iraqi Freedom (OIF) where he performed his duties heroically.

We had gone to visit Rob at West Point in September 1997 and that Christmas; he came to visit us in Huntsville as Marilyn was visiting with my cousin and her husband. Rob's senior year, Christina and I planned a second trip to New York to see the Army Navy game. Nana flew in and we rented a RV. We then drove to Blacksburg and arrived late in the afternoon. We took Mike to dinner and then went to a motel where Nana would sleep. Christina, Sean, and I were to sleep in the RV, which we parked the motel parking lot. One of the things I have trouble with is I tend to want to save things. God gives us stuff to use, not hoard. So that night, I decided that we were not going to use the heater in the trailer. It was very cold outside, and Christina suggested that we turn it on, but I said we would be ok. Around 1AM, it was so cold in the RV that we could see our breath. I got up and turned on the heater, lesson learned.

The next day we picked up Mike and headed to New York. The traffic got crazy, and we got on a toll road, heading for the camping spot that we had reserved. We had a talk as we approached the toll booth as to whether the RV was too high to fit under the covered toll booth and decided we could just make it. As we passed through the toll booth, I heard a scraping sound and we passed on through the toll booth. Mike was going to the bathroom in the little bathroom that was on the same side as the toll booth, and he got to say hi to the toll booth operator. Turns out we had left the cover for the AC unit on the top of the RV on the ground behind us. We would not fully realize this until we got back to Huntsville.

The next day we drove to Giant's stadium where the game was being held. We had bought groceries for breakfast and the idea was that we could have breakfast for Rob and a few of his friends. He was finally a firstie or senior, so our expectation was that he would have a little time before and after the game so we could visit. We had not heard from Rob, despite frequent requests for information. Rob showed up with a couple of buddies in a rush. Turns out he was on restriction for something, so he had to get back to the cadet area as soon as possible, he was taking a chance just coming to see us. The boys gobbled breakfast, Rob gave everyone a hug and off they went.

Nana and Christina both had the cadet issued parkas for the game. We were on a middle deck in the stadium and the wind howled through the stands. It was the second coldest I have ever been in my life. Christina worked on keeping Sean warm and I tried to help Nana stay warm. I remember a picture we took at the game of the four of us and you could just see how cold we were. Army lost the game, so it was kind of a depressing day.

We drove back to Blacksburg and left Mike off and headed for Huntsville. When we were about 40 miles from Huntsville, the engine started cutting out; it was sputtering. We were driving on rolling hills so I would gas it on the downhill and eek us up the uphill. When we got back to Huntsville, the engine was cutting out again, but I was nursing us along when I noticed a police siren in my rear-view mirror. We stopped and the officer told me that I had cut someone off. I apologized, I hadn't even seen the dude and explained that we were having some trouble with the mobile home. Just then, the engine backfired and we all jumped about 3 feet in the air. The policeman escorted us to the house which was only a few miles away. The next day we returned the mobile home to Enterprise when I realized that we had knocked the cowl off the AC unit on top of the vehicle. They asked me where it went, and I honestly told them I had no idea. They were so apologetic about the engine, they forgot about the cowl.

Mike and Rob were 2 ½ years apart, so when Rob graduated from West Point, Mike was finishing his sophomore year. We all went to the graduation including Nana and we proudly watched Rob's class graduate. Marilyn, my cousin Cathy, and her husband also attended. West Point is not a good place to hold family affairs. The little town outside West Point, Highland Falls didn't have any decent hotels back then, the Thayer was full because grads had preference, so we had nowhere to get together as a family. I had to leave after the ceremony as we had to return to Huntsville as I had a big review that following Monday. Rob was angry that we were not coming to the pinning on ceremony which I would have been proud to attend, but since I didn't know about the event, we left. It made Rob real mad at us and we didn't talk with him for 9 months. I really regret that I was not there, but you need to tell people what you want them to do. Good lesson learned-be respectful of other's schedules even though what you are asking is good for everyone. I can surely understand why Rob assumed we were going to be there.

Mike had a good experience at Virginia Tech and with the Corps of Cadets. We went to visit him his senior year and I went up to his room with him. He had to change uniforms and we talked, and I remember how impressed I was with his maturity. He truly had become a leader.

Rob went to Ranger school and later jumpmaster training. Like he always did on any kind of examination, Rob excelled at both; he graduated first in his jumpmaster class which many say is the toughest course in the Army, as the student needs to retain a lot of information and apply it. Mike went to Ranger also after he graduated, and he got recycled in the third and final phase of the training. Mike was on a patrol, the patrol leader got sick, and Mike had to take over. The lesson learned from this event is leaders need to share information. The PL had not shared the entire plan with Mike, so he got recycled. I was angry. My boys had 7 combat tours between them, and I have never been so worried about them as I was when they were at Ranger school. They both made it fine.

My Public Affairs Officer at Army Space was a fellow named Ed White. Ed had been part of the initial cadre that had formed the 1st Ranger battalion. When students graduate from Ranger school, they are given their first ranger tab which is called the "blood tab". When I left Army Space Command, Ed gave me his blood tab, a precious gift. I asked the boys for their blood tabs after they had both graduated and I had a shadow box made with all three. It has been lost, but it is a beautiful memory.

Mike graduated in December 2000, he had to take an extra semester to make up for his first semester in the engineering department. Mike was assigned to the 101st Airborne Division at Ft Campbell Kentucky, which was only 140 miles or so from Huntsville. I gave Mike a Ford Ranger pickup truck, which I thought was the perfect vehicle for an Infantry Lieutenant, who had to haul his field gear around all the time, but Mike was so-so on the truck; he appreciated that he didn't have a car payment, but the truck is not what he would have bought. I went up to visit Mike and was pleased to see he had a nice apartment, which he had furnished with the essentials, bed, dresser, recliner, TV, and kitchen stuff. He was squared away.

We had driven Saddam out of Kuwait during Desert Storm, but he started making noise again and President Bush decided that it was time to unseat him. Plans were drawn up for an invasion, or I should say updated for an invasion. The 18th Airborne Corps would support the mechanized guys who planned to advance very rapidly. Tanks are not good in cities but light units like the 101st are, so the light divisions had the mission of securing urban areas after they had been surrounded by the mech guys.

I thought the strategy was all wrong. I believed what we needed to do was secure the oil infrastructure, so Iraq would have revenue after the invasion and then surround the cities and let no one in or out until the residents had internally solved their problems.

There were several problems with my plan first -time; it would take a long time to wait them out, not the American Way of War and two, Americans would not tolerate attacking women and children. My solution to that issue is to just let the women and children out of the city and have holding camps near their city where the civilians would be cared for. Instead, we went back to conquer territory idea we had in Vietnam, even though winning the hearts and minds of the people was an objective.

General Garner had become a high-level advisor to the Secretary of Defense. He recommended creating 3 countries-one for the Sunnis, Kurds, and the Shiites. They had hated each other for 1000 years and it just made sense. Garner raised quite a fuss as he was prone to do and eventually the SECDEF called him into his office and told him he had to fire him. He then gave Jay a medal for outstanding service, and they walked next door to a press conference to announce the firing.

There were agendas in Operation Iraqi Freedom. General Shinseki my former acquaintance from Europe was now the Chief of Staff of the Army. He was asked how many soldiers he needed for the mission; he said 600,000 which would have doubled the size of the Army. The military had become politicized as no one would even consider a draft which was the only solution to raising that many soldiers. General S was dismissed as the Chief because of his recommendation. He retired and later would be appointed as the Chief of Veteran Affairs, which was clearly seen as a payback for an unjust action, where he did a lot of great things for us old timers.

The 101st flew into Kuwait and staged in camps just north of Kuwait City. Saddam learned of this and one night fired several scuds at the camps. Patriot was there and the system had been upgraded big time since Desert Storm, much more accurate, and they cleaned the skies. Mike wrote me a letter just before they headed north and commented on how happy he was at the Patriot's success. I shared his thought with several active duty and retired ADA Generals I knew, and I got back the reply "I know you are proud of your son." That wasn't the message that I wanted to convey; I wanted them to know a grunt appreciated Patriot. Air Defense for years stood ready and never got a chance. Now everyone was seeing what they could do, even my son, and I was proud of that, and Mike too of course.

The 101st went from Kuwait all the way to Mosul on the northern border of Iraq. Mike was leading an Infantry platoon and he and his boys were kicking down doors. I was so happy to see him when he got home.

Mike went from the 101st to the advanced course in Columbus Georgia. Before he went to Columbus, he called me and told me he wanted to buy a new car. He wanted a Toyota 4 Runner and had looked at one that had 70,000 miles on it. I advised him to find one with fewer miles say around 30,000 which he did. I asked him how he was going to pay for his $16,000 purchase. He replied "Cash". Stupidly I asked him where he was going to get the money, it seemed like he had been in the Army for 30 minutes. He explained the Army had a very generous savings program in combat zones where if the soldier contributed $10,000, the Army would match it. His truck was in storage, and he had turned his phone off, so he saved all his pay less a few dollars each month for shaving crème and haircuts. Mike would eventually go on 4 combat tours, and he would follow the same investment strategy on the next two, modifying it slightly for the 4th tour when he was married. He learned money sense from his mother.

We got to see Mike at Benning and he seemed to be having a great time. When it was time to get his orders, I was surprised that the Army was sending Mike back to another light Division, this time the 82d, Rob's old outfit. Almost as soon as he got there, Mike was assigned to a Brigade Staff and off they went to Afghanistan. This tour was uneventful, and Mike got home just fine.

In the middle of this, Mike had started dating a lovely girl named Jill Henry. Jill and Mike had met at Virginia Tech, had dated some, but it didn't seem like the relationship was going anywhere. We loved Jill and I talked to Mike: pull the trigger, ask her to marry you, she is a lovely girl etc. etc. Mike replied that he didn't want to do that; he didn't know when he would be going to be deployed again and he thought it was unfair to marry a woman and then leave her, potentially over and over.

Mike took command of an airborne company shortly after he got back from Afghanistan. Shortly thereafter, there was the big callup and the United States was going to send in forces to finish the job we had started with OIF years earlier. Mike's company got tapped to deploy, not a surprise with them being in the 82d.

I learned all this when he came home on leave, but Mike's company was given the mission to pacify a neighborhood in downtown Bagdad. Almost all the residents of this barrio belonged to the same Sunni tribe, so part of Mike's job was to establish a relationship with the Chief. They got to be pretty good friends to the point that the Chief suggested that Mike marry his then 12-year-old daughter when he came back, an invitation Mike tastefully sidestepped. The first six months were busy. I learned from Mike's Battalion Commander that every night Special Forces and British SAS commandos were in Mike's neighborhood, searching for enemy insurgents. Mike's Forward Operating Base, or FOB was 2 miles away and to get there, one left the neighborhood and turned right onto a main highway that ran by the FOB.

One platoon from the company was always in the neighborhood as a contingency. As he was leaving after a visit and was starting to turn right to return to the FOB, someone fired an RPG from a 3-story building across the highway. Mike's driver said duck sir and the thing missed his head by less than a foot. The gunner on Mike's HUMMV laid down suppressive fire with the onboard .50 Caliber M2 machinegun and Mike called for supporting fire.

When Mike was home for his midtour leave, he briefed me on the whole operation complete with satellite maps. I asked Mike what support he called for and he explained there was a hierarchy of responses beginning with the deployment of the company drone and escalating upward. I asked why they didn't call in the USAF and level the building, the response that my generation would have used; and he reminded me that they were trying to minimize "collateral damage" or the killing and injuring of non-combatants. He eventually called for a MLRS ATCMS, a precision guided missile that flew through the window to deliver a thank you. I still have pictures of when General Petraeus, the Commander in Chief of the Iraqi coalition, visited Mike's company.

When Mike got home, the Army told him he was going to have a "take a knee" job and he ended up going to Washington DC to work at the Military Personnel Command supporting the conduct of promotion boards, a skill that would help him later. Jill had come to Huntsville with Mike on his mid-tour leave and they announced they were going to get married. We were frickin elated. Mike reported into his new job and told me his boss was a female LTC from the Adjutant General's Corps. I sensed that situation might have been mixing oil and water, but Mike handled it well.

A date was set for the wedding, and we all showed up. Father Phil O'Kennedy who was our pastor at St John's in Huntsville, agreed to take a little vacation up to Virginia and marry the kids. They had met him at our house, so they at least knew him before the wedding.

The rehearsal dinner was held on the roof of the hotel where everyone was staying which overlooked the water and the theme of the party was Virginia Tech-all the party favors and decorations were VT or VT's colors. We had a great time. I felt responsible as a Dad to always give the boys their rehearsal dinners. Rob's had been at a ritzy restaurant in Manitou Springs which was lovely and while I wanted to do more for Mike, he was perfectly happy with what I did. The issue was equality, you always need to be perfectly fair with your kids.

The wedding was the next day at a beautiful chapel on Norfolk Naval base. I got into my tuxedo but was a little sore doing it as Ken, Jill's Dad, had all of us men over and we shot skeet the morning of the rehearsal dinner. After we were done shooting, my right shoulder was black and blue. Father Phil did a beautiful job with the wedding, and I was so happy and proud. Mike wore his uniform and Jill was a beautiful bride.

We then retired to a building about a mile from the chapel for the reception. It was a Navy recreation center, a building that was built for special functions. It wasn't fancy but we had plenty of room for the dinner and dancing after. Mike had rented an all-black band that played all the 4 Tops favorites, and they were good. Christina and I danced and danced. Mike and Jill moved into his apartment in Washington until his next assignment, which would really irritate me later.

Rob had a very active life once he was assigned to the 82d Airborne Division after the basic course. The world had changed: in 5 years with the Division, he was deployed 3 times. I never realized this, but after the Arab Israeli war of 1973, the US agreed to have an infantry battalion, 800+ men, in the Sinai continuously. It was an uneventful tour militarily, but interesting when we received post cards and letters from places like the Red Sea, which apparently is quite the tourist area.

Later he was assigned as part of the peace keeping force in Bosnia Herzegovina, the plan I had worked on years later. When he got home, I was horrified to learn that he had been assigned as the S-5 of his battalion and had ridden around the countryside with just his driver talking to local leaders. Thank God, there were no incidents, but when I had been doing the plan, we expected intense contact with the local population. His final deployment was to Afghanistan where he was a battle captain for his battalion and went on several patrols and earned his combat infantryman's badge and a bronze star.

Rob had married a girl he met in Colorado Springs who was a medical student before they were married. They were married at the Cadet Chapel at the Air Force Academy, and we had gotten them a time share in the mountains which they used for their honeymoon. We had taken all the wedding presents to our house and they planned to sort them all out after they got back to the Springs. A few days after their wedding, Megan's mother called us and asked if we knew where the kids were. We told her and she asked if we could get hold of them right away. When I asked "why", she replied that she had just received notification that Megan had been accepted to Wake Forest Medical School. She wanted to go to the med school at North Carolina and had even moved there to establish residency, hoping that would give her an edge for admittance. Right before the wedding, she had learned that she had not been accepted by UNC, but now she had less than a week to report to Wake. They came home, identified all who had given them all the gifts so they could write thank you notes. They then flew back to Carolina to get on with this next challenge in their lives.

I was worried about Rob in this relationship from the start. Megan had lost her father when she was a teenager, a man she adored, and it scarred her permanently. She felt betrayed that her dad had left her too early and developed a distrust of men. She had a very cold persona, but Rob really loved her, and I took satisfaction in that.

Rob ended his tour in the 82d and called his assignment officer to see where he was going and to request an assignment in the Southeast so he could be close to his wife who was finishing medical school at Wake. They had been separated during their whole engagement with Rob off on multiple deployments and Megan in North Carolina. His assignment officer told him that staying in the South was impossible and that he was going to Korea. Really frustrated and mad, he called me for advice. I still had some of my "sons" on active duty and some of them were in in high places, like LTG Bob Lennox who had a big position in the Pentagon.

I told Rob let me try to fix the issue, he said ok, and I called Bob who told me he would be happy to help. I called Rob back and he told me he was very angry, and he had decided to get out of the Army. By now Megan had graduated from medical school and had taken a position at the Veteran's Hospital in Denver. I talked to brother Mike, and we decided to offer Rob a job, which he accepted. He would work in Colorado Springs Monday through Friday and spend the weekends with his bride in Denver where they had bought a cute house in Washington Park.

Rob originally started working with Mando and me on THAAD. We were having frequent marketing meetings and Mike had developed a neat system to track opportunities. The Army Science Institute put out a contract for subject matter experts to help them with several things. Rob wrote the contract and we won; it wasn't enough money to pay Rob's salary, but it was a whole new line of business, which we all hoped would grow and it did.

Rob had several jobs where he would go to the Infantry school and be the interface for the soldiers with University educators who were doing studies on how soldiers learned. On two of these studies Rob worked with a PHD from Stanford University, and they hit it off. At the end of the second round, the Doctor asked Rob if he would be interested in attending Stanford to get his PHD. Rob replied he didn't know and was then told that his tuition would be taken care of, and he would receive a stipend for the first 4 years. Rob called me and asked what I thought, and I told him to follow his heart. Megan was not enthusiastic, but Rob hurriedly, as the semester was about to start, enrolled. He went to Stanford and after a couple of weeks flew back to Colorado to talk to Megan about moving out with him. He entered his house and was about to start the conversation when Megan handed him divorce papers. She was not going to California. She provided a generous settlement, but my heart ached as Rob was on his own again. It's hard to understand when one is doing everything one thinks is right-loving someone with all your heart-and understanding how they can just walk away. It takes hard work on the part of two people, frequently swallowing self-pride, to make a marriage work. I guess she had her life plan and didn't want to adapt. She worked with Veterans for years, so she did a lot of good.

I really didn't understand what a PHD involved. Rob took several courses that I thought were a little different, like rock climbing. He fell in love with Stanford football and regaled us with stories of his tail gating. I flew out one year and he and I got to watch the "Big Game" between the University of California Berkeley and Stanford. It had been the big game since my Dad had played at Cal. It was the second time that I had been in that beautiful campus stadium, and I enjoyed the ambiance a lot. I did have a little trouble adjusting to the antics of the Stanford band who are a unique group.

It would take Rob 7 years to graduate and when the scholarship money ran out things were tough. But he persevered and kept going. Rob told me that he didn't care if we came to his graduation, but he did want us to come to his thesis defense. Mike, Jill, and I flew out. Rob was to present a briefing on his topic to a group of 6 professors, who would then consult to determine if the contribution to the body of knowledge was sufficient and if Rob had proved his points. We rehearsed the pitch; Rob was still a little nervous, but Mike and I told him to go for the gold. The profs came in including Doctor Dan, Rob's mentor, who had gotten him into the program. Rob gave his pitch, and we were asked to leave while the panel talked.

We went outside on the beautiful Stanford campus and sat on a bench for a while. I then told Mike I was going for a little walk, and I walked down to the beautiful Stanford Chapel. I wanted to pray for Rob's success. It was close to noontime, and I was praying about halfway down the chapel whose floor sloped down to the altar. There was a section of the church to my right front that I couldn't see and as noon approached, I noticed people walking by me in that direction. I finally got up and went down there and there was a Catholic Priest all vested up sitting in a corner. I went up to him and asked if he was about to say mass and he said yes and he asked if I had any intentions for the mass. I told him about Rob and during the intentions, the priest mentioned Rob's defense. I was getting worried that I was gone too long, but Father said a mass that reminded me of some of the masses that I had gone to in the military-beautiful, but short.

I returned to the building where Rob gave his presentation and Mike told me that the profs were about to render their verdict to Rob. He passed; he had some cleanup on the presentation to do which would take several months, but it was over. He would be a "FUD" as we called PHDs when I went to college. Rob's fellow PHD candidates had arranged a picnic nearby and we all had a great time. Rob was walking around with a coffee cup that said: "Trust me, I'm a Doctor." The young men that organized the party were all super impressive young men. It was an honor to be with them.

Meanwhile, we did the training development for THAAD the same way we did GMD; first the task development to include the preparation of the dreaded TARS; then Program of Instruction development and finally we had to conduct the pilot course. The difference between the GMD and THAAD pilots was in the THAAD pilot we had a few guys as students who would eventually be operators; in GMD we had a no one who would eventually be a scope dope for the pilot course.

THAAD was an Army Air Defense Program, so we were going to teach the course at Ft Bliss. The post had reconfigured an old building in the 5000 area for our use. It was a long, narrow building with a huge patio which ran the whole length of the building. There were four classrooms and a lab where Lockheed installed the THAAD systems. There was an outdoor break area in the middle. I spent a lot of time in that building and have fond memories of it. Later, the Army would install several expandable vans which we used for teaching as well.

TRADOC was present for the pilot so our instruction as well as the course content was going to be graded. Mando was our interface with the TRADOC guys and all that went well. The course was 8 weeks long, so we all camped out in a motel just outside the gate. We all ate breakfast together and the boys would go do things after work. One Friday at breakfast I suggested that we all go to Mexico the next day; walk over the border to that same area-the Santa Fe bridge- where I had sent Tony Carpenter years earlier. One of the guys mentioned that he had read in the paper that there had been a recent shooting there and 3 innocent people were killed on the street where we planned to shop. We killed the idea of going to Mexico. Later, we decided one weekday afternoon to drive out to Fabens, Texas to a famous restaurant called the Cattleman's. It was about 30 miles east of El Paso and as we drove out there was a border guard vehicle every mile or so surveying the border. Life changed since I was at Bliss as a Lieutenant. It was sad, visiting Juarez had been a great experience in times past, it was always exciting. We had lost something due to the Cartel's hate and greed turning the nice parts of the city into battle zones to satisfy their unholy desires.

We just gave the course; the evaluators did not interrupt us. We had frequent AARs internally with ourselves and selected other soldiers. After every exam and before every class, we implored the soldiers to tell us what they really thought and they did, but everyone was incredibly pleased overall.

In some ways, the hardest part of any course is writing the test questions, so after every examination we would go over the results with the soldiers who would tell us if the question was vague or misleading. We had a test generator that housed our questions which could be modified very rapidly. It was called a generator because it would print out an exam after the parameters were inputted for the exam-number of questions, etc. We reviewed every exam before it was given and threw out or modified many questions after talking to the students. Nobody had an issue with the 90% standard to pass. Mando had devised a way of grading the final crew drills the students had to perform to the same standard. The final crew drill evaluation became a very competitive operation.

When the pilot course was complete, the TRADOC evaluator would not give us a go, deferring his final decision until after he returned to Fort Monroe and discussed things with his colleagues. The issue was the 90% score on tests. The widely accepted score and the TRADOC standard to pass exams again was 70%. Despite our arguments as to the importance of the mission and the operator knowledge and decisions which we evaluated in the course; he wasn't convinced. We talked to Chuck, and he said we would resolve the issue by having a council of Colonels with a representative from all the interested parties just like we had done in GMD. The group included a Colonel from Headquarters, TRADOC. They all agreed on the 90% standard, and we got our letter giving approval to the course a few weeks later.

Mando had argued that we needed to teach more on the alarms in the system and the messaging system. At one point, he recommended spending 40 hours on the messages and alarms and my recollection was we tried it in the pilot course. It was just too much, and we reduced that instruction to 4 hours. Mando and I resolved all our differences the same way. We got input from the users, if there was any, we argued back and forth sometimes for weeks, then I decided, we agreed to disagree. Leaders need to take the best information available and go with their gut decision sometimes. And if that decision is wrong, take corrective action as quickly as possible. I've tried to live by that code my whole life.

We were under contract to teach the initial core of operators. My remembrance is we taught 3 full courses. We continually improved the training and added little things as the instruction went on. Chuck approached me one day and told me there was a movement in the government to divest themselves of contractors who were doing what the prime contractors could do. Government supervisors were trying to reduce their span of control and simplify things. I went to see Roy Tate, a retired ADA Colonel that I had known since my first assignment in the Army. Roy was the training lead for Lockheed Martin. He and I had always been cordial, but I didn't know him very well. We had a friendly, productive meeting and Imprimis was given a contract to be a subcontractor to LM. We would run the THAAD training program. It began a great run of almost a decade where we worked with Lockheed on all kinds of things.

While Roy was the LM training manager, things went very well. Because we had conducted the GMD training program, when LM decided to take a run at winning the GMD contract, we were included as a subcontractor for that project. BG Jeff Horne had been hired by LM to be the chief of smoke, to energize everyone to do their best. I had met Jeff in the Army and he knew me, but we were not close. Because he was a retired Air Defender, the LM project manager let Jeff play in the training sandbox. We were trying to prove not only that we could do the job, but that we were totally prepared to begin the day we won the contract.

For example, all the GMD missile procedures for all phases of missile maintenance and operations had not been updated in 5 years. My boss came to me and asked if we could work with the people at Lockheed's missile production in Courtland, Alabama which was about 40 miles west of Huntsville. LM had some guys who had gone up to Greeley Alaska when the system was first fielded and helped solve some missile issues which was preventing the system from declaring itself combat ready. They literally pulled Boeing's feet out of the fire.

I would work at Courtland for 2 months. While we were bidding on GMD, I also had a cubicle in the LM office in Huntsville where I would do all my contractual work for security reasons. I would host a teleconference every day with the missile technicians at Courtland, safety people, quality control folks and others as needed, and we would go through the Boeing missile procedures line by line correcting or confirming what was there. I met some great people, including Richard Clary who had a unique personality but was one of the most creative people I had ever known.

We eventually all traveled out to the LM headquarters in Sunnyvale, California to spend the last month or so writing the final bid. Horne was in his element, demanding the impossible. For instance, he asked me to develop the total training program for the operators, maintenance people and others in a week. The issue was we didn't know which subcontractors were going to bid with Boeing or which were going to side with us. Until I knew who our teammates were and their capabilities, building a training program was impossible in any detail.

We worked 6 1/2 days a week. I remember I had to get a little firm when I told Jeff that I would not work on Sunday mornings as I had to go to mass. He reluctantly said ok. We finally submitted the proposal, and I flew back to Huntsville on New Year's Eve. If LM would have won, Imprimis would have added 38 employees and would have worked for them for years to come.

We lost because Boeing underbid us. We were paranoid about costs, but we bid what we needed. The rumor was we had a far better technical proposal, but the government could not get around to granting the contract to a newcomer when the previous prime could do the job at a lower price. Boeing poured on additional costs after they won the contract, ending up probably spending more money than we would have.

While I spent almost a year working on GMD, our contract with THAAD continued. When you hire people, one hires them generally at the location where they apply. We had by now offices in Colorado, Huntsville and in El Paso. We had the flexibility to do this because we all merged on El Paso to teach. By the time 2010 rolled around Mando and 3 or 4 other THAAD employees were in Colorado, we had 4-5 guys in El Paso, and I had myself and a couple of other THAAD employees in Huntsville.

Christina worked for the company for full time for about 3 years and then she decided she had better things to do. In addition to caring for our baby and our chocolate lab and taking care of a huge house, she decided she wanted to write books. She published two children's books which were historical fiction about the Revolutionary War and won awards for them. She then decided that she wanted to get back into Triathlons.

We had gotten into bicycling while we were in Colorado. We had our bikes set up in a room in the basement and we would participate in these videos of these skinny little women who would just kick your butt regularly. We then took a cycling course at Carmichael Training Systems which was headquartered in Colorado Springs. Chris Carmichael had been Lance Armstrong's coach when he won all those Tours de France. We would ride on weekends. There was a bicycle path that had been built with Colorado lottery money that ran from the south side of the Springs all the way to Denver. We often rode from the south side to the north side of the Springs, about 30 miles. Mike rode with us one time and even though he had not been riding at all, despite the brisk pace that I set, he hung in there. Like I said, he always was the superior athlete.

Christina and I rode the Tour of Tucson, Arizona in November of 2004, which was a "metric century", a 66-mile ride around the perimeter of the city. We finished fine, but our hotel did not have a jacuzzi and my butt was so sore, and I was so stiff, I suffered the afternoon after the race was done.

So, the climate was right for Chris to get back into Triathlons. She started doing what they call sprint Triathlons and moved up to Olympic Triathlons in 2002. In 2003 she moved up to half Triathlons. We took a trip to St Croix so Chris could do a half-triathlon. We rented a bungalow on the beach. After we had moved in, we went to the grocery store to stock up. They had a local beer there called Red Stripe and it was like $2 a case, so we stocked up on that as well. We had driven around the island, trying to let Chris see as much of the bike course as possible but we decided not to drive the entire bike route, assuming that the rest of the bike course would be like the beginning. Big mistake.

The day of the race came, and we all headed into Christiansted which was right on the Atlantic Ocean. Watching a triathlon is one of the most boring sports to watch as all an observer only can see the beginning and end of the events. At St Croix, we did get to see the entire swim. Christina swam in front of us all the way as the route paralleled a boardwalk that ran along the beach. We cheered her on as she transitioned to the bike and then we went to a bar to wait. One always has a feel about how long something should take, and she was late, very late finishing the bike.

She finally came in and reported to us that the bike route, which we had not driven, was a bear with many tough, challenging hills. She then started out on the run which consisted of running two 6.2-mile loops. The finish point was next to the bar, so I saw her when she was finishing her first loop. She scared the daylight out of me as she was beat red and looked so dehydrated. It was probably 100 degrees that day and it was so hot that where they wrote her number on her arm to start the race ended up sunburned into her arm for a week. I suggested she stop, which of course was a nonstarter. I gave her some water and poured some over her head and off she went. She finished like she always did no matter what she started. My wife is like that in all things in life. A fierce competitor who competes against herself every day.

Having survived St Croix, Christina continued her training. Through her Carmichael connections, she had met Lance Watson who was the Canadian Triathlon coach. Lance knew that since her time at St Croix was good enough to qualify for a full race, Mike got her into Iron Man Canada which would be held in Penticton Canada which was about 50 miles east of Vancouver. Christina redoubled her training. She was running so much that our lab, JT, who always ran with her started quitting on runs. He would just lay down sometimes only yards from the house. She would call me from her bike, 30 miles from Limon Colorado, which was 70 miles to the east of Colorado Springs.

I had a big In Progress Review the Monday after the race, so I couldn't go to the race. So, in August 2004, Roberta, Christina's mom, Sean, and Christina headed north, spending a couple of days in Vancouver which they told me was one of the most spectacular places in the world. They then drove over to Penticton and settled in their hotel. Penticton existed to support Ironman Canada. There was a huge lake south of the town where the bike ride of 112 miles and the marathon would take place. The people were helpful and friendly as this race was the town's annual major source of income.

Christina called me as she was about to start, about 7AM Colorado time. I wished her luck and thought about her all day as I puttered around the house. She called me at 10PM that night and told me that she had finished under the time limit to be termed an Iron Man. Sean had seen her coming in and ran the last mile of the Marathon with her which I am sure lifted her spirits.

Later she told me a cute story which sums up the people of Penticton. She had about 10 miles to go in the Marathon and was running along the lake, all alone, at night with a chem-light to help her see the road. Up ahead, she saw a parked car and several people sitting on lawn chairs. As she approached them a flashlight from the group shone on her chest where her number was affixed. The light went down and the next thing she heard was "Come on Christina, you're almost done, keep going." They apparently went out every year and knowing the spot where one was challenged to overcome the fatigue and pain of the day's exertions and they made themselves present just to give folks that final boost they needed. It really helped. Sometimes the best thing we can do is just to be present for people. That was the last Ironman Christina ran. She would stay active, doing the Pike's Peak Marathon in 2006 walking/running the 26 miles up and down Pike's Peak.

After his bland last experience with Hockey, Sean had decided he wanted to play soccer. Colorado Springs had a local Soccer Association called Pride Soccer and we signed him up. Pride had some interesting rules, one of which was coaches could retain players after a season. Most house leagues allow coaches to keep one or two players, but the roster essentially turns over every year. I was happy with the Pride policy; we could build something. Another thing I liked about the association is we would have a full schedule of games in both the fall and the spring, so I had lots of chances to make the boys better. The team was selected, and I had a parent meeting like I did before every season. Pretty simple rules: the coach coaches and the parents cheer, a lesson learned from my select league days in Virginia.

I would coach the same core group of boys for 8 seasons. We played all over Colorado Springs, but my favorite place to play was at El Pomar, which had been a retreat for the family that had founded Colorado Springs, on the extreme south side of the city. They had about 10 fields, there were trees all around, it was a wonderful place. I had a great group of parents, and

I designed a logo for the team, and we had T-Shirts and caps made which the parents enthusiastically purchased.

At one game the ref came running over to our sideline to ask the coach to have a parent run the line for the game to determine when a ball was out of bounds. Everybody had a team something on, so I had to be pointed out as the coach to the ref. I named the team the Blackwatch, after the English regiment that had fought at Waterloo and our emblem was the English Premier Lion, rearing up with his foot on a soccer ball.

I had a plan to teach the boys every soccer skill they needed to have and as they got older, we could teach more and more. When they started out as mostly 5-year old's, it was magnet ball with everyone yelling at them to spread out. By the end, they played a pretty good triangle, they could control and pass the ball and they were super competitive. I never had to worry about effort with that group of boys. I think the key to coaching is to make everything routine and habit. The boys would start every practice with the warmup routine we used for games and although we did some drills, all my skills teaching was in the context of game situations. Even at practice, the boys ran everywhere they went on the field, never picked up a ball so that every aspect of the game was routine and familiar to them. I think the key to the team was the parents and boys really liked each other and we had many parties at our house that were a blast. We eventually played in a national tournament at the Air Force Academy. It was all my guys with two new recruits; we came in 3d place.

I will always remember the parents and the boys well. Calvin and Ben, Sean's closest friends and their parents. Chris, the beautiful little boy who had a mental disability but who I would put in the game in certain situations, so he felt he was part of the team. His parents told me that just being on the team was enough, but we made sure that he played and when he would kick the ball, the whole sideline would erupt. Sports can be such a development tool for young people, but it needs to be done with humility. You need to drum into the kids that they are part of the team, and they should help their teammates and the important thing is to do your best and learn from defeats; to constantly try to get better. Sports can teach some valuable life lessons and I hope my boys learned them.

After we moved to Alabama, Sean and I would play one more soccer season when he attended St John's. The team was terrible, they had no skills and a lack of competitive juices. But Sean competed even though as our goalie, every game was like trying to stop a flood. But what I was most proud of was Sean remained super competitive and was angry at the rest of the team, not for losing, but for not trying to get better.

I went to referee school in 2003 and became certified as a soccer referee. I've discovered later in my life that I like to know how things tick, so I attended classes and then took the hardest written test I have ever taken in my life. I passed and was given my referee certification. I ref'd for 2 years, often 2-3 games a day and gained an appreciation for the nuances of the game and how to behave as a coach. A soccer ref controls not only the field but the area 100 yards around the field. I was refereeing a game between a team from Denver and a local team one day. The Denver coach was a TV personality in Denver and all through the 1st half he would make little snippy comments like "you blew that one ref". When the second half started, he kept it up. I stopped the game and walked over to his sideline and said "enough". And that was the end of that. He knew I could have cleared his sideline including him. I was in my late 50's when I was refereeing, and I remember how sore I would be after the games. I lost weight, but overall, it was a great experience, and I learned a lot about soccer.

In the summer of 2005, Christina and I went to France on vacation. We had hooked up with a cycling touring company owned by Marty Jimerson, who was the US National Cycling champion in 1999. In the competition to select the US Postal Bicycling Team for the Tour of France, he was competing against a young Texan who was an up and comer named Lance Armstrong. Although Marty was at least equal in the tryouts, US Postal went with Lance and Marty's career was pretty much over. Every cycling team has specialists-hill climbers, guys who can burn on the flats for extended periods of time and one all around guy whom the whole team supports to get the win. There wasn't room on the team for both Marty and Lance.

We flew into Paris with our bikes and were met at the airport by Marty and a couple of his guys. They loaded us into a van and took us to a hotel near the airport where they were assembling and tuning all the bikes prior to putting them on top of the van and taking us to our first hotel. We had picked the first week of the tour as the course is the flattest and our hotel for the first day was near the start point for the race. Marty wanted us to see it all-a start, a finish, a time point, a feeding zone-all aspects of the race. Marty knew people so he could get us on the course in advance of the race and we road 40-50KMs of the race route every day. We would then stop at a time marker, have lunch, and watch the race go by, up close and personal. Marty knew everyone and we got to meet several of the participants before and after the races. It really was a guided tour.

After a 3-hour bus ride, we arrived at our first hotel which was in a beautiful little cull de sac in a small French village. The town was quaint, cobblestone streets and beautiful trees. Marty announced that we were going for a 45-minute ride, and we had 30 minutes to get ready. I was tired, I had had my typical lousy flight going to Europe, not much sleep and sore from riding in planes and busses for almost 11 hours. We went off and I learned quickly that when riding in the back of a group of riders, when the group turned, they would accelerate, and you had to bust to keep up. It only took one turn to learn that lesson. It was lightly raining and here I was busting tail, not a happy camper. But when we got back to the hotel and took our showers, I felt great. Lesson learned: when you travel a lot, exercise at the end of the day is good for the body. After we cleaned up, we walked to a pizzeria a block away for dinner and as we passed by the garages lining part of the street, we noticed that Marty's bike mechanics were tuning up our bikes in two of the garages. I thought that was just fabulous.

Day one of the race was a time trail. We rode to the starting line; Marty talked our way onto the course and off we went. After a short distance, there was a bridge we had to cross that went up at a 45-degree angle for it seemed like over a mile. I was trudging my way up the hill and this old French guy came up beside me. We exchanged glances and you could just tell he was going to kill himself if necessary to beat me over that bridge. I gave him the win, frankly I was working as hard as I could just to keep going. Once I got to the top, it was about 10 km to the timing station that we were going to stop at to see the race. It was great fun. We were on the side of the road, less than 3 feet from the competitors as they came by. The guys started based on their ranking, 2 minutes apart. Lance was last and the guy next to last cyclist was a German named Jan Ullrich. Ullrich was one of those guys that was always in the hunt but never won. We watched riders for quite a while and as they came by, we could see their times, so we had an idea about how they were doing. I had stepped on the road a step or so after Ullrich went by, and Christina grabbed me and said look out. Lance had already overtaken Ullrich at our checkpoint and when he passed, probably approaching 40mph, the wind was visibly disturbed.

Part of the tour's benefits was fine dining and nice hotels. We stayed in a former convent for about 3 days and had wonderful meals. There was an old (12th-13th century) church there which had been abandoned. We all crawled around in it trying to assume what it once looked like. We rode a finish one day, observed the feed zone another and finally came the day we were all looking forward to: the team time trial where the teams were scored as a team rather than individually as in every other stage.

Marty divided us into a slow and fast group and Christina was kind enough to ride with me and the slow pokes. We formed in two lines side by side and the person in the right front would go as hard as he or she could until they were out of gas and drop off to the head of the left line. The person at the rear of the left line would move over into the last place on the right line and we would just keep rotating over again as long as we rode. Marty had given us team jerseys for the event, so we all looked the same. It was the 4th of July so one of our guys figured out a way to attach a big American flag to his bike. To the French, when the tour came through your area it was a holiday and they all went out to the race route hours in advance and had a picnic. As we went by, many would yell "Allez" or "go" in French.

After about 40 KM we rode into a French town, took a perpendicular right hand turn and stopped about 100 yards down the road at a bridge that had a time display. We sent folks out in the 4 cardinal directions looking for food. Christina continued the race route. There were no restaurants or delis, so she stopped at a garage to ask for help. There were two men in the garage and Chris tried to ask them where she could buy food and beer; I loved a beer after our ride. Christina always said she had no aptitude for languages, but she could always communicate. One of the guys heard beer and walked over to his refrigerator and pulled out a couple of beers. When she realized what was happening, Christina tried to get the man to understand that she didn't want him to give her a beer, she wanted to buy some beers. They came to a closer understanding, and he told her where the grocery store was, but he insisted that she kept the beers. I enjoyed them when Chris got back to the bridge.

We had taken off only an hour or so before the race started, so teams started to come by. Marty had the team rosters, and he would tell us which teams had Americans and we would then cheer them on by name. Floyd Landis, who would later win a tour and become the center of a big controversy about doping, heard us, looked up to find us and gave us a big wave.

As I said we were about 100 yards from the right-hand corner, and it was interesting to see how long it took the teams to get back into formation after the turn. Most of the teams were back in line 50 meters from the turn, some took almost to our location to shape back up. When Lance's team,

Discovery, came around they were back in formation within 20 yards. They won the time trial and in our little glimpse of the race, we could see why.

Another time we just rode out into the middle of the French countryside and watched the tour go by on a road that was probably a lane and a half wide. We rode out on the route and Marty had set up a nice lunch for us and we stood at the side of the road, literally less than 2 feet from the riders as they went by. After the caravan of team cars and race officials got by, we started out and we started riding toward the finish line. We were riding in a long straight line, not going too hard and a lady who was last in our line went off the side of the road and hurt herself. She needed help, an ambulance.

We had no communications, so Marty divided us up. He was going to take a couple of guys and ride for help while most of us would remain with the woman. He put me in charge, I guess he thought the old Colonel was the one he could trust the most. A team Codifis car came by which stopped. They asked what was happening and when we told them, the passenger said he would call for an ambulance. Sure enough, 15 minutes later an ambulance arrived and took the woman and her husband off. We learned later that she was fine. We now had two extra bikes, but we took it slow and the best riders in the group just pulled them along.

This trip was absolutely the best vacation I have ever taken in my life. I guess the lesson learned is when I exercise on vacation, I enjoy it much more. Marty is still in business as of 2020, and I wish him all the best.

CHAPTER
TWENTY-ONE

HUNTSVILLE, 2006-16 AND RETIREMENT

Christina and I moved back to Huntsville after six years in Colorado in 2006. Things were tense at the company, and I decided that I needed to give Mike space.

Christina and I bought a house on the extreme west side of Huntsville-Madison; in fact, it was in Limestone county. Madison annexed our area and much more. We paid our taxes to Madison, but we paid our utilities in Limestone. When we first got there, there were probably 6 or 8 houses in the development. Today there are 400. We originally had to drive some to buy our groceries until a Publicx was built just down the street from us. It was a nice home, 2000 square feet smaller than our home in Colorado, but it was all we needed.

We picked that area, because Christina and Roberta, who was a lifelong educator, had surveyed all the schools in

Huntsville and decided that Heritage Elementary was the best for Sean. Sean would attend Heritage until the 7th grade and then he went to St John's school which was in our parish and then to Liberty middle school for the 9th grade as a new high school, James Clemens was being built right next to our housing development.

Sean got into golf during this time frame. He had started playing in Colorado at Patty Jewett before we left, which was the oldest public golf course west of the Mississippi. When we got to Alabama, he decided he would play in the Redstone Golf club's annual tournament. The first year he played in the club championship he was 10 years old, and he beat several adults. This caused quite a stir as some were resentful of this kid was "embarrassing" adults, so a meeting was held, the rules were changed, and it was decided that one had to be 18 to play in the championship. The club pro then asked: "Well what is Sean going to do next year?", so they created a junior championship.

There were two divisions: 18 and under and 13 and under. When he was 11, he won the junior under 13 championship and dominated. The next year he came to me and said he wanted to play in the senior division of the juniors, even though he would only be 12. I cautioned him that he could be playing some high school guys and he might get beat, but he said he wanted to try anyway.

We showed up to the tournament and sure enough, Sean's foursome included a high school senior and a high school sophomore. The tournament had two rounds and after the first round, Sean was in the lead, but not by much. We talked that night and I told him he had to go out and dominate on the second day.

The next day, all of them bogied the first hole. Then Sean went out and parred the next eight holes in a row, creating a substantial lead. We made the turn and when we got to the 14th hole which is a par 3, the high school senior told me that if Sean got a hole in one, he was going to quit. Sean got a par but ended up winning by 20 strokes or so. It was a proud day when he received his trophy that night.

The second half of Sean's eighth grade year and the first half of his freshman year in high school, he got very sick. Christina took him to a slew of doctors, and no one could figure out what was wrong. He was in real pain; his intestinal system was not right, and the boy just suffered. Christina finally found an allergist who tested Sean for food allergies and found out he had a bunch of them. He had been tested for strep, but the previous doctors had only done a throat swab. The allergist did a blood test and confirmed he had it. Christina had suspected strep for some time, but she persisted in Birmingham, and she was right. No one knows your body like you do, or in this case, your mother, and you need to stick to your guns with your medical treatment; the doc knows best, but you know your body best.

Sean lost time with his golf but his 10th grade year he started attending James Clemens where they had a golf team. His coach was a faculty member who had played a year of college golf and one of the Dads did most of the coaching. It wasn't much. Sean was pretty much on his own. He studied golf videos and read golf magazines faithfully and he became in tune with the latest techniques in golf, but he was applying them in an environment where no one understood what he was doing. Sean played for Clemens his sophomore and junior seasons, but he graduated in December of his senior year, so he passed on playing his last year of eligibility.

We all felt comfortable with this decision, because Sean was playing in lots of other golf tournaments every year, in fact a double figure number of tournaments each year. He was playing a tournament almost weekly in the spring and summer as part of the Alabama State Junior league. Most of these tournaments were local, but we did travel on occasion. One time when he was younger, we played in a tournament about an hour away. It was a magnificent golf course, just beautiful and tough. Sean seemed not to notice. His next to final round he played the son of the Alabama Golf coach. It was a competitive match, but Sean lost. We were packing up in the parking lot when the coach came by and told Sean to keep playing, he had real talent.

Sean also tried to qualify for the US Open and the PGA junior championships. Later, it was always interesting to see Sean in a foursome with adults, some of which were professionals. He qualified for a slot to play in the Veritas championship in Los Angeles. Christina and Sean flew out and I met them there. Sean competed against guys from all over the world. He had a bad first day but played pretty good thereafter. Before the tournament, we went to a Los Angeles Angels game and we all sat in the top deck Those seats were so slanted, it scared me a lot. My balance was already starting to go, and I was uncomfortable.

In late 2008 I had an experience that changed my life. I went on a Cursillo weekend. I had a good buddy in Huntsville, Mark Richards, who I had served with in Korea who was big in the movement. Mark had married a Korean girl, Sue, from the area around where my Hawk Battery was in 1976. Mark had served at the Battalion Operations Center, and I didn't remember him much. He remined me that he had been invited to my promotion party to Major and had had a great time. We would eventually become the best of friends.

I hired Mark to work with me on the GMD contract and when he moved into his new office, the first thing he unpacked was a bible. Mark would eventually die way too young of cancer, and I was with him just a few days before he died and had a part in his funeral. The world is a worse place because Mark Richards is in Heaven.

The Cursillo premise was simple; provide an encounter with God and then follow up with weekly gatherings of men and monthly gatherings of men and women. Christina and I had been getting back into our faith for several years when we were in Colorado. We were attending mass regularly and to help a priest friend in Colorado, I became the President of the Parish Council for a small parish near the Southgate shopping center which was just down the hill from our house and Nana's which was mostly Hispanic.

When we returned to Huntsville, we started going to mass at our old parish, St John's which was only a few miles from our house. Father Phil O' Kennedy became the new pastor a year after we arrived back, and he hired Christina to be the director of adult education. She taught a class every Sunday between masses, which I never attended, and she worked there the rest of the week as well. Because we didn't need the money and because we had medical coverage through my retirement, Christina agreed to be paid part time, but the job was a full-time gig.

Father Phil was a genius. He was also impatient and had no time for sniveling. His manner was somewhat brusque at times but there was no question who was in charge. After I went to my Cursillo all the Cursillistas and anyone else who wanted to, attended 6AM mass on Tuesday mornings for years. Mary Ellen Roberts, who was a lovely woman and one of our choir leaders, was singing the Alleluia at Mass in the big church. She was an awesome pianist but had a weak voice, so she asked me to sing the Alleluia which I did with great gusto for years.

Fr Phil instituted a massive building campaign where a pastoral center, an office complex and a day chapel were added to our facilities. The early morning mass was moved to the chapel, and I sang the Alleluia there for almost a year when one day as Father was processing into mass, he stopped by me and asked why I was singing the Alleluia. I was shocked, I had been singing it for years, but he didn't want me singing it anymore. I'm sure I was too loud for the small chapel, I couldn't help it, but he just cut me off and Mary Ellen started singing it again. If you don't want someone to do something, have the courage to just tell them and if you are considerate of them, you will tell them why. Father didn't do that, he just insulted people-bad leadership.

Despite his faults, Christina was there to learn how to organize a parish which would serve her well later. Father Phil was a very spiritual guy and he later travelled with us to marry Mike and Jill, but I never felt completely comfortable around him.

Anyway, back to the Cursillo. Christina learned of the movement at church and put Mark on to recruit me. There was an old tradition in the Cursillo where the man was supposed to go ahead of the wife to the weekend. Christina would try to motivate me by saying she wanted to go but wouldn't until I went. Mark took a soft sales pitch, saying he would fix me up if I ever wanted to go.

I don't know what it was, but I finally decided to go. The weekend started on a Thursday night and the previous Sunday I decided that I would attend Christina's class at church after mass. I sat next to Mike Monis, an Army LTC who was a Program Manager whom I had worked with. The subject of the talk was discipleship. When Chris got done, I said to Mike, another cradle Catholic, "Mike where did this come from?" He replied "dunno, we were told that if we followed the rules we were going to Heaven." That was so true. The Catholic church I grew up in was an institution of fear. If I had a dollar for every time a nun told me I was going to hell, I would have retired 10 years earlier.

Up until high school, the mass was in Latin, although after the Vatican II conference, mass could be said in the native language of the area. The church of my youth was stilted, law bound and administered itself in a punitive manner. None of this was in line with what Vatican II wanted, my perception of the church wasn't too good. To be fair, I had not really gotten involved in any of our parishes in the Army as we kept moving. The only priest I knew at all was Father Ratigan from Saudi, and I really didn't know him that well.

Three guys came by to pick me up-John Kutsor, Wayne Sovocol and John Simmons- and we drove the 30 minutes to the Benedictine Convent in Cullman Alabama without incident. I was "in-processed", assigned a room with a couple of other guys whom I would chat with briefly, usually just before we went to bed late at night. That first night, we were supposed to have already gone to dinner, but we skipped that step. Normally the sponsor is the one who escorts the candidate to and from the weekend, but Mark, who was my sponsor, was on the team so he delegated that responsibility to the boys. I took me a while to get over the fact that here I was in Baptist Alabama, and I was in a large convent, which in its hay day could have housed 300 nuns and near a monastery which could house 50 priests right in the middle of the state.

We all stowed our gear and moved into a large meeting room. We were then assigned a table and tablemates which would be the only permanent aspect of the meeting. We had a table leader who was an experienced Cursillista, and I had two table mates. One guy was a banker from Birmingham and the other guy was a lawyer from Huntsville named Bob Becher. I chatted some with the banker, but Becher was quiet, almost evasive so I decided to leave him alone. We were given an introductory talk by the honcho, or rector and then we went to the chapel for a series of reflections on who we were. In the chapel, that first night we were sworn to silence until after mass the next morning.

I remember I didn't sleep well that night. We got up the next morning and went straight to the chapel, had mass, and went to breakfast. We all sang grace before meals and at first, I thought it was stupid, but all joined in, and we got better and better as we practiced 3 times a day. Becher showed up at the table and apologized for being so withdrawn the night before. He told us he was considering becoming a Deacon. I asked him "So what did you decide?" He replied he was going to do it, and Bob and I became dear friends from that point on.

Cursillo in Spanish means "Short Course" and that is what it was. We had 5 - 45 minutes classes a day on various aspects of the faith and the church. We were given a notebook and encouraged to take notes and at the end of each day we were told after dinner we would make a table poster on a topic given to us based on the talks of the day. I started organizing my notes so I identified the key points that would tie the thoughts of the day together. At first, I was a little reluctant about the poster business, but after that first night when all our competitive juices came out in a relaxed, communal sort of way, I got into it.

Something was happening. I was more relaxed and happier than I had been in years. Friday night we had confessions and I had not been to confession in 8 years. They had the priest who was with us on the weekend and 4 or 5 Benedictine Priests from the nearby monastery to hear the confessions.

The 20 minutes or so I had to wait my turn in the chapel was probably the worse time I have ever had in my life. I felt miserable; all the focus on self-introspection had pointed out a lot of things that I was not very proud of. Remembering my life-long experiences with confession, which frankly had not been that many, I decided I would blame it on the Army, the culture, the environment. Everyone would believe that soldiers are not saints and I wanted to fit in, right? I finally got my turn and nervously went into a big room that had been divided into sections where several priests were hearing our sins. I sat down and began..." Bless me Father I have sinned; it has been 8 years since my last confession; You know Father, I was in the Army for almost 28 years". I then heard "Infantry, 35 years." The priest I had drawn was Father Pat Eagan, a Benedictine Monk who was a lifelong bachelor and who had decided when he retired that he wanted to devote the rest of his life to God. Well, there it was, time to fess up. I had a pretty good confession, I mentioned all the sins but not in the detail that I should have. But when I left the room, I felt good, free somehow.

It's interesting that all through my Army career, I really believed in the value of the After-Action Review. In my spiritual life I had never thought of an AAR on my life choices and following Jesus that confession offered. I had an indelible mark since when I was a kid where we dreaded confession since it was always a butt chewing, sometimes for things that we really weren't guilty of. Vatican II had changed all that, and confession became reconciliation, squaring things up with God.

On the third day, I met my next challenge. We went out to a statue on a remote section of the convent and said a rosary. I hadn't said a rosary in 20 years and since our Lady appeared at Fatima, we were asked to add an additional prayer to every decade. One of the big take a ways from my Cursillo is I was ignorant of my faith. When I thought about it, I hadn't done any religious reading, with one small exception, or studied my faith since my religion classes in high school.

I resolved to fix this situation. I asked one of the veterans what I should read, and he told me he had been told by a highly respected Bishop, Bishop Foley, to read the Doctors of the Church, that small group of Saints whose writings were especially truthful and impactful. I didn't even know what a Doctor of the Church was let alone who they were, but I was determined to find out. I knew I needed to read spiritual books.

After each talk, we would have discussion at our table, and I discovered that the other guys had the same guilt and tendency to mess up that I had. I always had the feeling that I was alone with my temptations and failures to think of others; but

I learned everyone had the same problem. It came from original sin, and something called concupiscence where we all tend to admire sin and fall prey to it. But I also learned that God was like Vince Lombardi, He gives us chances to sin and suffer only so He can get our attention and teach us what is right.

Graduation came around, Christina couldn't be there because she wasn't a Cursillista yet. We all did our promises. I pledged to try to go to mass more than once a week and to pray a decade of the rosary every day. At the graduation, I got my commitment cross where I admitted to all present that Jesus was counting on me, and I was counting on Jesus. My life was changed.

We were told that we had to join or form a small group that would meet once a week to discuss our piety, study, and action. Bob and I decided to form a group which grew to the point we had to split it, but those two groups of men are still getting together once a week, almost 15 years later. Some of my very dear friends have come from those Cursillo small groups; men I really admired and accepted me for what I was, not what I did. We understood right away that every week that we had to talk about our spiritual lives and what we had read, so I really started reading.

The Monday morning after my Cursillo weekend, I got up an hour early to pray and say part of a rosary. I have been spending an hour with God every morning since. Stupid me, I asked Christina to get me a book on every religious order in the Catholic Church. I needed a model, a rule to follow if I was going to get this spiritual thing right. She laughed and asked me if I knew how many religious orders there were in the Catholic Church? She replied over 30, so I asked her to get me some books on the top 5 or 6, the Franciscans, the Jesuits etc.

While I was waiting for the books to come, she gave me an overview of the Catholic Spiritual tradition. At this point I was reading and not absorbing much, but I ran across a Saint that I had never heard of named Teresa of Avila. Her words just jumped off the page to me. Her relationship with God was respectful but real. She was always joking with God, yet her prayer life was at such a level that she was declared the Doctor of the Church for prayer. She was a practical, focused, inventive, resourceful, and powerful woman who founded a religious order that exploded once it got founded. I would go on to read all her books on prayer. She became my patron Saint, the one who got me started and who still challenges me each day.

I had a spiritual mentor, Deacon Jim Bodine, and we met once a month to discuss how I was doing spiritually. One day after I described the 3 books I had read since our last meeting, he said to me "Slow down-take time to absorb". It was probably good advice, but I kept reading like crazy.

<u>I read a bunch of books by Jesuit authors including Father Walter Barry. Barry wrote a book called God and Me which essentially was a practical treatise on prayer. I was so impressed with the book; I gave a copy to every guy I sponsored on a Cursillo. Christina and I went to a retreat held by Father Barry in Atlanta. He talked all weekend on how Jesus wants to be our friend. They had his books for sale in the retreat house's bookstore and I bought 10 copies, in addition to my original copy that I brought with me. They had a book signing and Father was a little surprised when I walked up with the 11 books that I wanted him to sign. I explained the first copy was mine and the remainder were gifts. He opened my copy with all the reminders and notes written throughout, and he</u>

smirked "so you really read it." To which I replied, "No Father, I inhaled it."

I read all Teresa's books and grew more and more fond of her. My perspective of my relationship with God was too narrow. Teresa was all in and I had to try to emulate her.

I especially enjoyed the practical, common sense approach of the Jesuits. I also loved the Carmelite spirituality, and I had an attraction to the Franciscans though I am not sure why. Many of the books I read on Francis were written for teens and some for children and Francis was always portrayed as this goody - goody two shoes who was perfect. I would learn later that that was certainly not the case, but he was a truly great man.

Over the years, I investigated with Christina's help, the Carmelites, the Dominicans. The Jesuits have no third order as they are pledged to the pope to deploy on literally a moment's notice, and they knew lay people had commitments that prevented that. Anyway, the Jesuits, other than their small retreat house in Atlanta had no presence in the southeast at all. I had a guy I worked with on the GMD contract who was a lay Carmelite and he advised me to stay away from the Carmelite chapter in Huntsville at that time. The Dominicans had no draw for me, I admired St Dominic, but in retrospect, I guess they were a little too intellectual for me.

It's amazing the way the Lord works when you are looking for it. Juan Ruiz, who was the Hispanic National Coordinator for Cursillo, went on EWTN, the national Catholic TV channel to explain Cursillo to the world. Juan gave an initial explanation and then the Franciscan priest who was hosting the show asked him "So Juan, a Cursillista could become a lay Franciscan if he wanted to expand his faith journey?" Juan was taken aback a little but responded, "Sure Father, in fact I think that is a good idea for those are inclined to join a religious order." It hit home for me.

A few days earlier, Bill Edwards a friend from Huntsville, called me and invited me to come with him to a meeting of the local Franciscan fraternity which met in Decatur Alabama, 20 miles west of Huntsville. The fraternity was rebuilding and barely had the 5 professed members needed to be a fraternity, but they hoped that Bill and I would be the new blood they needed.

Christina and I had served on the Cursillo Secretariat for five years and the divisive attitude of the local secretariat meant they were not going to consider any new ideas and that was frustrating. At the National level, Cursillo was trying to change, and I was tuned in with National on the changes. I introduced the new thoughts at the School of Leaders for the Cursillo in our Diocese. I was booed, yelled at, hated for what I was introducing. The climate was raw, argumentative, and hostile.

I had joined Cursillo because it gave me peace, I loved my group brothers. But the local Cursillo was filled with Pharisees like our Lord dealt with, people who lived by what they thought was right and to heck with everything else despite the truth being taught to them by multiple sources, not just me. Christina and I moved to the Cursillo team of the Southeast Region of the United States and served there for going on 5 years. When I left my Cursillo weekend, I had a strong feeling that I owed the program. I have now paid my debt.

The following Monday after the weekend, we had a meeting at the office and Mando called me after the meeting and asked "What changed? I told him I had gone to a Cursillo weekend.

I had forgotten to tell Mando that he had to cover the training in El Paso for me a week earlier. We had agreed that one or the other of us would be on site until the team got its feet on the ground. Mando had made plans for the weekend that I went to the Cursillo, big plans; he was going to get a car for his daughter. Instead, he covered the training in El Paso.

He had gone to mass the Sunday I was at the Cursillo, frustrated. The Hispanic priest who was going to say mass noticed his intense prayer before mass. When mass ended as Mando was leaving the padre asked Mando if all was well. Mando replied he was upset with a friend. The priest said: "Maybe he had something important to do or maybe he went on a Cursillo weekend." Mando replied that the friend in question, me, would never go to a Cursillo weekend.

Mando shared with me on the phone that he had been to a Cursillo right after he graduated from High School, but he had not done anything with the movement since then. Back then when he was so much younger the time was not right for his encounter with God. Everything is timing. You can talk to people until you are blue in the face and if they have not suffered and lived enough, they won't be ready to let God in. There are exceptions of course, Saints known and unknown who hooked up with God right from their childhood. But I think those people are the exception. Most people come to a real relationship with Jesus after they have experience life and lived a while and encountered something they cannot control.

Mando is now an ardent Catholic very faith filled, but he is not too enamored with the institution of the Catholic Church. My Dad was the same way. He was a man of great faith, believing that God had cured him of cancer when he was a young man. But he didn't take full advantage of the Catholic faith.

He went to mass regularly until he got sick a second time. but I think he did so in large part due to Nana's example.

I'll just get this out of the way. The church is lenient when it comes to recruiting priests. And so, for the church, like any large institution, there are good priests and bad ones. They all deserve respect because they alone can bring us the Eucharist, but some of them have horrible management and leadership. I have learned from talking to priests and seminarians over the years that the predominance of the curriculum at the seminary is on philosophy and theology. I get the theology, they need to understand the thinking around church tradition, but I think they get too much on philosophy. Seminaries need to, for a significant portion of time, to teach leadership; good practical leadership and how to manage people and money.

Mando and I did a little leadership study during the pandemic, that compared servant leadership, the so-called approved church leadership style, to Army leadership. And our conclusion was leadership was leadership, good leaders practiced the same traits and principles.

We need to pray for our clergy. They are learning from the school of hard knocks. We need to remember that no priest can mess up a sacrament, when they say mass, they facilitate the transformation of the bread into the body and blood of Christ and despite their potentially poor leadership and management, the sacrament is perfect every time.

We continued to train THAAD crews. I will always be proud of the fact that we continually assessed our products and made changes where necessary. Our biggest challenge continued to be creating tests and coming up with practical exercises that would reinforce what the students had been taught in the classroom. I was grateful to Rob who authored several PEs that in my opinion were flat brilliant. They seemed a little pedantic at face value, but I saw student after student understanding what we had taught them at a very high level resulting from Rob's work.

It seemed like we were always moving offices in both Huntsville and El Paso. Mike Richmond was our task lead there and did a wonderful job of finding us adequate, inexpensive office space. He would always have me down when he was looking, and one time there was office space available at a convent. There weren't many nuns at the place and the church was trying to keep the facility open. I could tell right away that the boys didn't like the idea of being in a convent, so I led them on a little, complementing the facility and continually bringing up the possibilities that the place had. They were very relieved when I told them I was just kidding. We were blessed with our instructors in El Paso who not only taught well but represented our company with real class.

Two of our employees went to work for Lockheed, our prime contractor. Roy Tate retired, and Kyle Koltoff left I2 and became the LM training manager. Right after Kyle took over, I was called on the carpet by a senior Lockheed Executive whom I knew from our GMD work and it became clear that our company and me, personally, were being accused of doing things that were flat untrue. LM then had our former employees start teaching some of the classes and then all training was transferred away from the LM people in Huntsville that we knew well to another division in Florida. Every LM division had a different philosophy on the use of sub-contractors. The space division, the folks we worked for, used subs freely, but the LM supervisors in Florida believed in having as many LM people on a contract as possible. We had a couple of years on our contract left, but I could see the writing on the wall.

We worked hard to get other work. Mike still was updating the marketing program that had us investigating training and engineering opportunities all over the country. It was this program that got Rob's work with the Army Research Institute identified and funded. Carlton Brewer, a great man, was hopeful that the Missile Defense Agency would develop a program for a Kinetic Energy Laser, and he talked to me about doing the training for that. The program was never started which was a big disappointment. We almost got the contract to develop a training program for Apache helicopter pilots to use the hammerhead radar which was mounted on the top of each aircraft. We chased that awhile, but in the end it fizzled. So, we had a busy, but exciting life, teaching full time, and chasing work all the time.

I continued with my Franciscan studies. Bill and I were advancing quickly. Our first formation director was a saint in New Hampshire, and we would VTC with her at least once per month. The Franciscan fraternity was on shaky grounds. They had exactly 5 members, only two of which were active. The Minister, or chief, was determined to keep the outfit alive. For some reason, we got on her bad side. I guess she thought that we did not have what it took to be a Franciscan. We kept asking questions about the road ahead and she really resented it as in retrospect I do not think she knew the answers. We were going so fast with our formation, that she started adding requirements for us to take the final step toward being a Franciscan.

We went to the annual regional gathering of the Franciscans. She was so upset with us she arranged a meeting with a member of the regional Franciscan organization and Father Linus, our regional spiritual advisor. It was a heated conversation; Bill was so mad he was almost out of his mind. Father and I just tried to keep things calm while Bill and Beth, the minister screamed at each other. It seemed at the time that we finally ended a 15-round fight, and they called a truce. Fr Linus finally summed things up when he said to me and Bill: "You two are high speed guys, I understand your concerns, have patience." And that ended our attendance at the Annual Regional Gathering until later.

We returned to Huntsville and shortly thereafter Beth told us she was disbanding the fraternity. She was tired of keeping something alive that really had no future. She told us that we could transfer anywhere but had no recommendations. I think she wanted us to quit. We met several Franciscans from a fraternity in Chattanooga, Tennessee at the ARG and they seemed like they had good outfit. So, we applied to move to there.

Bill and I drove to Chattanooga and attended a meeting and were invited back for a second. But there was something wrong, nothing was said but we sensed a problem. Turns out that our former minister had destroyed all our records, the proof of our progress. Bill and I both had big 3 ring notebooks with all our work, which we submitted for the formation director's review. We were told that there would be a 3-month delay while they decided whether they would accept us or not. We could continue our formation, but we were in a conditional status.

They explained all the delays, the conditional status etc., was by the book. Formation went well and over time we convinced them that we were not the terrors Beth had proposed we were.

We were finally professed as Secular Franciscans after 4 years of formation, a year longer than the normal timeline. All was well. Interestingly, our long formation had taught us little on Francis and Clare. So, my free time for the next few years was reading as much as I could on those two great saints.

The THAAD contract finally ended. LM was going to use their own people. A while before that fatal day, Christina had come to me and asked for me to retire. Retirement appealed, but I did not think I had enough money. She then came in with an itemized accounting of our expenses and income and proved that we did have enough money. So, I decided to quit. I am sure Mike thought I was letting him down like he did when we moved back to Alabama. He was going to keep the company going, but I was tired and like they told us in the Army, you will know when it is time to quit. 28 years almost in the Army and 21 in the defense contracting world was enough work in one lifetime. It was time to move on.

A priest we had known from his time at St John's, Fr Mark Spruill, was now the pastor of a small country church in Ft Payne, Alabama about 90 miles from Huntsville. Christina knew him from her time at St John's where she had helped him out with some projects. A friend of mine from Cursillo, Kevin Genelin, was from that parish and had died very unexpectantly from a heart attack at the age of 57. Kevin was super involved in the parish, head of the pastoral council, the head knight and he took care of the church and grounds. He had been painting a bathroom in the church when he started feeling poorly, just two days before he died. A leadership vacuum now existed in the parish and Father Mark expressed an interest in Christina and I moving to Ft Payne and filling the void.

Christina did not push it and I was initially a little uncomfortable. I had been to Ft Payne a couple of time as part of Cursillo team building but I did not remember much about the place. My friend Kevin Genelin had hosted the meeting and it had been very pleasant. My recollection of the church was it was plain, but when I heard the story of how the people had fought to get the church built and had persevered for almost two decades to get it done, I was impressed. Father Mark was the first full time pastor which everyone considered a great blessing. The church in some form had been in existence for 55 years when we got there, and they had gotten their first pastor around year 50. Real commentary on the shortage of priests.

I had made a deal with Father. I wanted to do three things: serve as a "surrogate" deacon in his words, lead a men's prayer group and at Father's insistence, manage the maintenance of the parish. I was told he had plenty of help; my job would be just to get the supplies, coordinate the events and overwatch what was happening. That turned out to be an error; guys had helped Father, but they all had physically demanding jobs and family responsibilities, so getting help from the Anglo population turned out to be difficult from the start.

The interior of the church needed painting badly, it still had the original paint, so my first project was to paint the parish hall, the kitchen in the parish hall, the vestibule and eventually the sacristy. To create interest, we had a contest at all the masses to pick the color for the hall. I had picked a light green, a beige (my choice) and a light yellow as the three options. The green won in a landslide. My perception was our budget was limited, so we only had enough money for one coat of paint. I have learned even when you are painting a wall the same color, you need two coats to really make it look good.

Christina had asked Father to work with the adults as she had done at St John's and for a while she was listed as the adult formation coordinator in the bulletin. Then one day, that entry was removed so she decided to help our part time Director of Religious Education by taking over the confirmation program. The program separated the boys and girls for the instruction and men to taught the boys and women the girls. I was recruited early on, and I taught confirmation for five years, trying to get the boys to love Jesus as I did. Sometimes it seemed like an impossible task. We have subsequently learned that the church is revising its whole approach to administering the sacraments and I think the new program will be a lot better. Teaching people to love is an exceedingly difficult job.

Maintenance was really needed. After we finished painting the church, Father had raised the money for a new Religious Education Building. I had been invited to the final planning meeting, but everything was about done, and I had very little input. By now I had a work buddy, Charles Czajkowski, a transplanted New Englander who had worked in the south most of his adult life. Charley and I spent weeks and weeks hanging white boards, bulletin boards, installing shelves in the storeroom and various other chores in the new RE building. We were working over 10 hours a week; quite a lot for a couple of volunteers.

Many things were reaching the end of their life cycle. I convinced Father to replace the AC system in the church and we contracted with Rise Air Conditioning to do the job. Sean had heard me talking of the AC project and Clint Rise, his high school buddy, was now working for his Dad. We called them and they came out for a quote and gave us a price 1/3 less than an AC outfit in Birmingham had quoted to Father. When that was done, we fixed the drainage around the church and finally totally remodeled the Parish Center, the old church, to include creating a large conference room which previously had been a real need.

Christina and I tried extremely hard to befriend the Latinos, who were 95% of the parish. Talking with them at church and having them over for a meal, we learned that they did not feel that they could get a room for their many activities. Father put me in charge of facility planning, I wrote an SOP that I coordinated with the Parish Council, and I started getting the Latinos the space they needed. Father had the bands moved into an area that had been the old visiting priest's quarters which had a unique lock. Father had one key issued for the five bands, yet we had 6 keys sitting in the key box. So, I issued the boys the remaining keys, so every band had a key. The climate with the Latinos was one of fear, everyone was petrified to make a mistake, but I decided that I would take the hit which never came. Our Latinos followed the facility rules better than the Anglos.

Although his Spanish was decent, I don't think Father Mark every felt comfortable with the Latinos. Our parish lacked spirit; everything was done with the thought someone was looking over your shoulder. It was not a happy situation.

I tried to get guys to do a Cursillo group with but after spending time with them I think I intimidated them a little, so nothing happened. Christina and I remained on the Regional

Team and gave talks at several regional encounters. We remained detached from the Cursillo in our own diocese.

Southerners can be vengeful people. In Alabama there was an election for governor one year when we were in Huntsville and the candidate who won ran on a platform of starting a lottery to help underprivileged kid get a college education. I was walking out of the office on the Friday night before the election and I commented to a native Alabamian "Hey Royce, guess we are going to have a lottery on Monday". He replied, "No way" and he was right. Every Baptist preacher in Alabama got on the pulpit the Sunday before and told their congregations that the lottery was the devil. The resolution was crushed. The only city in Alabama that voted for the lottery (80-20% for) was Huntsville.

Southerners also can be insular. The same guy I had asked about the lottery, and I had a long discussion where he accused me of being a carpetbagger, an outsider who came to Alabama to take advantage of the work in the Missile Defense Agency. That conversation petered out when I asked him if his family had fought for the south during the Civil War. You should have seen his eyes when I told him mine had.

The first three years in Ft Payne, I devoted most of my time to improving the facility. When Father Mark left, I was satisfied with what we had done but I was disappointed at the same time. Progress almost universally means pain, discomfort, getting out of one's routine and I just felt that there was more we could have gotten done, like painting the sanctuary of the church.

Ft Mark left in July 2019 and his replacement was Father Rick Chenault, whom Christina knew some as he was the director of vocations for the diocese. Father showed up to move in and came out to meet the boys who I had enlisted to move his stuff into the rectory in a t-shirt, shorts, and an Auburn visor cap. He was a big guy, a former offensive guard in high school, but he was a little overweight and he and I had many discussions about physical fitness. We had two Auburn grads in a row as pastor; there are opportunities for penance everywhere!

Father came to dinner soon after he arrived and apparently Father Mark had told him to talk to us early. He humbly asked for advice as this was his first parish and I told him that I would help him if we had total transparency. To this day we talk straight to one another although Father is such a caring person, he will sometimes give you a vague reply to trivial things if he thinks his answer might offend you.

The Catholic church has been around for 2100 years, and I am convinced the only reason it is still in business is the presence of the Holy Spirit. Priests are not trained to lead or manage which constitute most of their challenges.

Father Rick was ready to meet the challenges and he began by instituting regular staff calls. I did an organizational assessment of the parish staff duties and procedures which seemed to help our new office manager, Cecilia, some. Father had other meetings; the Liturgical meeting led to the resignation of the lady who had been the chief sacristan for decades; but while she was a dear person, she was just too old to keep up. The normal Pharisees popped up using the argument that they had been doing this or that for decades and in most cases, Father just let those things ride; there is a time and place for everything.

Father approved getting the sanctuary painted, started frequent holy hours, and heard confessions incessantly. I have never been in a place where it has been so easy to go to confession and that is how it should be. Father is a natural leader; he has worked very hard to build cohesion amongst his staff and key volunteers and he has not been afraid to make hard decisions. In late 2020, he hired Christina quarter time as the Coordinator of Ministries. As usual there were parishioners who did not like Christina, I guess she was too straight forward with them, but I am confident Father, with the great staff he has, will continue to grow our efforts in northeast Alabama. And its showing; despite the pandemic, mass attendance is pretty good, and collections are up, both signs of a vibrant parish. We are becoming community because Father cares about every person in the parish and while he cannot help everyone, that does not mean that he does not try. I admire this guy almost as much as any person I have known in my life, and I have asked him to bury me, and I hope he can. He is a caring, humble servant of God, an example to all priests.

Certainly, part of his success is he hired bi-lingual staff. When we arrived, we had a great parish secretary who had been at the church for years, but she didn't speak Spanish. So, if a couple would come in with a question, communication was difficult, if not impossible. Miss Cecilia fixed all that. Now anyone who comes in can ask and get their questions answered in English or Spanish. Cecilia was a little uncomfortable when she first took over, but Christina and I have helped her a little and now she runs the parish, to include the budget, which in most parishes is a separate person. Her present partner, Carolina Vargas, does nothing but add value. Father learned something I learned years ago: any leader is much better when he/she has good people working for them.

ADVICE FOR GRANT AND ANY OTHER GRANDKIDS THAT MIGHT COME LATER

Grant, I started this book from February 2020 and finished it in July 2022. I have not met you yet, you are not quite two years old, but always know that your grandmothers and I love you very much, just as you are, always.

My first thought for you is always respect other people. As you will learn, your Step Grandmother, Christina, and I are ardent Catholics. We believe that God made all of us good and bad. There is good in everyone although in your life you will meet people that will make you question that fact. Your Great, Great Grandfather Archie once told me "Paul, always leave a man with his dignity". It was the best advice I ever got. When I was in the Army, I was famous for the way I would chew people out, just ask your Uncle Rob who was present for one of them. But I always tried to end a counseling with something positive like "You are better than this, you can do better. I know you can."

Respect other people always even though it may be hard at times. Try to understand always where they are coming from; are there pressures on them to meet some goal, or do they have an inflated image of themselves where they are trying to be something they are not. There are a lot of people in the world like that. If you understand them some, it is easier to bear them and leave them with their dignity which could be something as simple as saying nothing.

Always forgive. There are a lot of people, even some in our family, that have trouble forgiving. If you do not forgive, it will eat on you. When you think of that person you will get angry and resentful while the other person who may or may not know you are angry with him/her is oblivious to your feelings. So, it is hurting you more that it is hurting them. And even if the other person was wrong, real wrong, if you tell them that you forgive them, it will impact them in a remarkably interesting way. This is because you have taken the high ground, you are doing what is right and people have real trouble dealing with the truth sometimes. Remember, all of us are sinners, we all make mistakes and when you keep this in mind, forgiving will be easier. When I was in the Army early in my career, there was a publicity campaign that was titled "Zero Defects", meaning no mistakes. Everyone makes mistakes, it is part of being human and remembering that will help keep you grounded.

Always be positive. Be a source of energy to those around you. Many people get depressed worrying about the future and obsessing about something they did in the past. Sure, you should learn from you mistakes and try not to repeat them, but the past is gone, and the future isn't here yet. Live for the present and always be grateful for what you have whether it is a lot or not much.

The thing that you should be most grateful for is your family. You are BLESSED having the parents you have and all the experience in our family. Always love your family which includes being present to them even when you are in your twenties, when you think you have things figured out. Our kids are our greatest gift, and I will tell you there is no one that I would rather hang around with than with your Dad and your Uncles Rob and Sean. In my old age, my wife and my family are truly my greatest joy. Remember, they will not be here forever. And remember, all families have arguments, but you be an ambassador of peace like you Father is.

<u>Remember, your life is not about you. Sure, there will be situations where you are put in charge and people are counting on you and you need to have confidence to perform the best way you can. But that does not mean that any or all successes are because of you. You are part of a team, and everyone contributes. When I was in my battalion, I thought I was pretty much in control of things. But when I looked back and saw the number of officers in that battalion that had great success as Army officers and the Non-Commissioned Officers who went straight up in rank, I realized it was our success, and we were successful because of all of us.</u>

As you grow up and work you will have success and you will develop an ego. As I said before, there is nothing wrong with being confident. But if you find yourself being offended by things people might say about or to you, you need to think about it. Remember, most of these comments and accusations are just words. If there is something there, fix it. But the bigger the ego, the easier it is to be offended.

Look at your life realistically and honestly. When you are wrong, and you will be, admit it. I got angry a lot when I was younger, and it solved nothing. When you are angry, you are not thinking correctly. There is righteous anger, when getting upset is correct, but always treat others with their dignity.

Think, then act. Be honest with yourself and others. Tell the truth, politely and respectfully, but stand up for what is right including your conduct. This is the mark of a man, my grandson.

Do your best at all you do: in your job, being a good husband, raising your kids. Never quit, try hard all the time. Try every day to be a better employee, husband, and father.

Be generous with your time, treasure, and talent; all is a gift to share, not hoard. The Catholic Church defines the sin of greed as not only trying to get more and more money but also holding on to what you have. I am not recommending being crazy here, but you should always live below your means. That is, you should spend less money per month than you earn. Your Dad is an excellent example of a person that always lived well within his means. I think he learned that from you Grandmother, Marilyn. But when we have extra money, share it with a charity or your church, some worthy cause; the rewards I have found are tremendous.

I am sure that God will bless you. Always have an attitude of gratitude. Success is not measured by what you have although some people look at life that way. So be grateful that you and yours are dry, have something to eat and are safe. Start there.

Life is measured by what you do, and your children do to make our world better. The standard in everything is not perfection which many people seem to think is the answer, but better. Just try to make things better than when you found them. I heard a speech one time by a General and he told the audience that when you walk by a mistake, it becomes your standard. In other words, if you see something that is not right and make no effort to correct it, then that becomes what you accept. You may not be able to fix wrongs, realize you are not totally in charge of anything. But try to make things right, be a person people can count on.

We learn from others. Always be grateful to those who help you. Try to find one or two good friends with whom you can share everything. People who you are totally comfortable with but who will tell you the truth. You will have friends who will try to ingratiate themselves to you for their own gain. True friends are with you because they care about you, and they will tell you the truth. You may not like it sometimes, but I guarantee it is the best thing for you in the long term.

Remember the key to life is physical, intellectual, and spiritual balance. As I write this, I am 75 years old, yet I work out hard at least 4 times per week. Your Dad and Mom are diligent in their workouts. Your Dad was voted the most outstanding all-round athlete in his school. Your grandmother Christina is an Ironman. Uncle Rob was a great soccer player. Uncle Sean was a particularly good hockey player and golfer. Your great - great grandfather, Gomp Gomp was an all-American football player whose team won a national championship, and he was drafted by the Cleveland Browns to play pro football. Your Uncle Mike was an outstanding football player and pole vaulter in track. Your Physical fitness is important to our family; stay in shape, devote the time. Do not make your work your life. As you might deduce from reading this book, that I did that way too much. Balance all aspects of your life. Remember, just spending time with your kids is important.

Find sources to find the truth-the world, life and spiritual. I am sorry to leave you a world where people would rather talk about their agenda rather than tell the truth. You see it everywhere, especially in the news and politics. Find you sources of the truth of what is really happening. Your Dad was great at that, talk to him about it.

And lastly stay with God. Our whole family was raised Roman Catholic but while that is my strong preference, there are other churches. The Catholic Church is human, there are some priests who are not good guys. But even a rotten priest delivers all the sacraments perfectly all the time. So, go to church, marry a girl that believes in God and make God the center of your life and your family. I will tell you that I was not always close to God, but once I confessed my sins and let Jesus in, my life is SOO much better. The sacraments give grace or help from God, and I recommend you take advantage of them.

So, partner, this wraps it up. I am not sure that we will get to know each other well, as I will probably be with the Lord before you graduate from High School. But always know your grandfather loves you with all his heart and has been, and will be, praying for you every day both here and in heaven. Have a great life.

ASSIGNMENT TIMELINE:

- 69-70 Ft Bliss; C/V Battalion Activation
- 70-73 3d Armored Division Budingen Germany
- 73-74 Advanced Course Ft Bliss, Student
- 74-76 Tactics Department Ft Bliss-FAW Instructor
- 76-77 Korea 38TH ADA Brigade, Commander A Battery 1/44 ADA (Hawk)
- 77-80 USAFA Colorado Springs Colorado; Military History Assistant Professor
- 80-81 US Command and General Staff College, Ft Leavenworth, Ks, student
- 81-86 Ft Stewart Georgia and Hunter Army Airfield Ga; operations officer, City Manager and Battalion Commander Ft Stewart and Hunter AAF
- 86-87 Pentagon ODCSOPS
- 87-88 Army Fellow to the Center of Military History
- 88-91 Director Tactics Department Ft Bliss
- 91-92 Commander, 10th ADA Brigade Darmstadt Germany
- 92-Summer 94 ODCSOPS USAREUR, Heidelberg Germany, ADCSOPS
- Summer 94-96 Commander US Army Space Command
- 96-2000 Contractor, Huntsville Alabama
- 2000-2006 Contractor, Colorado Springs Colorado
- 2006-2016 Contractor Huntsville Alabama

2016-Present Retired; moved to Ft Payne Alabama

Family Photo at Nana's Funeral 2018
Back Row, Left to Right: Sean, Michael, Jill, Rob, Kriss, Matthew, Shannon, Damon, and Sara
Front Row, Left to Right: Christina, E Paul, Mike, and Cheryl

Michael and Grant, Opening Day, 2021

www.ingramcontent.com/pod-product-compliance
Lightning Source LLC
Chambersburg PA
CBHW051417290426
44109CB00016B/1340